The American University of Beirut

The American University of Beirut
Arab Nationalism and Liberal Education

Betty S. Anderson

University of Texas Press ◆ Austin

Requests for permission to reproduce material
from this work should be sent to:

    Permissions
    University of Texas Press
    P.O. Box 7819
    Austin, TX 78713-7819
    utpress.utexas.edu/about/book-permissions

The paper used in this book meets the minimum requirements
of ANSI/NISO Z39.48-1992 (R1997) (Permanence of Paper). ∞

Library of Congress Cataloging-in-Publication Data

Anderson, Betty S. (Betty Signe), 1965–
    The American University of Beirut : Arab nationalism and liberal
education / by Betty S. Anderson. — 1st ed.
       p.   cm.
    Includes bibliographical references and index.
    ISBN 978-0-292-74766-1

    1. American University of Beirut—History. 2. Education,
Higher—Arab countries. 3. Education, Humanistic—Arab countries.
4. Nationalism—Arab countries. I. Title.
    LG351.A72A76 2011
    378.5692'5—dc23   2011025372

To families and friends

Contents

Acknowledgments

I first visited the American University of Beirut (AUB) in June 2000; in that short visit, both Beirut and the school tantalized me sufficiently that I knew I had to return to learn more about them. I made it back in summer 2004, via a Fulbright Hays Faculty Research Abroad Grant; I have continued to return every year since. Whenever I walk through the Main Gate, I still get the same catch in my throat I did that first time.

In the long list of AUBites who helped me with this project, I extend warm thanks to Saouma BouJaoude, Peter Dodd, Ann Kerr, Samir Khalaf, Tarif Khalidi, and Samir Seikaly. Jean-Marie Cook has been a fount of information about AUB and Beirut and a good friend over these last few years. During my many visits to campus, I often affiliated myself with the Center for American Studies and Research (CASAR). Former director Patrick McGreevy and assistant to the director Nancy Batakji Sanyoura gave me support and a friendly home while on campus. I spent many an hour listening to Patrick's fascinating perspective on AUB, American Studies, and Beirut; he also happily listened to the many crazy ideas I had about this book. Nancy is a brilliant administrator and a wonderful friend. I could not have done any part of this research without the help of the librarians working in Jafet Library's Special Collections. Month after month, hour after hour, I sat at my corner table in the basement of the library, reading, photographing, and typing from the school's immense collection of documents. I thank Samar Mikati Kaissi, Iman Abdallah, Kamelia Kassis, Nadine Knesevitch, Abeer Medawar, and Dalia Najiya for all the help they gave me. Former president John Waterbury kindly invited me to teach a class about the history of AUB in the spring 2006 semester, and this enabled me to spend yet another few months doing research on campus. I also used the class as a tool for working out the different themes I planned to cover in the book. I thank President Waterbury, the students, and the class auditors for the opportunity and for their input. The current AUB president, Peter Dorman, has been equally supportive of my project and I thank him for that. Ibrahim Khoury, former AUB information director in Beirut, and Ada Porter, director of AUB communications in New York, granted me access to the alumni and gave me information about the school's history. Philip Khoury, the current chairman of the AUB Board of Trustees, offered me invaluable aid during the research and writing of this book as well as throughout my career; I thank him for his gracious help.

When I told people at AUB about my research project, they often asked when the "definitive" history of AUB would be produced. I hope someone takes on that task, but this book is *a* history of AUB and only one of many stories that can be told. In the following pages, I have tried to do a service to this school and to the many AUB denizens who told me their stories, from those who gave formal interviews to the many people I spoke to time after time whenever I was on campus. In no instance did any member of the AUB community ask that I censor or change my text; any errors or mistakes contained within are entirely my own.

While that trip to Beirut and AUB in 2000 sparked my interest in the topic, a conference at the University of Erlangen-Nürnberg, Germany, in 2005 started me on the road to actually writing the book. The topic was "The Roots of Liberal Thought in the Eastern Mediterranean," and I gave my first paper on the development of liberal education at AUB. I am grateful to Christoph Schumann for inviting me: participating in that conference gave initial shape to the thesis of my book. Participation at a number of subsequent conferences, where organizers challenged me to think about AUB and its history in new ways, gave me the opportunity to develop my thinking still further. Israel Gershoni and Amy Singer invited me to participate in a Middle East Studies conference in Istanbul in 2007; I found that theories about the international student movement of 1968 opened up new avenues for thinking about student agency in the university civic space in times of quiet as well. My participation in three CASAR conferences on America and the Middle East challenged me to think through what the programs of "making men" and making women meant for student lives at AUB. Salman Hameed's conference on Darwin and evolution in the Muslim world at Hampshire College in 2009 compelled me to rethink not only the importance of the 1882 Darwin Affair at the Syrian Protestant College (SPC) but also the very means by which knowledge is discussed and analyzed in the liberal education classroom. I thank all of the organizers for helping me hone the themes of this book.

Over the years, I benefited from the hard work of many research assistants—in Boston, Washington, Beirut, and Amman—and would like to thank Ahmad Barakat, Samuel Dolbee, Aaron Faust, Andrew Naramore, Matthew Pierce, Hannah Schmidl, and Mohammad Tannir for all their wonderful work. Special thanks go to Makram Rabah, my chief research assistant throughout the entire project. He organized all of my interviews, conducted them with me, and searched for research material whenever I asked, all the while serving as my best source for information and insight on Lebanese politics. Thank you, Makram, for help that I would never have been able to get from anyone else and for becoming a wonderful friend in the process.

I want to thank Barbara Diefendorf, Marilyn Halter, Nina Silber, and Diana Wylie for their unstinting support throughout the time I have been a member of the History Department of Boston University. Jim Dutton deserves special thanks for everything he does for me and for the friendship he extends to me. Israel Gershoni, Herbert Mason, Roger Owen, and John Voll have offered invaluable advice and support over the last few years. My Skype buddies, Ellen Fleischmann and Heather Sharkey, have read numerous versions and drafts of this text; I thank them for helping me make this a better book and for being such good friends. Ussama Makdisi offered insightful suggestions about adding historical context; Kate Seelye provided invaluable information about her family. Emily Luckett continues to give me the best advice I can get anywhere and I thank her for that.

I dedicate this book to the many families and friends who give me homes and anchorages whenever I need and want them. I thank Fida Adely, Abla Amawi, Sally Bland, Louise Cainkar, Jennifer Lindsay, Roberta Micallef, Amy Schmidt, and Jenny White for always going on adventures with me. The Lindsay-Janke, Adely-Haddad, Macdonald-Martin-Jones, and Micallef-Nilsson clans have all made me an honorary member of their families. It is wonderful to know that all these doors are open to me and that I seem to be able to stay as long as I want. Larry, Carol, and Mark, we lost our parents far too early but I am very glad I still have you on my side. To my parents, Joyce and Elroy Anderson, the person I am today is the person you encouraged me to be.

The American University of Beirut

1 | ADMINISTRATORS AND STUDENTS
Agency and the Educational Process

"The great value of education does not consist in the accepting this and that to be true but it consists in proving this and that to be true," declared Daniel Bliss, founder of Syrian Protestant College (SPC; 1866–1920) and its president from 1866 to 1902, in his farewell address.[1] President Howard Bliss (president, 1902–1920) said in his baccalaureate sermon in 1911, "In a word, the purpose of the College is not to produce singly or chiefly men who are doctors, men who are pharmacists, men who are merchants, men who are preachers, teachers, lawyers, editors, statesmen; but it is the purpose of the College to produce doctors who are *men*, pharmacists who are *men*, merchants who are *men*, preachers, teachers, lawyers, editors, statesmen who are *men*."[2] Bayard Dodge (1923–1948) stated at his inauguration as president of the newly renamed American University of Beirut (AUB; 1920–   ), "We do not attempt to force a student to absorb a definite quantity of knowledge, but we strive to teach him how to study. We do not pretend to give a complete course of instruction in four or five years, but rather to encourage the habit of study, as a foundation for an education as long as life itself."[3] The successors to these men picked up the same themes when they elaborated on the school's goals over the years; most recently, in May

2009, President Peter Dorman discussed his vision of AUB's role. "AUB thrives today in much different form than our missionary founders would have envisioned, but nonetheless—after all this time—it remains dedicated to the same ideal of producing enlightened and visionary leaders."[4]

In dozens of publications, SPC and AUB students have also asserted a vision of the transformative role the school should have on their lives. The longest surviving Arab society on campus, al-ʿUrwa al-Wuthqa, published a magazine of the same name during most academic years between 1923 and 1954 and as of 1936 stated as its editorial policy the belief that "the magazine's writing is synonymous with the Arab student struggle in the university."[5] From that point forward, the editors frequently listed the society's Arab nationalist goals. In the fall 1950 edition, for example, al-ʿUrwa al-Wuthqa's Committee on Broadcasting and Publications issued a statement identifying the achievement of Arab unity as the most important goal because "it is impossible to separate the history, literature and scientific inheritance of the Arabs" since "the Arab essence is unity."[6] Toward this end, al-ʿUrwa al-Wuthqa pledged to accelerate the "growth of the true nationalist spirit" among the students affiliated with the organization.[7] In describing education as an activist pursuit, the statement declares, "To achieve political ideas which are aimed at our nationalism it is necessary for we as students to seek information by many different means."[8] In this call, the AUB Arab students must take on the task of studying the Arab heritage as thoroughly and frankly as possible so that when they graduate they can move into society with solutions to the many problems plaguing the Arab world.

Since the school's founding in 1866, its campus has stood at a vital intersection between a rapidly changing American missionary and educational project to the Middle East and a dynamic quest for Arab national identity and empowerment. As the presidential quotes indicate, the Syrian Protestant College and the American University of Beirut imported American educational systems championing character building as their foremost goal. Proponents of these programs hewed to the belief that American educational systems were the perfect tools for encouraging students to reform themselves and improve their societies; the programs do not merely supply professional skills but educate the whole person. As the quotes from al-ʿUrwa al-Wuthqa attest, Arab society pressured the students to change as well. The Arab nahda, or awakening, of the late nineteenth and early twentieth centuries called on students to take pride in their Arab past and to work to recreate themselves as modern leaders of their society;

the Arab nationalist movement of the twentieth century asked that students take a lead in fighting for Arab independence from foreign control. The students streaming through the Main Gate year after year used both of these American and Arab elements to help make the school not only an American institution but also one *of* the Arab world and *of* Beirut, as the very name, the American University of Beirut, indicates.[9] This process saw long periods of accommodation between the American-led administration and the Arab students, but just as many eras when conflict raged over the nature of authority each should wield on campus; the changing relationship between the administration and the students serves as the cornerstone of this book, for it is here where much of the educational history of SPC and AUB has been written.

American Education

The American University of Beirut (AUB) is an institution of higher learning founded to provide excellence in education, to participate in the advancement of knowledge through research, and to serve the peoples of the Middle East and beyond. Chartered in New York State in 1863, the university bases its educational philosophy, standards, and practices on the American liberal arts model of higher education. The university believes deeply in and encourages freedom of thought and expression and seeks to foster tolerance and respect for diversity and dialogue. Graduates will be individuals committed to creative and critical thinking, life-long learning, personal integrity and civic responsibility, and leadership.[10]

The liberal educational system extolled in this April 2007 mission statement describes a program long in development on campus. In opening the school, Daniel Bliss and his colleagues pledged to unite together the teaching of the most modern of literature and science with a commitment to the principles and beliefs of Protestantism. In 1866, this combination did not pose difficulties; the schools after which Bliss modeled his program struggled to connect similar elements within what was considered the American classical educational program. While Harvard, Yale, Amherst, and other East Coast Protestant colleges did not seek to convert their students in the same way SPC hoped to do, they did teach a curriculum that enveloped all knowledge within Protestant denominational precepts. They believed in a unity of truth that taught students knowledge as a holistic concept; religious precepts confirmed science, the humanities, morality, and ethics. In this arena, Julie Reuben states, "the term *truth* encompassed all 'correct' knowledge; religious doctrines, common-sense beliefs, and scientific theories were all judged by the same cognitive standards. Religious truth was the most important and valuable form of knowledge because it gave meaning to mundane knowledge."[11] In combination with the extensive in loco parentis regulations imposed on every campus, the old-style American Protestant colleges enclosed students, mind, body, and soul, within the campus walls, within the school's religious theology, and within a curriculum circumscribing what the schools' leaders considered the only knowledge valid for higher education. Teaching within a unity of truth meant teaching for conformity. Students passed when they reproduced what they had been told; they excelled when they explained why something was true.

When Daniel Bliss opened his school, he followed the model of his colleagues back in America by establishing a fixed curriculum that left little room for debate, critique, or analysis; rather, professors taught students how to understand the truth proffered to them. Eschewing the Greek and Latin classics prevalent in American colleges of the day, Daniel substituted English and French, and delivered the whole program in Arabic. He required that all students, regardless of religious faith, attend Christian services and Bible study classes. The school converted almost no students, but the students were immersed in evangelical Christianity; no part of the curriculum contradicted the school's Christian precepts. As Bliss declared in his farewell address in 1902, "belief without knowledge may become a degrading, wicked superstition; with knowledge, it becomes a rational faith, soaring far above the knowledge from which it started in its upward flight."[12] Bliss did not attempt to compel religious conversion, but he did hope the students would embrace Jesus Christ as their role model.[13]

Difficulties arose, however, as changes bombarded the colleges back in America; in the second half of the nineteenth century, new scientific discoveries and pressures from the increasingly industrialized society forced schools to broaden their course offerings and rethink their pedagogical theories. New Land Grant universities opened in America after 1862, offering a mixture of professional and academic courses and serving as competition for the old-line Protestant colleges. To remain relevant in American society, the older colleges had to remold their structures and redesign their goals. What emerged was a new American liberal education system based not on teaching a fixed body of knowledge, but on the inculcation of the skills required to analyze data. The history of SPC and AUB reflects this pedagogical transition. When the school became the American University of Beirut in 1920, its Christian proselytizing mission officially ended; liberal education henceforth defined the fundamental aims of its program and served as the focal point for most of the debates and conflicts that occurred between the administration and the students throughout the rest of the twentieth century.

In liberal education, students succeed when they learn how to validate and produce knowledge on their own; the professor's job is to demonstrate the tools for doing so. As such, liberal education espouses methods for scholarly discovery, constructed in discussions of opposing viewpoints; an event may certainly have happened, but it can be examined from, for example, a Marxist or a gender perspective. The foundational notion that great men produce history starts to crumble when one begins to analyze how women or people whose names do not appear in the written record have influenced local or national events. Even scientific subjects requiring verifiable facts have techniques for generating new questions through discussion, analysis, and experimentation. As a 1945 Harvard University report summarized, the primary goal of liberal education is to teach students how to think; "by *effective thinking* we mean, in the first place, logical thinking: the ability to draw sound conclusions from premises."[14] In the words of the report, "The objective of education is not just knowledge of values but commitment to them, the embodiment of the ideal in one's actions, feelings, and thoughts, no less than an intellectual grasp of the ideal."[15] Students must be active participants in their own educational experience; in its new liberal iteration, education could no longer mean conformity.

To actuate the culture of free expression necessary for this new pedagogy, the course of the late nineteenth century saw American Protestant colleges officially break religious denominational bonds; once the parameters of truth had become unbound from religion, professors sought to teach their students the tools necessary for constructive debate, discussion, and critique. Potentially any topic could be tackled in the classroom provided the participants understood the rules of tolerance and respect needed to engage it. Even though the SPC religious requirements remained intact until the school changed its name and status in 1920, the school's offerings became increasingly secular under Howard Bliss's tenure. The new liberal educational program and its insistence on free inquiry meant that a religious ethos could no longer validate and bind knowledge together. SPC, as with its American counterparts, could no longer declare all knowledge compatible with Christian precepts.

To foster this classroom atmosphere, the goal of proselytizing for Protestantism at SPC transformed into one of proselytizing for modernity; throughout the course of the twentieth century, the leaders set "making men" as their primary conversion program. When women arrived on campus with coeducation in the 1920s, the discussion expanded to include the proper roles for women in modern society. This transition from religious conversion to a program of character building fit perfectly within the parameters of liberal education because the new program was premised on the belief that with freedom comes responsibility. Only men and women of superior character could truly understand the tasks they were undertaking in the educational realm. As a result, liberal education cohesively integrated tools for validating knowledge, aspirations for professional achievement, and lessons in character development. SPC and AUB delivered not just a curricular program but a comprehensive blueprint for living. In their writings, the Americans at the school made modernity and civilization tangible concepts, their elements universally recognizable, rankable, and unalterably Western. American prophets—President Abraham Lincoln, missionary leader John Mott, politician and orator William Jennings Bryan, oil magnate John D. Rockefeller, and the Blisses themselves—guided followers to what amounted to a successful and modern faith in American educational progress. These men's lives exemplified the honest, hard-working, and innovative skills necessary for success, the essential commandments of an SPC and AUB modernity. If students could live lives as these men had, imbued with strong Protestant American values, they would inevitably succeed, regardless of whether or not they signed on the dotted line of Protestantism. Historian Richard Hofstadter famously wrote that "the United States was the only country in the world that began with perfection and aspired to progress."[16] The Americans at SPC and AUB presented the school's curriculum as a perfect amalgamation of the American religious and educational structures; they tasked their students with understanding that education meant working for perpetual personal progress.

Arab Education and Activism

The opening of the school in 1866 coincided not only with the emergence of the American liberal education system but also with a pivotal moment in Arab and, more specifically, Syrian and Lebanese history.[17] The nine-teenth century had dawned in 1798 with Napoleon Bonaparte's occupa-tion of Egypt for three short years. A joint Anglo-Ottoman force defeated the French in 1801, but the invasion had the long-term effect of catalyz-ing action in both the Ottoman Empire and Egypt; the two governments hoped the introduction of westernizing reforms would forestall any such European incursions in the future.[18] The Ottoman sultans in Istanbul and Governor Muhammad Ali in Cairo trained new conscript peasant armies using European guidelines, opened Western-style schools for specialized military and professional training, and codified new secular laws follow-ing European models. The Ottoman Empire also instituted the Tanzimat reforms, which sought to break down the traditional millet system. In it, each of the many religious groups living in the empire had its own legal court. The sultans and their advisors hoped the Tanzimat reforms would equalize the legal status of the religious groups of the empire. By so doing, they envisioned the emergence of a new kind of Ottoman citizenship.

In neither region did these programs work as intended. The British occupied Egypt in 1882, and the French conquered much of the rest of Ottoman North Africa during the same period. The European powers militarily and economically infiltrated the Ottoman Empire during the course of the nineteenth century; World War I caused its final demise. The millet system was replaced not with a shared Ottomanism but with a fractured nationalist landscape. In Egypt, a protonationalism began to emerge among graduates of the new schools and recruits in the new military; by the 1870s, supporters had gathered behind Colonel Ahmad ʿUrabi's revolt against the authoritarianism of the Egyptian government. Thereafter, a vibrant Egyptian nationalist movement fought against Brit-ish rule. In the Ottoman Empire, national identities formed among all the ethnic groups, with the predominantly Christian Balkans region proving particularly contentious. The area that would become modern-day Syria and Lebanon in the twentieth century, and the birthplace for the majority of the students attending SPC and AUB, saw violence break out in the massacres between Muslims and Christians in the 1860 civil war. Muslims fought against what they felt were the disproportionate benefits accruing to Christians because of Ottoman reforms and European intervention; Christians struggled to gain an equality promised them by the Ottoman sultans but still elusive in practice.

In response to these atrocities, the societies and governments of Syria and Lebanon followed divergent national paths. In Damascus, the 1860 civil war catalyzed an intensified local and Ottoman effort to build schools and open up career opportunities for Muslims, matching the effort already begun among the Christian populations by foreign missionaries. Subsequently, young educated Arab Muslims and Christians formed the backbone of the *nahda*, an Arab nationalist and intellectual movement that began in the second half of the nineteenth century. Students of SPC and AUB became active members alongside colleagues educated in comparable institutions. In Mt. Lebanon, a system of political sectarianism rather than national cohesiveness emerged. A decade-long occupation by the Egyptian government that began in 1831, followed by the European and Ottoman decision to partition Mt. Lebanon into Christian and Druze Muslim sections, disrupted the power balance and helped catalyze the 1860 civil war.[19] Henceforth, Mt. Lebanon would receive special administrative status within the Ottoman Empire under the protection of European supervision. Religious affiliation would determine political access; the large numbers of religious groups represented in Mt. Lebanon translated into a dispersion of power to many different actors and agencies and little to the staff itself. In terms of AUB's existence in Beirut, this development limited governmental control over the school in Lebanon.[20] AUB's administrations have had to negotiate with the Ottoman, French, and Lebanese governments over the years concerning accreditation issues, but otherwise have experienced few real threats to the school's independent status.[21]

New national and sectarian identities in the Middle East could not have arisen without another of the unexpected consequences arising from the Ottoman and Egyptian reforms; out of the new institutions emerged a new elite stratum, a "bureaucratic bourgeoisie," to use Fatma Müge Göçek's term.[22] New types of schools not only provided the practical training this group needed as it forged new positions within the reforming states, but also helped its members gain a consciousness of their vanguard status in an era of rapid change. Prior to the onset of the nineteenth-century reforms, Selçuk Akşin Somel reports, "the educational aim of the pre-modern Islamic school system at the primary level was the inculcation of basic religious knowledge to students, particularly the learning of Qur'anic verses by heart," while at the next stage, in the *madrasas*, students extended their study of religion, taking courses in Arabic grammar, arithmetic, Qur'anic commentary, and Islamic philosophy.[23] For further religious study, a small number of students moved on to Islamic universities such as al-Azhar in Cairo; government schools in Istanbul provided specific skills training for future military leaders and civil servants. Little in this educational structure required students to produce knowledge for themselves; the focus at most levels was on the memorization of data already accredited by either religious or military scholars. Graduates funneled into preset occupational paths based on their educational experience. Once the Ottoman and Egyptian governments launched their westernizing reforms, these schools quickly proved inadequate for the training required for the many new positions created. Memorization of the Qur'an no longer served as sufficient primary education; students now needed advanced linguistic and scientific skills to gain access to the geography, mathematics, history, and military tactics so necessary for leading modern governments and armies.

In this pursuit, the Ottoman government allotted heavy resources to primary and secondary schools; in fact, Selim Deringil goes so far as to write that "in the second half of the nineteenth century the Ottoman Empire came into its own as an 'educator state' with a systematic programme of education/indoctrination for subjects it intended to mould into citizens."[24] The premier secondary school, the Galatasaray Lycée in Istanbul, once also known as the Mekteb-i Sultani, opened in 1868 and gradually became a twelve-year preparatory school.[25] Its curriculum followed the French lycée system, with courses on natural sciences, law, philosophy, and classical European languages taught in French. Arabic, Persian, and Ottoman Turkish literature; religion; Islamic and Ottoman history; geography; and calligraphy were taught in Turkish or the languages under study.[26] In 1909, the Mekteb-i Mülkiyye-i Şahane, originally the Imperial Civil Service School, became a special university faculty.[27] More generally, the Ottomans opened *idadiyye* schools, which provided three to seven years of secondary schooling for students in such cities as Damascus and Beirut.[28] The Ottoman state opened fifty-one secondary schools throughout the empire between 1882 and 1894.[29] The Ottomans also opened schools specifically designed to educate girls for the modern era, although at a slower rate than for the boys. At the private level, religious leaders and merchants established schools to educate their own constituencies in the new style. One of the most famous in the Arab world was the National School in Damascus, the Mekteb 'Anbar, which educated many members of the new Arab bourgeoisie in the nineteenth century. It became a *tajhiz* (preparatory school) in 1918, and, according to Philip Khoury, it served as "one of the principal centers of nationalist activity during the 1930s"; in addition to modern science and Western philosophy, "the history of the Arabs and their fundamental contributions to the progress of world civilization was taught in the most exacting national terms."[30]

State and private actors built up an impressive array of schools in Beirut in the second half of the nineteenth century, making the city a particularly active center for education and intellectual discourse and an ideal location for SPC and later AUB. Butrus al-Bustani, a Maronite Christian convert to Protestantism, opened al-Madrasa al-Wataniyah, the National School, in 1863, with the hopes of bringing all of Lebanon's religious groups under one educational umbrella.[31] In the first years of SPC's existence, al-Bustani's school served as its official preparatory school. The Ottomans established a branch of the Sultani Lycée (Mekteb-i Sultani) in 1883 and soon enrolled the sons of the most prominent and wealthy Beiruti families.[32] al-Madrasa al-ʿUthmaniyah, the Ottoman College, opened in 1895, providing a curriculum ranging from religious studies to introductions to astronomy and the natural sciences, all taught in Arabic.[33] Beginning in the late nineteenth century under the rubric of the Maqasid Islamic Benevolent Society, Sunni Muslim notables in Beirut organized a series of schools for boys and girls as "a modern Arabo-Islamic alternative to the mission schools."[34]

The problematic nature of the aims of the nineteenth-century Ottoman and Egyptian reform programs was reflected in the educational system. As Benjamin Fortna writes, "The late Ottoman state assigned education the conflicted task of attempting to ward off Western encroachment by adapting Western-style education to suit Ottoman needs."[35] Education of this type was built upon "the principle that education was inherently a powerful commodity, able to transform society either for good or bad, depending on whose education was being provided."[36] Furthermore, as Göçek explains, government leaders saw their schools as mechanisms of control over the students passing through the classroom. The Ottoman leadership hoped the educational experience would facilitate a blurring of the lines between the old religious millets and encourage the graduates to work together to aid the sultan in his reform efforts.

In fact, the opposite occurred for many of those so educated. As Göçek notes, "The main distinguishing trait of this bourgeoisie was its ability, for the first time, to wrest resources away from the sultan's control."[37] While Göçek is speaking specifically of the new bourgeoisie's relationship with the Ottoman sultan in Istanbul, her words also apply throughout the Arab provinces, as new students found they were not beholden to old feudal, tribal, and commercial leaders in the same way as in the past because of new job opportunities available to them. Mimicking Western curricular goals translated into a delegitimization of older forms of knowledge and with it expressions of loyalty to those who had been the purveyors of the older styles of intellectual authority. In all of the new schools, state and private donors followed much the same path that American education took in this era; their curriculum fractured the religious unity of truth that had dominated Middle Eastern schools for centuries. The graduates of these schools had skills few others had obtained; these skills in turn gave their owners leverage against the state and, in many cases, the traditional leaders, who no longer held the same level of influence in the Ottoman provinces. Given the proliferation of Western commercial and consular contacts, increasing numbers of graduates did not have to look to the state or to the old guilds or merchant houses as the proper realms for their careers; they now had many more opportunities completely disconnected from these agencies. Graduates could sell new products to the Europeans, work for European firms and consulates, and, with European loans, open their own silk or textile factories without resorting to the strict rules set down by the guilds. Even when graduates took government positions, their skills gave them a degree of independence their predecessors had not experienced. As a result of these opportunities, new educational institutions did not produce a united Ottoman citizenry but a bureaucratic bourgeoisie that sought opportunities wherever they could be found.

Foreign missionary activity in the Arab world both supplemented this local educational effort and accelerated its effects. Local agents followed the standards for modern education set by the missionaries; mission schools helped expand the ranks of the new bureaucratic bourgeoisie, particularly among the Christian populations of the region. Catholic missionaries had long worked throughout Mt. Lebanon; they extended their influence as the nineteenth century began. The American Board of Commissioners of Foreign Missions (ABCFM) set up a station in Lebanon in 1820, followed by the American Presbyterians in Egypt in 1854. The British Church Missionary Society (CMS) was established in Egypt in 1825, later spreading its mission to the Ottoman Arab provinces in the Eastern Mediterranean. The missionaries immediately introduced elementary schools and, by the 1840s, had opened secondary schools as well. In mid-century, the missionaries started founding colleges, with Robert College opening in Istanbul in 1863 under American aegis and the Université Saint-Joseph established in Beirut in 1875 by the Jesuits. Roderic Davison reports, "By the eve of World War I an unofficial count put French Catholic schools in the Ottoman Empire at 500, American schools at 675, British at 178. The French schools enrolled 59,414 students, the American schools 34,317, and the British 12,800," not to mention the smaller enrollments for German, Italian, Austro-Hungarian, and Russian schools.[38] Adding to these totals, American Presbyterian missionaries launched the American University in Cairo (AUC) in 1920.[39] The Beirut Female Seminary, founded in 1835, had evolved into the American Junior College for Women (AJCW) by 1927.

All these schools galvanized young Arab students and graduates to form the intellectual backbone of a nineteenth-century movement in the Arab world trying to articulate an empowered Arab identity. This Arab nahda challenged young Arabs to take pride in their historical and linguistic heritage while simultaneously preparing themselves for a modern world dominated by the West. As Albert Hourani says of the shared consciousness this Arab bureaucratic bourgeoisie espoused, "There is a new self awareness and, linked to it, a new and more active interest in the political process, a new concern to take part in the movement of change and determine its direction."[40] As enunciated in dozens of newspapers and journals published in Damascus, Beirut, and Cairo, Arab writers called on their brethren to reclaim their history and language as pivotal elements defining who they were. At the same time, European power could not be ignored; these writers grew up in a world infused with potent Western models. As a result, a contradiction of sorts lay at the foundation of the nahda; its proponents extolled the Arab past as the key to keeping Arabs together in the present while often elevating Western guides as the most influential for their futures.

A typical narrative trajectory produced by nahda writers took the Arabs from the pinnacle of civilizational success in the medieval period to a long fall into backwardness, ignorance, and servility under Ottoman rule.[41] The nineteenth-century exposure to Europe made them acknowledge their weaknesses and forced them to articulate solutions, often of Western origin, to the many problems weakening Arabs and the Arab world. In regard to the awakening many writers defined for this period in the Middle East, Reinhard Schulze states that the nahda "required a concept of cultural decadence, for how else was the claim to cultural renewal to be justified?"[42] Stephen Sheehi attributes what he calls the "obsession of Arab and non-Arab thinkers" with "failure" to the very definition of modernity used in the late nineteenth century.[43] In this iteration of "cultural decadence" and "failure," Arab writers explained that the encounter with the West had prompted the Arabs to realize that their society had fallen behind on the historical continuum; modernity itself required that there be a progression from backwardness to progress.[44] Nahda writers held to the belief that the

Arabs needed to find the correct mix between Arab historical pride and Western civilizational dynamism. Each writer balanced these competing forces differently, but all sought to write a prescription for building a successful Arab society for the future.

This was the era of the American self-made man, whose fictional narrators, as Tom Pendergast notes, "referred not to a static figure but to an entire narrative of becoming."[45] All over the Middle East, too, Arab writers provided guidelines for individual Arabs trying to determine who they ought to become given the Arab and Western models on display. As Elizabeth Kassab reports, "On the whole, Nahda thinkers were eager to grasp the secrets of progress, to understand what lay behind Europe's advancement and superiority in the hope of adopting it to their own societies" while also asking, "How was one to define Egyptian, Arab, or Muslim culture with respect to European culture?"[46] Keith Watenpaugh identifies a middle-class penchant in Aleppo for "being modern," as its claimants "incorporated into their daily lives and politics a collection of manners, mores, and tastes, and a corpus of ideas about the individual, gender, rationality, and authority actively derived from what they believed to be the cultural, social, and ideological praxis of the contemporary metropolitan Western middle classes."[47] Furthermore, "by being modern, its members declared their intention to take a preeminent role in the production of knowledge and culture, not just for themselves, but for society at large."[48] Beth Baron reports that the women's press in Egypt in this era, dominated by Syrian and Egyptian women, articulated an ethos for "improving the domestic environment"; in this iteration of a woman's proper role, "young girls had to be formally instructed in an age of science to run a home properly and raise children well, tasks that were no longer meant to be entrusted to others. Domestic work became professionalized with its own schools, texts, journals, and a jargon."[49] As a result of these articulations, Arab men and women writers of the nineteenth-century nahda generated a shared consciousness of the need for dynamic change within themselves and Arab society at large. They wrote guides for the modern leaders they felt they and their colleagues ought to become.

As the twentieth century dawned, the European powers increased their colonial encroachment throughout the Middle East, forcing Arabs to face yet another era of negotiation about their individual and national identities. The British and French had already colonized North Africa and Egypt prior to the end of the nineteenth century; after World War I, they divided up and colonized much of the rest of the region, arbitrarily handing out national identities without consideration for the relationships already existing in the Arab world. The West had for decades provided the guideposts for modernity; European civilization had dominated the imaginations of the young people going through schools like SPC. The new colonial realities after World War I diminished that appeal and forced the newly colonized to evaluate yet again the relationship between Arab and Western civilization.

During World War I, the quest for a new Arab identity took political form in the Arab Revolt Sharif Hussein and his son Faisal led against the Ottoman Turks.[50] Faisal and his Arab army liberated Damascus from the Ottoman forces in October 1918 and set up an Arab government there, but the colonial powers had different plans for the region. The British government had promised Hussein, in the Hussein-McMahon correspondence of 1915–1916, that an independent Arab government would arise if the Arab Revolt succeeded in defeating the Ottoman army. However vague the British may have been in their promise to Hussein, the end result came as a betrayal to the Arabs who had supported the revolt. Instead of an Arab state, Britain and France chose to colonize the Eastern Arab world, working under the aegis of the new League of Nations to establish colonial mandates.[51] French troops ousted Faisal from Damascus, captured the Syria mandate, and broke it up into provincial segments, following a divide-and-rule policy. Along the coast, France combined the old provinces of Mt. Lebanon and Beirut with areas to the north and south to create Greater Lebanon. Britain took the Palestine mandate and quickly divided it into two, with Palestine to the west of the River Jordan and Transjordan to the East. In Palestine, Britain applied the Balfour Declaration of November 2, 1917, promising the establishment of a Jewish homeland there. Britain united together the provinces of Basra, Baghdad, and Mosul to form the new country of Iraq, bringing Faisal in to serve as its new king. Britain and France both maintained their colonies in North Africa and Egypt.

Suddenly, by colonial fiat, Arabs became Lebanese, Jordanians, or Syrians, but those particular nations had no historical narratives, no flags, no anthems, and no unique ethnic, religious, or linguistic structures. No one in the new mandates had demanded that these political arrangements be made, but the interwar period saw the introduction of institutions associated solely with these new state structures. Despite the artificiality of these new areas, new state institutions did succeed in bringing people into the national projects during the mandate period; vested interests became indebted to these borders and institutions and so worked to solidify them. These borders have never been permanently erased and national identities have formed within them. Over the course of the twentieth century, new national definitions gradually differentiated Lebanese from Jordanians from Syrians.

Even as these new loyalties were slowly forming in the interwar period, the larger pan-national Arab identity did not disappear, but in fact became a potent tool of political opposition against the mandate governments. Activists in every country heaped approbation on local leaders who had agreed to work with the colonial powers and who, by so doing, maintained their power and wealth despite many calls for a more equal distribution of resources. Students served as particularly enthusiastic actors lobbying for Arab political unity as the best possible solution to the problems existing in all the new Arab states. Young people at schools like AUB and the newly founded Egyptian University (1908) and the University of Damascus (1923) joined political parties such as Hizb al-Istiqlal (Independence Party) and the League of National Action, calling for Arab unity to destroy the weaknesses wrought by colonial political divisions.[52] Arabs also became fervent proponents of Palestinian rights during the 1936–1939 Arab revolt in Palestine. Palestine, in this iteration, was a cause all Arabs should support because it was the beating heart of the Arab body; political divisiveness could only facilitate Zionist ambitions. In their writings, these young men and women envisioned a united Arab world that would harness its collective powers to alleviate poverty, break down the autocratic nature of governments, and force the Europeans and Zionists out of the Middle East.

When Egypt and the other Arab countries achieved political independence at the end of World War II, young activists attacked their governments for continuing their elitist policies and accused them of losing Palestine to the Israelis. Young and progressive leaders like Gamal Abdul Nasser of Egypt sparked passionate feeling when they mobilized their populations to support the political and socioeconomic revolutions they fronted.[53] The Baʿth Party of Michel Aflaq and Salah al-Bitar, as well as a series of Arab nationalist parties, articulated the intellectual rationale for replacing the separate countries with a united Arab nation.[54] All these leaders rallied their citizenry to support the recovery of Palestine and the continuing liberation battles being waged throughout North Africa, all of them articulated through the perspective of Arab nationalism. Educational systems expanded, and professional and technocratic job opportunities proliferated. Supplementing the universities already in existence,

Lebanese University (1951), Baghdad University (1957), and the University of Jordan (1962) provided new opportunities for higher education throughout the Arab world. Arab students all over the region enthusiastically protested on behalf of Nasser's policies and against those imposed by the West, with the United States slowly displacing Britain and France as the chief obstacle to Arab progress. People throughout the Arab world saw the 1950s as an exciting moment in history, when the Arab world could truly claim its independence. Fayez Sayegh, a political science professor at AUB in the 1960s, writes of the brief union of Egypt and Syria between 1958 and 1961:

> For the first time in centuries, *Arab forces* have now appeared on the stage of Arab life ready and able to remake Arab history. For the first time in many centuries, Arab leadership has asserted itself as the principal actor on the stage of Arab life, abandoning alike the observer's seat and the spectatorial role formerly assigned to it. No longer is Arab society content with reciting a script written by someone else, or with suffering meekly during a performance, supposedly its own but actually designed neither for its enjoyment nor for its edification. At long last, the Arabs have now emerged, in their own homeland, as the makers of their own history.[55]

This message could have been articulated ten or fifteen years earlier, for it expressed the young Arab desire for empowerment over Western imperialist policies and reactionary Arab governments.

When Israel occupied East Jerusalem, the West Bank, the Gaza Strip, the Sinai Peninsula, and Golan Heights in the June 1967 war, leftist students turned away from leaders like Gamal Abdul Nasser, who had fronted the Arab nationalist movement of the 1950s, but continued to maintain their enthusiasm for the Arab revolution he had promised. In this new phase, they looked instead to the Palestinian *fedayeen* groups now taking the lead in the fight to regain Palestine and foment the Arab revolution. The different Palestinian militia organizations—Fatah, the Popular Front for the Liberation of Palestine (PFLP), the Democratic Front for the Liberation of Palestine (DFLP), and others—took the lead in militarily attacking Israel. They did so from formal and informal bases in the surrounding Arab nations; in the process, they came into conflict with the Jordanian and Lebanese governments, which were opposed to such military exercises. They also gained enough credibility to take control over the Palestine Liberation Organization (PLO), founded in 1964 but dominated by Nasser until the 1967 defeat. University students all over the region, such as those at AUB, passionately supported the Palestinian efforts.

Student Agency

Generations of students at SPC and AUB brought these individual and Arab national identities on to campus as they negotiated their relationship with the school's administration. Year after year, they embraced the school's programs; while doing so, however, they never served as passive actors, imbibing unconditionally the educational programs proffered to them. As at any educational institution, students do not participate in most of the discussions about the curricular program. However, throughout the long history of university life around the world, students have demanded of their administrators that they receive the right to engage with the educational process and its decision-making bodies.[56] In these instances, students have seen discrete successes over the short term but much larger gains over the long term. As Philip Altbach explains, "There is often a tendency to judge student movements on the basis of the direct impact that students have. But this is too simplistic; the impact of student activism is often less direct and less immediately visible. Students might contribute an idea that does not yield results until years later."[57] Altbach points to student success in breaking down in loco parentis regulations on American campuses by the 1950s and early 1960s as one example. Furthermore, "As students mature, they frequently bring some of the values and orientations learned on campus to the broader society. It is virtually impossible to quantify these less dramatic trends, but they are nonetheless quite important in assessing the impact of student activism."[58] Students may be the consumers of a product constructed by others but only they can gauge the success of the programs thus enunciated, only they can determine whether the administrative aspirations for them have been met.

In the case of SPC and AUB, the students extolled the freedom of thought and expression so integral to the American conception of the educational program; they also enthusiastically used the tools acquired in the classroom to analyze their own shifting society. In just one exemplary quote, Munif al-Razzaz could report of his experience as a student in the 1930s:

> Our minds were opened, but not only by reading books and articles.
> This was a cultured air . . . [and the encouragement of] participation in
> all elements of life, things not obtainable in the classroom alone. There
> was an air of discussion, in all possible discussions, and in all world top-
> ics. What we understood and what we did not understand, the inter-
> change between all types of study and specialties and the interchange
> between students from most areas of the eastern Arab world, with some
> inoculation of foreign students. . . . All of that left in myself a new
> influence. It took my life and ideas and my mind into a new direction,
> similar to what happened to many of the other students.[59]

The educational project of SPC and AUB encouraged such intellectual
exploration as the only viable path for individual educational attainment.
From their first protest in 1882, students took the lesson of active participation presented to them in the classroom and catalyzed the transformation
of their relationship with the school's authority figures; they wrote their
own educational coda on the pillars the school's leaders built. Students did
so in petitions during the Darwin Affair of 1882 and the Muslim Controversy of 1909, in their own magazines as of 1899, and then as they took their
debates into West Hall, the Milk Bar, and Faisal's Restaurant throughout
the twentieth century.[60]

For many years, the school's American leaders posited that the pri-
mary reason for opening the school was to impart their superior culture to
a group of students in desperate need of their enlightenment. As Ussama
Makdisi writes, the American missionaries arrived in the area in 1820 with
a preconceived notion of a chasm "between an advanced, tolerant 'Judeo-
Christian West' and its intolerant Islamic antithesis."[61] Makdisi notes,
"The idea of American missionaries as pioneers required that the Ottoman
Empire be seen as an extension of the fabled American frontier, a semi-
barbarous landscape in need of colonization and enlightenment by rugged
'American' individualism, liberal education, and above all religious toleration."[62] Presidential speeches and writings indicate that this vision of the
dichotomy between East and West flourished at the school and survived
well into the twentieth century. For example, SPC president Howard Bliss
said of the Syrians at the Paris Peace Conference in 1919,

> They are intelligent, able, hospitable and lovable, but, together with
> the sure defects of a long oppressed race—timidity, love of flattery,
> indirectness—they also have the defects of a people who are face to

face with the results of civilization without having passed through the processes of civilization. They lack balance; they are easily discouraged; they lack political fairness, they do not easily recognize the limitations of their own rights. They must therefore be approached with sympathy, firmness and patience. They are capable of nobly responding to the right appeal, and they will grow into capacity for self determination and independence.[63]

Given these impressions, the early presidents of SPC and AUB frequently expressed their hope that the school's graduates would become student missionaries, spreading the Protestant American civilizational template to their own backward societies.

The students initially accepted this civilizational construct; between 1899 and the mid-1930s, students wrote their own narratives of modernity, building on both the civilizational template disseminated by the Americans on campus and the Arab writers of the nahda. Their focus was on the Western traits they, as modern men and women, should acquire. In their publications, they debated the characteristics of masculine and feminine modernity, seeking out the path to progress so many of their colleagues outside the Main Gate likewise sought. The students looked to the American leaders of the school as unique authorities over the proper blueprint for modernity. With a reenergized Arab nationalism guiding them by the 1930s, the students still sought out character transformation but no longer favored the old Western models; they increasingly emulated heroes from their own society. By the 1950s, students pushed to have Arab political and national identity become part of their educational experience. As a result of this long negotiation between the administration and the students, the school still models the American liberal educational structure, but it has become an Arab institution as well.

In 1866, all the students enrolled at SPC came from Ottoman-controlled Syria (the modern states of Syria and Lebanon). Students from the area officially designated as Lebanon after 1920 have comprised the largest individual group of nationals on campus in any given year, usually representing between 40 to 50 percent of all students. Syrians, as a separate category, have typically made up about 10 to 15 percent of the student body.[64] Egyptians registered as about 19 percent of the students in 1904–1905, but gradually dropped in number thereafter.[65] By the 1950s, Egyptian students accounted for only about 1 percent of the student body, in large part due to the increase in higher education opportunities in Egypt as well as a strong

Egyptian nationalist ethos which encouraged students to study at home.[66] Palestinians gradually took the second spot, increasing their enrollments from 11.3 percent in the 1920–1921 academic year to an average of 29 percent in the 1930s. In the 1950s, Palestinians and Jordanians together accounted for 22 percent of the student body.[67]

The dominant student discourse throughout the school's life has been pan-Arab, reflecting the Arab origins of most students and the intellectual milieu which evolved over the course of the school's existence. When students wrote about how they wanted to be transformed by their educational experience, they generally spoke of themselves as individuals or as Arabs. The longest running organization representing the Lebanese students was Rabita, the Lebanese Student League, founded after the 1958 Lebanese crisis and functioning on campus through the 1970s.[68] Even with this organization and the large numbers of Lebanese citizens represented on campus, Lebanese concerns never held much sway in the campus space until the outbreak of the Lebanese civil war (1975–1989).[69] When specifically national issues came to the forefront, particularly those related to Palestine from the 1930s forward, or those related to Gamal Abdul Nasser in Egypt starting in the 1950s, the call to aid their causes came wrapped up as an Arab one. The Americans encouraged the construction of a space of tolerance for all religious and national groups represented on campus; liberal education necessitated breaking down any such barriers that might impede freedom of speech and discussion. Elie Salam ('50) said of the school in his era, "It was a very exciting period and we all came from [a] very provincial background, all the students at AUB. The good thing about AUB is that for the first time a Christian Orthodox from this area meets a Sunni Palestinian or a Sunni Beiruti or an Iraqi and they are all searching for their identity and for their dreams, and so it was a very intense acculturation period for the students at AUB."[70] The students turned this situation into a space where Arabness diluted the differences between students; Arabness recognized common problems and solutions for the Arab world as a whole. The students, as Arabs, wrote about the need to gain the education necessary for leading their countries to independence and political unification. As a result, when examining the most common political positions in the nineteenth and twentieth centuries, students wrote most frequently as Arabs, not as Lebanese, Syrians, Palestinians, or Egyptians.

University Writings and Writers

Between 1866 and 1920, the faculty and the administration were one and the same; after that point, when the administration began to take on a separate corporate identity, individual faculty members holding positions within the administration spoke in the name of that administration in all formal university documents and statements. Individual faculty members have left few of their views about the school, the administration, or the students in the written record.[71] As a result, this book primarily addresses the relationship between the administration and the student body, for only their voices provide sufficient coverage for analysis. In this book, the terms *administration* and *leaders* designate the dominant ideology emanating from the administration at any moment in the period under study, by definition reflecting the opinions of the faculty members who chose to accept administrative posts. Only those students who put names to bylines, held student office, wrote memoirs, recorded interviews, or are otherwise readily recognizable have been identified by name in this book. Over the years, student publications queried many a student about his or her opinion; those students have not been individually singled out in this text. Memoirs and oral interviews have been used sparingly because they tell the story of the school with the benefit of hindsight, not contemporaneously. Examining the evolution of the educational process requires an analysis of its elements as they were taking place, not as graduates think back and reminisce about their school days. With these considerations in mind, throughout this book the term *students* applies to the most active and prolific of the writers, political leaders, and demonstrators on campus, while also denoting large and often majority support for the ideas they expressed. Most of the book examines the realm that began as the Literary Department, became the Collegiate Department, and is now the Faculty of Arts and Sciences, because the school's core pedagogical elements developed there.

To analyze the prevailing administrative opinions, this study investigates the many presidential speeches archived at the school. The speeches cited at the beginning of this chapter are useful and necessary because they spell out the meta-narrative of the school's identity. These statements encapsulate the public persona of the institution and provide a framework for the gradual and smaller changes that occurred on campus year to year. In the case of SPC and AUB, they posit the need for students to be holistically transformed by the school's program, guided by Protestant and American educational models and their progenitors on campus. In these statements, the presidents articulate what they hope the school will bestow upon its students.

Faculty meetings, presidents' reports, letters to the board of trustees in New York, course catalogues, and the alumni journal *al-Kulliyah* lay out the actual process by which SPC and AUB shifted its program from proselytizing for Christianity to proselytizing for an American template for modernity, transitioning from the remnants of the classical American educational system to one based in liberal education.[72] These documents illustrate how these developments took place and focus on such decisions as those that expanded elective offerings and established separate departments for each discipline. These decisions, while small in and of themselves, allowed for the teaching of new tools for validating many truths rather than the understanding of one; they created the liberal education system when they opened many legitimate gateways to knowledge. These sources also lay out a picture of the ongoing and changing relationship between the administration and the students, because every major event on campus makes an appearance in these texts. Under Daniel Bliss, discussion of the intersection of religion and science in the Darwin Affair appears alongside lists of the many punishments meted out for students breaking curfew and climbing over the walls. Under Howard Bliss, during whose tenure Muslim and Jewish students walked out of chapel and Bible classes in spring 1909, these documents illustrate the search for the basal elements of the school's educational program. Under Bayard Dodge, speeches lay out the man the students ought to become as a result of their AUB experience. And under Samuel B. Kirkwood (1965–1976), annual reports detail the many moments of student rebellion. In general, these documents are aspirational rather than expositional in that they outline the programs the authors hope will enhance the educational experience for the students; they do not illuminate how the students actually responded.

For sources on student opinions, the school's archives contain dozens of publications. Students published a magazine or newspaper for part of almost every year between 1899 and 2010, failing to do so only in the years 1918, 1921, 1922, 1947, 1948, and between 1974 and 1997. From 1899 to 1932, students—individually, in small groups, through the venue of student societies, and as class assignments—issued handwritten and then typewritten magazines. In 1906 alone, the students published sixteen different papers, the largest output in any given year of the school's existence. The longest running magazine of this era was the *Students' Union Gazette*, published by the elected Students' Union and issued irregularly between 1912 and

1932.[73] The *Union* had as its aim "the cultivation and development of public speaking and parliamentary discipline among its members."[74] The earliest of these papers were in Arabic, but increasingly appeared in English; a small number of editors chose to publish in French or Armenian. Several papers combine two or more languages. Christians began this era comprising almost 90 percent of the student body; they ended the period representing about 50 percent of it.[75] Because of their dominance on campus in this era, Christians make up the largest group of identifiable authors of these early student magazines. Students typically produced two copies of each issue, with one copy left at the library and one available for distribution among the student body.[76] The AUB archives contain very few complete runs of these early publications because many have been lost to time; however, in total, the library collection includes issues from sixty-three separate student magazines published between 1899 and 1932. From 1933 to 1946, students issued *al-Kulliyah Review*; the Arabic Society, al-ʿUrwa al-Wuthqa, published its own magazine from 1923 to 1930 and again from 1936 to 1954; from 1949 to 1974, *Outlook* served as the primary student newspaper, with the Civic Welfare League (CWL) contributing *Focus* from 1952 to 1965.[77] *Outlook* reappeared in 1997, filling a campus publishing gap left empty since 1974.

Faculty advisors supervised all of the student magazines and newspapers, but this does not negate the student agency displayed within them. Student writers used these papers to articulate their views of the school and the role they hoped to play in the dynamic world outside the Main Gate. Between 1899 and 1932, faculty censors could not have persuaded the students to be so effusive about SPC and AUB aspirations for them if the students had not ascribed to the same ideas. The years of constant attack against the school's administration in the pages of *Outlook* could not have occurred if faculty censorship had weighed too heavily on the paper. If the faculty had dictated the goals of these papers, the students would not have been so enthusiastic in using them as an outlet for articulating their political, national, and educational identities. Further, the students did not produce narratives marginalized from the larger debates developing outside the school's confines. Students found affirmation for their analyses in the newspapers published throughout the region, many of which treated the quest for modernity and national identity just as the students were doing. Faculty censors assuredly played a role in these papers, but the world which the writers produced for their readers comes primarily from the pen of the students. Since 1899, these student writers have offered a cohesive written narrative of the issues affecting their academic lives by laying out guidelines for their own individual and group ambitions. Their goals frequently matched those set by the administration, but the students just as often wrote narratives of their futures independent of those mapped out by the school's leaders. As a result, the students present themselves as strong voices of authority concerning the educational experience they were imbibing and also, in their minds, constructing. Empowered by the school's educational programs and their own Arab concerns, they demanded that they be accorded respect as equal citizens of the institution. As these student publications show, students have for a century and a half forged their own way of fulfilling the motto emblazoned across the Main Gate: "That they may have life and have it more abundantly".[78]

Conclusion

In 2009, President Dorman said of the school, "Although it's possible—superficially—to view AUB as a collection of buildings and people and classes and research labs, it is in essence a series of dialogues, relationships, and interactions."[79] This book examines these "dialogues, relationships, and interactions" to show how they influenced the evolution of the school's educational program; embedded in this story is the evolving debate about the nature of authority wielded by American and Arab interlocutors on campus and off. In the long periods of accommodation between the administration and the students, as well as the relatively short periods of conflict, all the actors generated change in the educational programs at SPC and AUB. Study of the school's educational history proves how adaptable the school's pedagogical focus has been. Alterations in American education shifted SPC from classical to liberal education; changes within Arab political and intellectual spheres forced AUB to become an institution perfectly fitted for Beirut. Administrative and student voices helped make these transitions take place.

THE UNITY OF TRUTH
Classical and Liberal Educational Systems

The first prospectus written for the future Syrian Protestant College (SPC) declared that the school would be "conducted on strictly christian [*sic*] and evangelical principles"; its 1871 catalogue confirmed, "This college was established in order to provide for Syria and its surrounding areas higher education in the mathematical and literary sciences and that it would be in their language."[1] The school's leaders registered the program with the state of New York under "An Act for the Incorporation of Benevolent, Charitable, Scientific, and Missionary Societies."[2] As per the original documents, a board of trustees was set up in New York while a local board of managers helped supervise the campus in Beirut. The former still exists today; the latter was dissolved in 1902, when the trustees determined that communications improvements had eliminated the need for it.[3] On November 18, 1920, fifty-four years after the school had opened its doors in 1866, the Regents of the University of the State of New York amended the charter of the Syrian Protestant College, renaming it the American University of Beirut (AUB). On February 4, 1921, the school held an assembly to inaugurate its new name. The alumni journal *al-Kulliyah* quoted Philip Hitti, recently returned from America with a PhD in Semitic languages from

Columbia University and ready to take up a teaching post at his alma mater, as saying that for him, this day marked the end of a fifty-year "theory of education as mere mental discipline" in favor of an educational ideal that saw the teacher as "an original investigator of truth" and the student seeking "creative, scientific scholarship for social service."[4] In a few short words, Hitti managed to identify the pedagogical differences between the American classical and liberal educational programs.

Amherst College, as well as Harvard, Yale, and Columbia Universities, served as the primary ideological ancestors for the school's changing educational structure. The most direct lineage comes through Amherst College, which graduated Presidents Daniel (1866–1902) and Howard (1902–1920) Bliss, in 1852 and 1882, respectively, as well as many of the school's early faculty. Daniel Bliss, in preparing the first program for SPC in 1862, wrote to W. S. Tyler, his old Amherst professor, "If the Institution is favored of God & of man it *shall be* the Amherst—or the Yale of the Orient."[5] Amherst College serves as a case study for the changes taking place more widely within American Protestant higher education, as well as at SPC; every major tradition and innovation came up for debate within its walls while the Blisses and their colleagues attended and led classes there, and each new arrival at SPC and AUB carried the resulting pedagogical elements to Beirut. The SPC founders and early faculty did not, by and large, graduate from Harvard or Yale, but their alma maters accepted these schools' leadership over educational developments. All of these schools entered the nineteenth century offering a classical curriculum framed by a belief in the unity of truth; they entered the twentieth century in the midst of a shift to a liberal educational program that encouraged students to analyze data rather than memorize and recite it. All but Amherst had become universities, with all the offerings associated with such institutions. AUB followed a similar trajectory as it shifted from a missionary college to a secular university and as it came to exalt freedom of inquiry over the Christian ideal.

In the process of adopting liberal education as their standard, these universities also developed a new Western civilizational template as the foundation for teaching students how to take on the task of thinking and analyzing for themselves. As enunciated in Columbia University's contemporary civilization program, the prototypical program of its kind, study of the great books of Western literature and history actuated students' analytical skills. The program delineated the general knowledge necessary for anyone educated in the American higher education system, providing them with the information and skills essential for continuing into more specialized or professional studies. The basic structure called for American colleges and universities to supply a general, or liberal, education to their students in the first years of study, in preparation for more advanced studies in the final years. AUB moved gradually in this pedagogical direction, beginning in the 1904–1905 academic year and culminating in the years between 1950 and 1952, with the establishment of a two-year general education requirement modeled after the civilizational coda of the Columbia program.

Classical to Liberal Education

The classical curriculum taught at Harvard and Yale at the dawn of the nineteenth century focused on a close reading of Latin and Greek; educators believed that only through a study of these languages could students learn the mental discipline to apprehend the truth. In a very practical way, this truth translated into a prescribed curriculum heavily weighted to the study of classical languages and literatures, with students judged and ranked based on their ability to accurately recite the information proffered to them in class and text. Memorizing the elements of truth meant learning how to shine the light on them, not to question them. As an example of one such classical curriculum in 1852, the year Daniel Bliss graduated from Amherst College, students gained admittance to the school upon fulfilling the following requirements: "Candidates for admission to the Freshman Class are examined in the Grammar of the Latin and Greek languages, Virgil, Cicero's Select Orations, Sallust or Cæsar's Commentaries, Writing of Latin, Jacob's, Colton's, or Felton's Greek Reader or an equivalent, English Grammar, Arithmetic, and Algebra through Simple Equations."[6] These topics dominated the preparatory schools in exactly the same way they did the colleges. Upon admission, roughly half of each semester was taken up with studies of ancient Greek and Latin, with the other half devoted to topics such as algebra, calculus, geometry, English grammar, rhetoric, and zoology, with an option to take French or German. As the authors of the seminal Yale Report of 1828 explained of the goals of college education in this era, "The two great points to be gained in intellectual culture, are the *discipline* and the *furniture* of the mind; expanding its powers, and storing it with knowledge."[7] Study of the classics remained the centerpiece of this type of program because "familiarity with the Greek and Roman writers is especially adapted to form the taste, and to discipline the mind, both in thought and diction, to the relish of what is elevated, chaste, and simple."[8]

Professors tested students primarily through oral declamations and, in fewer cases, by written translations of texts or through oral debates. The declamation, or recitation, "was not a discussion group in the twentieth-century sense; it was utterly alien to the spirit of Socratic byplay. Rather it was an oral quiz, nearly an hour in length, held five times per week throughout the academic year."[9] To give an example of the process occurring within just one field of study, George Callcott reports that "in 1807 the typical history textbook still called for every student '*to commit all the historical facts to memory* and at the end of every section to repeat the whole of what has been learnt,' and as late as 1840 another called for the student to recite 'exactly in the language of the textbook.'"[10] In terms of any kind of vocational training, this curricular structure aimed at preparing students for work in the local ministry or the overseas mission. For those students eschewing the religious life, a college education failed to provide any particular guidance or help besides general training to be an educated gentleman. Schooling meant conforming to a prescribed norm, in terms of both the curriculum taught and the in loco parentis regulations enforced.

The Amherst curriculum of Bliss's final year exhibits a few of the innovations then current in American academia, for it was only in the previous quarter century that Greek had gained equality with Latin and schools had begun to offer electives to the students, however minimal. Roger Geiger explains that in the Yale Report, "the study of Greek was rehabilitated and broadened beyond the New Testament to Greek literature; and both Latin and Greek literature were extended into the junior and senior years."[11] Bringing ancient literature into the classroom was itself an innovation, for the older classical curriculum had focused solely on the languages themselves. Concomitantly, new pedagogies entered the classrooms alongside the new emphasis on literature. "The masterpieces of Greek and Roman literature, once presented as little more than a series of pegs on which to hang grammatical rules, now came alive in the minds and hearts of many students."[12] The new structure "involved the thorough study of Greco-Roman culture in order to place the students' classical reading into its proper historical context, to motivate them to greater diligence in their linguistic study, and, most important, to infuse them with the very 'spirit of Greece and Rome.'"[13]

The basic elements of the classical curricular structure survived into the mid-nineteenth century largely intact, but new American realities bombarded university leaders thereafter. Laurence Veysey notes that a wholesale revolution occurred in American education between 1860 and 1900: "The complexity of the university made the former college seem a boys' school in contrast."[14] In 1862, the United States Congress passed the Morrill Land Grant Act, which established state-run public universities. At the same time, prodded by professors who had studied in German research universities, American colleges evolving into universities in the latter half of the nineteenth century began introducing German research methods and agendas, accepting the idea that higher education was not designed solely to impart knowledge but also to produce it. No longer could college leaders legitimately tell students that they held ownership over the only viable knowledge base; no longer could knowledge gatekeepers keep up with the new research being produced all around them. Thus, as Protestant colleges entered the twentieth century, they faced significant challenges. Scientific innovation, industrialization, American imperial expansion, and competition from new kinds of state universities had shattered the unity of truth espoused by Protestant colleges and invalidated the classical system of education that had reigned supreme in America.

Scientific research of all kinds challenged the pedagogies attendant to the unity of truth; new innovations called on professors and students alike to be active participants in the new research project. "The recognition that knowledge itself was fallible and progressive cast doubt on the legitimacy of venerable doctrines," Jon Roberts and James Turner report, and "colleges and universities became identified as institutions imbued with the faith that the only knowledge really worth having is obtainable through rational, 'scientific' inquiry."[15] Professors and students could not, as in the past, merely observe and record natural phenomena; they must experiment with the phenomena in order to find new ways to analyze knowledge in their classrooms. The work of Charles Darwin serves as an apt example of how scientific research and pedagogy changed in the American classroom in the second half of the nineteenth century. Alongside the publication of Darwin's *On the Origin of Species by Means of Natural Selection* in 1859, a number of scientists had begun to investigate issues that eventually came under the rubric of evolution and the theory of transmutation. Jon Roberts states that while it is impossible to determine exact numbers of opponents and supporters, or even of ascertaining the theological beliefs that were most likely used to support one side or the other, "in the short period between 1875 and 1880, most religious intellectuals came to realize that scientists had rendered a clear verdict in favor of the theory of organic evolution," even if many remained skeptical of Darwin's particular theory about it.[16] Almost by definition, the professors tackling this contentious topic could not rely on the older pedagogical methods of memorization and recitation because an understanding of evolution, as well as the expanding field of scientific research, demanded that followers approach the data and the processes involved with an activist eye. Scientists of the era drew, as Roberts and Turner report, "on the post-Darwinian view of intelligence as active and functional to emphasize the 'aggressive dynamic,' and experimental aspects of scientific investigation."[17]

The example of Amherst College demonstrates the uneven and uneasy adoption of new analytical and scientific concepts on college campuses in the second half of the nineteenth century. President Edward Hitchcock (1845–1854) embodies the older generation, which saw science fitting neatly within theological confines. He taught geology during Daniel Bliss's residency on campus as "a vehicle for religious instruction." Thomas Le Duc notes that "the enslavement to theology demanded a logic that would fit observed evidence into a fore-ordained scheme."[18] In these types of courses, professors such as Hitchcock posited that no research would ever upset the divine inspiration for nature. Instead, as Julie Reuben comments, "natural theology assumed that knowledge derived from the study of nature helped people live moral lives"; no scientific research could overturn God's truth because God had created it all.[19] Neither William Augustus Stearns (1854–1876) nor Julius H. Seelye (1876–1890), Hitchcock's two immediate successors, approved of Darwin's ideas.[20] Seelye even published *A Criticism of the Development Hypothesis, as Held by Charles Darwin, Thomas Henry Huxley, Alfred Russel Wallace, Herbert Spencer, and the New School of Naturalists* in 1888.[21] However, both presidents also believed in academic freedom of thought, and so allowed professors under their charge to teach the topics they preferred. By the time Howard Bliss attended Amherst, at least two professors, Benjamin K. Emerson (1870–1932) and John Mason Tyler (1879–1929), had already introduced their students to the study of evolution.[22] The prospectus for Tyler's course reads, "The course in Biology, as formerly, will comprise a study of the development of the animal kingdom from the lower forms up to man."[23] This introduction of biological evolution did not translate into an immediate and wholesale change throughout the Amherst science curriculum, however. In fact, professors of other sciences at Amherst, especially of chemistry, physics, and astronomy, typically "retained a purely descriptive approach, partly vocational, and vaguely disciplined."[24]

comparatively sheltered college world, freedom is dangerous for the infirm of purpose, and destructive for the vicious; but it is the only atmosphere in which the well-disposed and resolute can develop their strength."[37] To institutionalize this educational philosophy, Eliot expanded the elective system to unprecedented levels and abolished most elements of the in loco parentis program previously dominating student lives. By the second half of the nineteenth century, Harvard imposed virtually no requirements on the students; they could build their own programs with few restraints.[38] Students needed to learn how to govern themselves so that they could truly understand the responsibilities attendant to freedom; that kind of person would be Eliot's lifelong searcher and a good future citizen of his nation.[39]

This process of educational reinvention necessarily involved breaking the Protestant denominational bonds that had dominated the university space throughout American history. Gradually, over the course of the late nineteenth and early twentieth centuries, Protestant universities eliminated their obligatory religious requirements, transferred faith-based activities into voluntary religious associations, and invalidated religion as a framework for enveloping knowledge. Knowledge no longer came packaged within a religious paradigm; religion became just another branch of study. Elective offerings allowed students to construct their own educational programs, unconstrained by the old prescribed curriculum. In essence, these reforms instituted a separation of church and state on most previously Protestant university campuses.

Amidst the ideological chaos, university leaders refused to completely abandon the concept of a unity of truth. A possible new path for this project appeared in the form of Western history. If in the past the classical world validated the religious present, the late nineteenth century saw American academics seeking a Western civilizational rationale for their country's modern success. For example, by the 1880s and 1890s, the academics writing such histories "shared their civilization's faith in progress and pride in the relative merits of their own generation"; "history was viewed as a vast panorama of human events which would be looked down upon from the heights of the nineteenth century and seen in its true perspective."[40] James Harvey Robinson, history professor at Columbia University, wrote the most widely read European history text of the day; in *An Introduction to the History of Western Europe*, he traced a continuous line of progress leading up to the mid-nineteenth century. Martin Luther's act of protest inaugurated "a fundamental revolution in many of the habits and customs of the people"; the reign of King James I of England gave the world the work of

William Shakespeare, "generally admitted to have been the greatest dramatist the world has ever produced"; Voltaire inculcated free criticism by waging a "relentless attack upon the most venerable, probably the most powerful, institution in France, the Roman Catholic church"; "The French Revolution, in the truest sense of the term, was a great and permanent reform" because the humblest peasant recognized that the "institutions in the midst of which he lived appeared to him to be *abuses*, contrary to reason and humanity"; and the Declaration of the Rights of Man opposed the "crying evil of long standing against which the people wished to be forever protected."[41] History professors at SPC adopted this textbook in the 1906–1907 academic year and used it for many years afterward.

Over time, this historical narrative formed the cornerstone of a new holistic pedagogy that brought the literary, military, political, and historical elements of Western success together. Columbia University produced the prototypical program in its freshman contemporary civilization class. It rejected both the previous American focus on education based on the Greek and Latin classics and a recent call for teaching solely in the professional fields. Instead, as history professor Harry J. Carman declared, "In introducing the general survey course, Columbia has operated on the assumption that it is not the fundamental business of the College to turn out specialists in a narrow field, and that an individual is, after all, not well educated unless he or she has at least some conception of the broad field of intellectual endeavor."[42] In an internal memo written during the preparatory phase, Dean Herbert E. Hawkes observed, "The underlying purpose of the course is to make the students citizens who can participate in national affairs with clear judgment and intelligence."[43] The great books of Western civilization were used as a means for laying out why that civilization had achieved such success by the twentieth century. Over the following decades, course requirements expanded to two years in order to include literature humanities, music humanities, and art humanities, and more of a world civilizational truth, rather than a merely Western one, cohered within the program. This decision solidified what the Yale Report of 1828 had recommended almost one hundred years earlier; its writers had suggested that an American college education delineate a general civilizational and intellectual program for the early undergraduate years in preparation for the more focused and specialized training at the higher and graduate levels.

The President's Commission on Higher Education for Democracy of 1947 summarized the consensus American education had reached by the mid-twentieth century, saying that "general education should give to the

students the values, attitudes, knowledge, and skills that will equip him
to live rightly and well in a free society. It should enable him to identify,
interpret, select, and build into his own life those components of his cultural heritage that contribute richly to understanding and appreciation of
the world in which he lives."[44] Teaching students to think, and to think
with an open mind and critical eye, gives them the potential to be the
innovative searchers of knowledge that Charles Eliot desired to inspire.

Education at the Syrian Protestant College

Daniel Bliss arrived in Beirut in 1856 as a missionary for the American
Board of Commissioners for Foreign Missions (ABCFM); he joined colleagues already in Syria trying to bring the light of evangelical Protestantism to the Muslims and "nominal" Christians of the Middle East.[45] In the
decades after the first American missionaries arrived in Syria in 1820, they
and their successors applied the majority of their resources to educational
endeavors because the more direct proselytizing efforts, such as distribut-
ing the Bible and preaching the Gospel, had achieved little success. When
the schools also failed to produce many converts, Rufus Anderson, corresponding secretary for the ABCFM, voiced opposition to these tactics.
In 1844 and 1856, he made tours of the Syria field and, upon returning to
Boston, wrote in 1844, "I never so much felt the incomparable importance
and value of the DIRECT AND FORMAL PREACHING OF THE
GOSPEL, as during my residence among these missions. No other means,
comparatively speaking, seem to have spiritual power, except in connection with this; and all others should be kept in strict subordination to it."[46]
In the Andersonian view of the missionary project, schools were useful
only if they served as zones for direct proselytizing and if the curricula
included only those subjects necessary for training future Protestant pas-
tors.[47] Anderson also stressed the necessity of teaching and preaching in
the native language. He derided efforts to use the English language for
conversion; the result, he said, "was to make them foreign in their manners, foreign in their habits, foreign in their sympathies; in other words,
to denationalize them."[48] This opinion resulted in decreased funding for
the American missionary enterprise in Syria, just at that moment when
a post-1860 Syria demanded new educational opportunities. The opening
of the Syrian Protestant College in Beirut signified a rebellion against
Anderson's policies in that its founders purposely proclaimed their right

to use education as a vehicle for proselytizing. When the school opened for its first sixteen students on December 3, 1866, it did so as an institution separate from the ABCFM, although affiliated missionaries served on its local board of managers, and all involved considered the school a virtual child of the mission.[49]

When Daniel Bliss inaugurated his new school, it stood at the pivot point of the American educational transformation; not surprisingly, its first curriculum reflected aspects of both old and new. In the first section of the school, the Literary Department, Daniel Bliss acknowledged the demands of his students and the changing educational tenor of American education; Greek and Latin received only minor attention and only in the third and fourth years. Unlike their American counterparts, Arab students received little instruction in the classical languages in their preparatory training, so could not have followed the same curriculum as that set up in American colleges. Instead, in the SPC curriculum, English and French took the place of the classical languages, offered alongside ancient and modern history, rhetoric, physics, mineralogy, chemistry, astronomy, geology, and physiology.[50] Bliss taught the capstone moral philosophy class, as did his fellow American Protestant presidents, first with his own notes and textbook, and then with Mark Hopkins's *The Law of Love and Love as a Law: Moral Science, Theoretical and Practical.*[51] However, except for some flexibility in the choice of English or French, the curriculum was comprised of a set of prescribed courses that every student had to complete for graduation; the language of instruction was Arabic. As at Amherst, the testing format relied almost exclusively on the oral declamation format, with only a few tests taken in writing. In 1867, one year after the school's founding, a medical department opened with its own set of prescribed courses; the School of Pharmacy launched in 1871. Religious teaching remained rooted in evangelical principles and all students, regardless of religious affiliation, attended Bible classes as well as daily and Sunday chapel services. Strict in loco parentis regulations maintained control over students' comportment and activities.

At his own graduation from Amherst College in 1852, Daniel Bliss stood halfway between the classical and liberal pedagogical standpoints. He believed that education was about using the proper tools for apprehending the truth. In this view of education, a truth certainly exists, yet education is also about teaching students to find their own way; recitation alone would not necessarily enable students to perceive the truth presented to them. Bliss gave an oration at his graduation ceremony from Amherst

College, doing so as the first of the "second-class" orations, meaning that he was "seventh in scholarship out of a class of forty-two."[52] In the speech he gave, called "Agitation," he declared that "when God first breathed into man the breath of life, he became a sentient, feeling, active being."[53] Man, in turn, must accept that "truth and error, in nature opposite, are strongly commingled in all that is human, and it is the life-work of man to separate the one from the other. Truth will conquer. Error must be exiled."[54] In this battle, "Truth has ever been the aggressive and Error the conservative principle. And why not? Truth can lose nothing by agitation but may gain all; and Error can gain nothing but lose all."[55] As a specific example of this activity, Bliss said, "There will be agitation in religion till superstitions and forms and dogmas shall give way to piety and sound doctrine—in morals till the lion and the lamb shall lie down together—in politics till aristocracies and oligarchies and democracies shall end in one grand Theocracy."[56] In his worldview, truth and error unquestionably existed, and education's goal was to show students how to differentiate between the two.

Reflecting his pedagogical stance, Bliss favored a system at SPC whereby "greater effort was made to educate the students rather than simply to instruct them."[57] As Bliss wrote in his 1902 farewell address, education was designed to prove "this and that to be true."[58] He expressed the view that "facts are the seeds of thought and like seeds in the vegetable world are of little value garnered up; but under the power of reason, will and conscience are made into ideals and laws that govern matter and mind."[59] In essence, he called on his students to discipline their minds to reason out for themselves a truth already known; for example, he reported, "in the Bible classes no attempt was made to combat error or false views, but we followed the method by which darkness is expelled from the room by turning on the light."[60] Only an upright, moral man, using his mental discipline, he said in his farewell address, could be taught how to follow the Apostle Paul's preaching, to "prove all things" and "hold fast to that which is good."[61] Bliss relied on this principle throughout his tenure as president of SPC because, as he said, new ideas and theories constantly bombarded the students of this era. "The wise Educator will help him to distinguish between the good and the bad, and induce him to gather the good into his life and to cast the bad away," he wrote in his 1896 "What Should Be Expected from Schools of Higher Education with Reference to Christian Life in the Country."[62] In his most famous speech, at the laying of the cornerstone of College Hall on December 7, 1871, Daniel Bliss declared:

tolerance but Christian message [handwritten margin note]

This College is for all conditions and classes of men without regard to colour, nationality, race or religion. A man white, black or yellow; Christian, Jew, Mohammedan or heathen, may enter and enjoy all the advantages of this institution for three, four or eight years; and go out believing in one God, in many Gods, or in no God.[63]

However, Bliss also said he expected the students to understand the truth of the college's Christian message. This was not Charles Eliot's lifelong seeker of truths, but someone taught the skills for understanding the light of truth shown to him. When a man acquired the skills for looking at the world through the lens of Jesus Christ, his reason could guide him through any field of endeavor.

Bliss enunciated such an educational policy because he felt that true modern education could only be successful if enveloped in Christian precepts. As he explained in "What Should Be Expected from Schools of Higher Education," the school that "cultivates devotion and fosters a love of divine truth whether revealed in nature or in God's word is a glorious means for promoting the Christian life in a country."[64] Bliss did not want SPC to serve as a theological seminary, focusing solely on religious training; rather, he saw literary and scientific studies as being compatible with Christian precepts because Christ's life bequeathed to students a guide for discerning that which is good while discarding that which is bad. "The learned professor can make his students understand and know the truth and the right but unless his own life is permeated with the Spirit of Christ in the classroom and out of the classroom, the heart and the life of the student will be untouched."[65] While Bliss felt that schools in America and England could successfully move toward a more secular curriculum, since Christian families regularly taught religious precepts in the home, he believed that in "heathen, Mohammedan and nominal Christian lands" religion needed to be the glue that kept all other subjects together, since no education was truly complete or modern without Christianity guiding it.[66]

As the school developed during the first decade, Bliss and some of the faculty members began to feel that special topics should be taught in English rather than in Arabic. Proponents of the change pointed out that few textbooks were available in Arabic and it was difficult to constantly translate English-language texts. While these issues were important considerations for the faculty, members who favored English over Arabic stressed the specific benefits accruing to the students from study of English language and literature.[67] The Yale Report writers characterized

Greek and Latin as capable of disciplining the mind to tackle educational inquiry; the SPC faculty positioned English in the same way. As one faculty statement said, English was "permeated with the spirit of progress in all departments of life."[68] In the mid-1870s, some of the professors experimented with teaching natural philosophy, history, and moral philosophy in English because, in the faculty's words, "we have taught English with the double object of disciplining the mind of the student and of furnishing him with the knowledge of the language whereby he could have access to the thoughts of the wisest and best men."[69] However, faculty members soon began to worry that even this expanded use of English failed to properly train their students. They feared that when the students left college they would quickly lose the benefit accruing from this work because the exigencies of their jobs and lives would not allow for continued study. "The American or European student, although he suffers a great loss in neglecting his ancient classics and his French & German[,] has access through his own language to nearly all that is valuable both old and new. But our graduates when they lay aside their English studies have little access to the thoughts of the great men of our age; they are shut up to the worst part of the dead past."[70] Given the richness of texts produced in English, "it is equally if not more important to give them a practical knowledge of the English language so that they may find something to write about and to teach."[71] If they read only their own language, they "are confined to books, saturated with errors in religion, morals[,] politics, medicine and social life."[72] Bayard Dodge (1923–1948) repeated this rationale when he wrote in 1928, "Though the Arabic language was marvelously adapted to poetry, religion, philosophy and history, words to express scientific ideas were lacking and scientific terms used for instance in Egypt were not always adapted at Jerusalem or Damascus. Further, those who studied science in the Arabic language were unable to profit by western journals, reference books, and post-graduate courses."[73] Without this training, "doctors, for instance, could not keep abreast of the progress of medicine because they could not read French, English or German publications and could not derive benefit from short courses at centers like Vienna or Paris."[74] In Dodge's perspective, modern science could best be disseminated through the European languages. Historian A. L. Tibawi presents a counterargument, writing that "the teachers qualified in Arabic ([John] Wortabet, [Cornelius] Van Dyck and [George] Post) were in the medical department. Not only could they fall back on good textbooks in their respective subjects produced in Egypt since the first half of the century, but they themselves were actually producing their own new textbooks."[75] In his opinion, the professors pushing for the change were those in the Literary Department, who were less qualified in Arabic.[76]

In 1878, those favoring instruction in English won the debate; SPC relinquished its "long cherished theory of teaching through the Arabic language [as] the best means of Christianizing and civilizing the East."[77] The school's faculty successfully lobbied the board of managers to allow English to be used as the language of instruction in the Literary Department as of the 1879–1880 academic year. This decision came solely from the English-speaking faculty, for only they had voting rights in the general faculty; none of the native Syrian tutors employed on campus had any institutional influence over this change.[78] The professors in the Medical Department successfully resisted the change for at least a few years, continuing to teach in Arabic.

In 1882, Bliss's efforts to maintain SPC's unity of truth clashed with the new questions and pedagogies being raised and introduced in American university classrooms. The spark for the conflict came when Professor Edwin Lewis gave a speech in Arabic at that year's commencement, which launched what would come to be called the Darwin Affair.[79] Lewis began by praising Charles Lyell's work in geology; it demonstrated that the "earth was not created in its present stage" and that man is able "to trace back the history of this earth stage by stage and acquaint himself with its conditions since it was brought into being by God up to the present."[80] Lyell was not a Darwinian because in a strict sense he was, according to Lewis, "convinced that variations were supernaturally directed." His ideas, though, had become contentious enough over the previous years that any mention of them could potentially generate opposition.[81] Lewis went further by commending the work of Charles Darwin. Lewis recognized that many opposed the theory Darwin formulated. "Whether or not this theory fulfills all what is required of it," he said, "there is no doubt that it is based on a sound scientific principle and that it has promoted many minds and revealed several facts."[82] On the other hand, because of the complexity of the theory, "we are unable now to give a final verdict, as there are still many things to be investigated, scrutinized, examined and established, before we can give a final opinion thereon."[83] While praising Darwin for his research and the means by which he reached his conclusions, Lewis also recognized the still popular but slowly receding academic belief that nature and the divine reinforced each other. Lewis touched on the basic theory underlying this natural theology when he said,

But if we know God by the light of the inspiration which He sends down upon us and then we look at nature, we will find in it the knowledge which we cannot find otherwise, we will penetrate its depths with keener insight and clearer light, and we will know that the laws of nature are the laws made by the Creator. And if we find the truth we will know through our souls that we are in the sight of God of Truth; the True of God and Creator of all.[84]

He moved into his conclusion by declaring, "Therefore, you must not despise any science nor disdain any knowledge, but let all that increases our knowledge and education be a miracle coming from God through His acts, just as the miracles of His sayings came to us through His inspiration."[85]

Lewis had not been the first to discuss Darwin's ideas on campus, but the forum he chose was so public that Bliss and the boards of managers and trustees had to react just as publicly themselves. Nadia Farag and Shafiq Jeha credit William Van Dyck, son of the longtime professor of internal medicine and general pathology Cornelius Van Dyck and himself a lecturer on materia medica, hygiene, and zoology, as the person who brought Darwin directly on to campus.[86] When Van Dyck arrived to take up his teaching post in 1880, he brought with him *On the Origin of Species* (1859), *The Descent of Man* (1871), and *The Expression of the Emotions in Man and Animals* (1872). He passed these books around, urging his students and colleagues to read them. Van Dyck also conducted an experiment in the Darwinian mode on the laws of genetic selection in the dogs of Syria. He sent his finished article to Charles Darwin on February 27, 1882; Darwin promised to publish it in the journal *Nature*, but died on April 19, 1882, before he could do so.[87]

And, years before Lewis gave his infamous speech, *al-Muqtataf*, a journal founded by two SPC graduates and lecturers, Yaᶜqub Sarruf ('70) and Faris Nimr ('74), had published pieces on Darwin and evolution. The very first volume, in 1876, contained a series on "The Origin of Man"; subsequent issues detailed debates about the theory of evolution and an issue in 1882 contained an obituary of Darwin. Consistent with Le Duc's observation that those on the opposite ends of the classical/liberal spectrum at Amherst College coexisted partly by ignoring each other, neither *al-Muqtataf* nor William Van Dyck's activities excited any noticeable attention from Daniel Bliss. The issue of Darwin became a problem when Lewis brought it to commencement, with its audience of students, parents, faculty, administrators, trustees, and board members.

Bliss's first written reaction to the speech was a short line in his diary on the day of commencement, Wednesday, July 19, 1882, saying, "Dr Lewis address much out of taste. An apology for bible truth & an acceptance as science unproved theories."[88] In a February 1883 letter to his sons, Howard and William, he wrote, "At Commencement Lewis gave an oration in which he praised up Chas. Darwin and gave the impression that he (L.) was a Darwinian and that man descended from the lower animals."[89] In the same letter, he said that William Booth, chairman of the board of trustees (1863–1896), would not accept the teaching of Darwin on campus. Throughout the summer and fall of 1882, al-Muqtataf published a copy of Lewis's speech, a series of the claims and counterclaims about Darwin, and information about the actions taking place on campus. When the new school year commenced in October, Lewis resumed teaching as normal and even gave the chapel sermon on November 5, 1882.[90] However, when the controversy did not subside, Lewis decided to send a translated copy of his speech to a respected clergyman in the United States for a judgment on its acceptability. The letter was sent to either Reverend Sell at the Union Theological Seminary or Julius Seelye at Amherst College. Farag supports the former claim, Jeha the latter.[91] Both scholars agree that the recipients accepted the speech as being in accordance with Protestant precepts. Jeha reports, "Seelye was firm in his reply about the irreproachableness of the speech with regard to religion."[92] When this support proved insufficiently persuasive to the board of trustees and Daniel Bliss, Lewis sent his resignation letter to Booth; a telegram accepting it was received in Beirut on December 2, 1882.[93] Most of the medical faculty, including both Van Dycks, resigned in solidarity with Lewis and in opposition to the actions of Bliss and the board.

A large number of students protested against Lewis's resignation; the following Sunday, they filed into chapel but refused to sing the hymns. The next day, the medical students and two literary students boycotted their classes. During the month of December 1882, the medical students sent a series of petitions to Daniel Bliss and the local board of managers asking that their grievances be addressed.[94] As Jeha notes, the issue of having evolution taught on campus was not the centerpiece of the students' complaints.[95] Students protested the fact that SPC had not done enough, in their opinion, to alleviate the problems posed by the 1882 decision of the Imperial College in Istanbul, the only accreditation service in the Ottoman Empire, to change the language of the medical examination from Arabic to Turkish. They also contested the requirement that they take final examinations both in Beirut and in Istanbul. Finally, the students demanded that SPC make available training in all the topics being tested in Istanbul, including zoology, disease diagnosis, and histology.[96]

Throughout the letters, the students also opposed the circumstances under which Lewis resigned. They respected Lewis's teaching methods and resented the fact that he and the other popular medical professors felt forced to resign in the face of administrative intransigence concerning both Darwin's ideas and Lewis's actions. As they explained in one letter to the administration, "This pious excellent man have you [sic] suspended suddenly in a way that violates his rights and ignores his excellent and pious services to the College and country for twelve years, and did not give him a year to arrange his affairs, [is] an unheard of thing."[97] The school, they insisted, was not living up to the contract the students had signed when they matriculated, which had promised that the professors under whom they sought to study would remain on staff throughout the academic year. Of these, Dr. George Post was the only one who had not resigned. As the students asked in their first letter, "Why then have you violated this agreement without informing us at the beginning of the year before we entered, not during the term of our studies? What is there to prevent our hearing after a couple of days of the suspension of another, and after a month of another[?] What sort of an affair is this?"[98]

In their last letter, the students laid out their position about student rights on campus. "You refused to listen to students whose acts did not convey any sign of rashness and who claimed their just rights."[99] In addition, the students wrote, "Sirs, we thought that presenting our requests to noble, pious American people who came to serve our countries in the name of the good and the right would assure us about all that we are struggling for. We resumed classes and met the requirements of each professor on the assumption that you, members of the administration, would bring justice to us."[100] Instead of respecting the rights of students, the letter stated, "without any examination of our case, the president of our school threatened, restrained and expelled us. He gave orders to deny us our beds and things. He also asked the services department to forbid us from taking our belongings or to be given any meal. We complied with the orders and endured all these hardships."[101] The students concluded by asking whether their rights would be protected if they signed the apology demanded of them by the administration. Jeha explains that this letter "was neither a plea nor an apology. It was, rather, a trial of the Board of Managers and the faculty and a clear condemnation of their position. It revealed the students' resentment over the manner in which their case was resolved and expressed their anger and disgust for the cruel way in which they were treated."[102] In the administrative responses to the students' complaints, the students are portrayed as recalcitrant children who must apologize for their transgressions so they can return to the fold. Despite their unanswered questions, the majority of participants in these protests did eventually sign the apology and reenter the Medical Department.[103] Twelve students continued their studies informally under Cornelius Van Dyck, took a local examination administered by a committee set up for the purpose, and then went on to Istanbul, where they were successful in getting their medical degrees from the Ottoman government.[104] Seven others never returned to SPC, including Gurji Zaidan, who later founded the journal *al-Hilal* in Cairo.

This student protest set a precedent for the next century of student-administration relations on campus. As these letters suggest, the students involved felt their rights had been violated by the actions of Daniel Bliss and the boards of trustees and managers; implicit in this call was the belief that students indeed have rights and can demand that those rights be protected by the administration. Proponents of the new American educational structure, at this point present at SPC in a merely fragmentary way, portrayed the program as a way of life that respected rights and opinions, even encouraging participants to engage with these concepts in real-world settings. As the final letter suggests, the students felt free to attack the administration for not fulfilling the ideals attached to American education in the Middle East, a tactic their successors returned to repeatedly throughout many a twentieth-century protest. The students did not win, as Zaidan explained,

> but the movement with which the students of the College came to the fore is worth recording because it started a new awakening amongst the students of the schools in the East. The merit for this is again due to the education in this very college, since it educated its students towards freedom of thought and speech and accustomed them to individual freedom and equality of rights, so much so that a student would complain about his teacher to the faculty, *'umda*, if he thought that he had overstepped the proper limits in his conduct. The faculty would establish his right even if he was the weakest student. This spirit distinguished this school from the schools of the East and had a great impact upon the education of the mind of the Syrians during this *Nahda*. It was this education which enabled the medical students in this year to complain to the faculty because they were convinced of the correctness of their act.[105]

In their letters, the students demanded the most modern scientific course-work so they could be adequately prepared to pass their medical examina-tions. They defended the rights of the Van Dycks and Lewis to teach them; their work, the students insisted, was more relevant than that presented by George Post.[106] As Zaidan said of their favorite medical professor, Corne-lius Van Dyck,

> Dr. van Dyck was a God-fearing man, his convictions being based on understanding and thought. He cared little for the details and triviali-ties to which some religious zealots cling and which have absolutely nothing to do with religion. But he held fast to the essentials of the Christian religion, unmindful of its external aspects and its superficiali-ties if they contradicted the principles of science. When a new theory of scientific thought appeared and presumably contradicted these superfi-cialities, he would nevertheless respect it and examine it from the point of view of scientists as, for instance, the evolutionary theory and similar theories of the philosophy of natural scientists.[107]

By supporting those professors who advocated teaching Darwin's ideas, and by implication the scientific methods of inquiry attendant to them, the students were demanding that new kinds of knowledge be allowed inside the Main Gate. They particularly supported those professors who had tapped into the new theoretical and pedagogical positions established in America.

Once the medical professors had left campus and the student protests had died down, Bliss imposed the Declaration of Principles on all new professors and required them to

> pledge ourselves to the inculcation of sound and reverent views of the relation of God to the natural universe as its Creator and supreme Ruler, and to give instruction in the special department assigned us, in the spirit and method best calculated to conserve the teachings of revealed truth and demonstrate the essential harmony between the Bible and all true science and philosophy.[108]

This pledge allowed Bliss to censor those topics and methods he found objectionable to the stated religious beliefs of the school. Under written contract, professors had to abide by a unity of truth written and delimited by Daniel Bliss and the boards of managers and trustees. Over the next few decades, new professors would remain on campus an average of only four and a half years, as opposed to twenty-nine for the earlier generation. This translated into an inordinate amount of influence over all aspects of campus life for long-timers like Bliss.[109] New professors saw their work at SPC as a brief interlude in careers otherwise practiced elsewhere.

Ramifications

Bliss's actions during and immediately after the Darwin Affair laid the groundwork for the school's developments for much of the next twenty years. In one very important result, Arabic and Arabs were marginalized at SPC. The resignation of almost all the Arabic-speaking medical professors hastened the move to English as the language of instruction in their department because their replacements did not have the same knowledge of Arabic. At the same time, the school's leadership used the Darwin Affair to officially move away from Bliss's initial goal of establishing an Arab leadership for the school. On March 18, 1862, in Bliss's first official letter seeking the support of the ABCFM in Boston, he said he wanted to turn over management of the school to the "native Arab element" as quickly as possible.[110] However, from among the Syrian natives teaching on campus in 1882, only John Wortabet, an Armenian convert to Protestantism, had received a professorial title.[111] Yaʿqub Sarruf and Faris Nimr had been hired upon their graduation as native tutors. On December 16, 1882, the board of managers voted that two adjunct professorships be offered to them, to take effect in October 1885; the former was to teach chemistry and physics, the latter mathematics.[112] When the faculty agreed to this future promotion, Sarruf and Nimr were teaching Arabic, mathematics, and a series of science courses. Both had pressured the administration to allow them to teach science and mathematics only, without the burden of Arabic, and with the promotion to a professorial rank.[113] On June 28, 1883, Sarruf and Nimr signed contracts to that effect, with the proviso that either side could cancel the contract with three months' notice. In July 1884, three months before the appointment was to take effect, the boards of managers and trustees voted to terminate the contracts of Sarruf and Nimr, rescinding the offer to make them adjunct professors. In making this recommendation, the board thanked the two men for their service; the board members "bear cheerful testimony to your ability and assiduity in teaching and express their deep regret that the exigencies of the Institution call for this separation."[114] Without further explanation for the termination, both men left campus and moved *al-Muqtataf* to Cairo, where it thrived until 1956.[115] The college made a gesture of apology to the two men in 1890, when it awarded them the school's first honorary doctoral degrees. Neither chose to attend the ceremony.

The decision to withdraw the promotion offer to Sarruf and Nimr had wide-ranging ramifications for the dominant discourse disseminated to the students in the classroom, for it valorized knowledge coming from an American and English world, while failing to acknowledge Arabic or Arabs as respected and equal intellectual ancestors for the students. The textbooks henceforth used at SPC and AUB reinforced a Western cultural framework by communicating a time line of history that found little of substance or progress outside of Europe.[116] When the language of instruction was Arabic, the school offered a yearly required course in Arab history; with the switch in language, Arab history disappeared from the curriculum until 1914.[117] In its stead, European history dominated from the 1880s forward, and especially during the era of the Arab nahda and the writing of the first generation of student publications. For example, in the 1901–1902 course catalogue, the history course extended over three years, starting with ancient history in the sophomore year, "including some references to the arts, sciences, and literature of the ancient nations."[118] In their junior year, students studied "medieval and modern history"; "a set of ten historical maps showing the political development of Europe and Western Asia is employed to illustrate this course."[119] Even though maps of "Western Asia," presumably the Middle East, entered the curriculum, they clearly did so as an adjunct to the main narrative of historical progress. Seniors studied constitutional history, with a focus on England, "which aims to gather up the threads of the whole course and weave them into a general view of all human history."[120] By 1904–1905, the constitutional history course had expanded to include Turkish history.[121] The purpose of studying history had contracted, however, for it was no longer the purpose to weave together all human history, but "to set forth the meaning of history and point out the chief lessons to be derived from it."[122] This history, whatever its parameters, meant European accomplishment; students had to figuratively place themselves in Europe to rationalize how the march of history related to their own educational experiences.

As A. L. Tibawi describes it, "The native cause was thus very badly served by the Lewis incident," and "native participation on equal terms was still unattainable."[123] Daniel Bliss had made explicit years earlier that only English could open a gateway for Arab students to study the great men of literature, that only the English language disciplined the mind. After 1882, the school experience took the students out of their world and placed them within one defined by the English-speaking administration, faculty, and text. Students, as seen in their own writings from 1899 forward, initially embraced this flight to the West because they sought to enter the world of modernity laid out in the English-language curriculum. Few new professors remained in Beirut long enough to learn Arabic or much about the culture and history surrounding the school. They had no reference points for the Arab world through which to articulate their ideologies and messages. The fact that the school's leaders relegated Arabic-speaking teachers on campus to tutoring and lecturing positions meant that the information they taught competed unfavorably with that imparted by the more prestigious English-speaking, Anglo-Saxon professors. In the switch to English, Arab tutors also lost their influential positions as translators and writers of Arabic textbooks for the school.[124] Even when the trustees voted in 1909 to allow Syrian teachers to become full professors, they refused to allow them voting power in the general faculty, and they maintained a discriminatory salary scale.[125] These professors could lead departments, such as the Arabic Department, but could not influence any policies instituted outside their own narrow domains.

Only as Arab professors gained equality of tenure and status, and as Arab nationalism gained ascendancy in the interwar period of the twentieth century, did students begin to question the English-speaking world in which they had been enveloped. Arabic teachers achieved that institutional equality with their Anglo-Saxon counterparts when the school transitioned from a college to a university in 1920. While the decision came as part of the transition to the university structure, it also resulted from pressure exerted from men like Philip Hitti, who had a PhD in Semitic languages and sought a professorship rather than a lectureship, as had normally been given to the Syrians. A number of the other Syrian teachers were searching for employment elsewhere, in reaction to the low salaries they were paid after the end of World War I; AUB had to make concessions in order to keep them on campus.[126] In October 1919, the general faculty to the collegiate committee voted unanimously to grant a chair in Semitic philology to Philip Hitti and, if he rejected this offer, to establish and offer him a chair in Arab history.[127] The committee also recommended that Asad Rustum ('16) be granted a permanent position in the History Department, with the expectation that he receive a chair in the future. Acting president Edward Nickoley (1920–1923) reported to Howard Bliss on February 18, 1920, that a general faculty meeting had been held to discuss the issue of Arab professorial appointments.[128] Participants felt that the school had been too quick to grant tenure and permanency to the Anglo-Saxon professors, doing so to compensate them for the sacrifice involved in moving from America to Beirut. "In this connection it was also pointed out that the security of tenure enjoyed by our permanent men has a deadening effect, that it does not make for efficiency, &c."[129] In subsequent meetings of the faculty, a clear consensus emerged favoring the equality of Syrian and Anglo-Saxon faculty members in terms of appointment; in spring 1920, the faculty voted unanimously to support this position.[130]

After Howard Bliss died on May 2, 1920, Nickoley continued to serve as acting president until Bayard Dodge took up his position on June 23, 1923; his letters lay out the change in status for the school and its Syrian staff as the American University of Beirut was born. In writing to David Stuart Dodge, president of the board of trustees (1907–1922), on August 1, 1920, Nickoley questioned the board's initial decision to grant only some of the professorial rights demanded by the Syrians.

> The full cooperation of the Syrian professors cannot be gained unless we place them on full equality so far as responsibilities and opportunities are concerned. *We must get rid of the color line.* The action of the Trustees, as I understand it, moves the color line upward but it retains it just as definitely as it has ever existed. As someone of our Faculty expressed it, "Yes, we have invited our Syrian brethren to the feast but we have taken the precaution of first removing some of the choice dishes from the table."[131]

When the New York Board of Regents of the University of the State of New York authorized renaming the school the American University of Beirut, it followed Nickoley's advice and agreed, "Hereafter no distinction shall be made between Anglo-Saxon and non-Anglo-Saxon teachers and administrators in regard to ranks or categories of promotion, but all, having once been given an indefinite appointment, shall be expected to pass through all subsequent categories in normal course of advancement with a longer or shorter occupancy of each grade as qualifications and preparation may indicate."[132] All professors, regardless of national origin, had institutional equality and voting rights within the general faculty. When new Arab professors joined Philip Hitti and Asad Rustum, they reconnected AUB to activities surrounding the campus walls. In the 1950s and 1960s, Arab professors began to gain numerical ascendancy over those hailing from the United States; by at least the 1965–1966 academic year, Arab faculty outnumbered American faculty.[133] Today, the president remains an American, a practice broken only between 1954 and 1957, when Constantine Zurayq served as acting president, and during the Lebanese civil war, when resident Arab professors took on positions as deputy presidents.

Liberal Education

The school opened the Department of Biblical Archæology in 1887 and the Department of Commerce in the 1900–1901 academic year, but in the newly named Collegiate Department, the curriculum remained largely the same between 1882 and 1902 with the exception of a small number of electives introduced in 1900. Daniel Bliss acknowledged the problem in his final annual report; of the curriculum, he said, "It needs a thorough overhauling and a systematic readjustment to meet present conditions."[134] Bliss recognized that the school had to adapt its curriculum to the real needs of the students so that they could graduate with the skills required for their future careers. "It has been a favorite educational theory that education and culture are in themselves sufficient spurs to urge students on to effort, and it cannot be denied that they form the noblest aim."[135] Yet, "the Collegiate course, above the sophomore year which admits to the medical course, leads nowhere except to an academic degree; and in no other place in the whole institution is the work of the students themselves so desultory and unsatisfactory."[136] For Bliss, the moment was propitious for change because of the new realities in the Middle East; in particular, he saw the recent British colonial successes in the region as a catalyst for students to study English. Bliss asked, given this situation, "Shall we disappoint them?"[137] In answering his own question, Bliss admitted that the school did not have the resources to open new programs immediately, but "we can legitimately plan to develop our History and Economics courses towards practical law; our Mathematics towards engineering; our Philosophy and Psychology towards theology or the science of teaching."[138] Particularly in medicine, he called on the board of trustees to adopt the practices being introduced in other schools throughout the region; they must improve their own program or lose students to the competition.

Ironically enough, one of the small additions made to the curriculum during Bliss's last years was the introduction of the teaching of one element of the theory of evolution. Starting in the 1891–1892 academic year, natural science professor Alfred Day adopted Joseph Le Conte's *Compend of Geology*, using it until at least the 1911–1912 academic year.[139] Le Conte was by then a professor of geology and natural history at the University of California; Andrew Lawson opines, "His strong advocacy of evolution as a principle running through all nature may be regarded as the most fruitful of his life's labors."[140] It is impossible to determine exactly how Day taught his geology course, for the catalogue merely states that "the course consists of recitations from Le Conte's 'Compend of Geology,' and lectures on the Geology of Syria, illustrated as far as possible by fossils and other specimens in the museum."[141] However, Le Conte's support of evolution was so well known by the 1880s that the choice of this text had to indicate Day's sympathy toward the idea of evolution. In this era of SPC's history, the general faculty had to vote on every new textbook adoption; Le Conte's text had to have passed through the same process and have received Bliss's blessing.

Although the Syrian Protestant College General Statement of 1897–1898 declared for the first time that "the Collegiate Department gives a liberal education in language and literature, science, history, and philosophy, leading to the degree of Bachelor of Arts," it was only under Howard Bliss, Daniel's son and successor, that the first tentative steps toward the inauguration of the new liberal education program on campus took place.[142] In many ways, Bliss's embrace of change reflected his own educational experiences at Amherst. By the time he graduated from Amherst in 1882, Latin and Greek still took up about half the time of the freshman class program, but lost ground in the following three years to far more emphasis on chemistry, mathematics, modern history, mineralogy, modern languages, biology, psychology, and English literature.[143] Amherst had expanded the number of elective courses, but to nowhere near the level Harvard had done under Eliot. As noted, Professors Emerson and Tyler offered evolution as an elective course. In loco parentis regulations loosened as well, particularly in the Seelye administration, when authoritarian rules gave way to the so-called Amherst system. In it, the students signed a covenant to observe the school's rules in something of a self-regulated honor system.[144]

Howard Bliss continued the school's expansion by opening the School of Dentistry in 1910, while increasing the list of course electives in the Collegiate Department and professionalizing the fields by dividing disciplines up into separate departments.[145] He gradually broke down the in loco parentis regulations that had circumscribed student activities throughout his father's presidency. In the 1904–1905 academic year, Bliss set up a special sophomore class to provide general training to those students who wanted to go on to study in SPC's professional schools, although students could still enter them by passing a series of examinations. Bliss found, however, that as late as 1912 the number of students studying in those two years was still relatively small, as students had not yet come to see value in this type of general education.

> But the numbers will grow, slowly in all probability, but surely, for more and more the desire to secure an education preliminary to professional studies that is sufficiently broad to put one in touch with "the best that has been thought and said" will send men to this School of Arts and Sciences, for here they can find to-day a thorough and varied course of elementary studies conducted by competent men who supervise the students' choice of electives, who are alive to the dangers of superficiality and intellectual dissipation, but who believe that a man who has not had a cultural training has lost a large opportunity for gaining happiness, efficiency and intellectual vitality.[146]

At the same time, the school's leaders made attempts to make the courses more intellectually stimulating for their students. In the July 1906 annual report, Robert H. West, the first dean of the Collegiate Department (1905–1906), soon to be renamed the School of Arts and Sciences, saw a dramatic change among the students in the junior and senior years because of the introduction of an extensive array of elective courses: "The result has been marked: the dilettante, desultory work which formerly was almost universal in these two years has largely disappeared, and has been replaced by an eager appreciation of the opportunities offered."[147] Starting in the 1908–1909 course catalogue, the school's leaders defined the method of instruction as follows:

> The primary aim of the college programme throughout all departments is to develop the reasoning faculties of the mind, to lay the foundations of a thorough intellectual training, to free the mind for independent thought. The permanent influence upon character exerted by the persistent requirement of thoroughness, seriousness, and diligence is more highly prized by the College than a brilliant show of a mechanical mastery of detailed information. In this sense, no course in the institution is

considered to be an end in itself; it is rather the aim of all instruction to train the individual student to meet the highest requirements of his life in society.[148]

Even this early in Howard Bliss's tenure, the school's faculty members were beginning to emphasize the element of freedom of inquiry that called on students to discuss and debate, with tolerance and respect, differing political, ideological, and religious views. As Howard Bliss wrote in his last published article, in 1920, "In all our classes, and especially in our Bible classes, there is a tradition of absolutely untrammeled inquiry; and woe be to the teacher who gives the impression that he is suppressing or fumbling question and answer, however blunt, embarrassing, or indiscreet the inquiry may seem to be."[149] In this atmosphere, the knowledge, per se, was not as important as instilling the tools needed to critically analyze the information received.

Howard Bliss's introduction of liberal education's curricular elements came to fruition with the school's name change in 1920; new programs were expanded and a research agenda was inaugurated. As Edward Nickoley wrote in his annual report for that year, "To the members of the Faculty the new name constitutes a twofold challenge: first, to a broadened field of work, to the branching out into new departments; second, and far more important, the new name imposes the obligation of producing a higher grade and better quality of work."[150] Echoing the discussion scholars had conducted in the Protestant American universities of the nineteenth century, Nickoley wrote, "As a university it not only becomes the duty of the institution to impart instruction but also to conduct and encourage research and investigation in new and original lines."[151] He hoped that "the American University of Beirut may become a university in fact and in deed as well as in name."[152] The name arose, as the faculty explained, because "it is the name the people use. They have taught us to think of ourselves as 'The American University,' although catalogs, handbooks, and stationery print 'The Syrian Protestant College' on almost every page. It has not been assigned by any ceremonial act. It has grown out of a half-century of educational ministry."[153]

Structurally, by this point, the concept had been accepted that in the first year or two of the students' educational experience, AUB provided pre-major and pre-professional training. As of the 1923–1924 academic year, the administration scheduled general education courses in the freshman year, with students then entering the School of Commerce, Pharmacy,

Dentistry, Pre-Medicine, or any major within the School of Arts and Sciences.[154] The concept of training students in general skills remained true to the Yale Report of 1828; as the faculty minutes report, students received "a broad foundation of culture" in that freshman program.[155] In the 1927–1928 academic year, the school introduced a sophomore orientation course entitled "Introduction to the Social Sciences"; "as the name implies, this course is intended to offer a comprehensive study in the various branches of social study for those students who plan to specialize in these studies in the last two years of the Arts course. Inasmuch as it is required of all sophomores, it serves also to provide a course in Citizenship and Social Relations for those students who plan the following years to take up the more highly specialized studies of the professional branches."[156] In fall 1927, *al-Kulliyah* reported that the course opened with six lectures by William Van Dyck; having resigned in 1882, he had resumed teaching at SPC in 1915. The lecture series was titled "The Biological Background of Man," and in it he "pictured the epic of the human animal, aided by charts, diagrams, bones, and fossil remains."[157] Not only had Darwin been admitted to campus, but the study of biological evolution had become a requirement for all students attending the sophomore class. Later topics covered in the course included psychology, religion and ethics, economics, political science, and sociology.

In the 1950–1951 and 1951–1952 academic years, the school revised its curriculum to more formally establish first the freshman and then the sophomore year as the stage for general, or liberal, education so that students would be prepared for their more specialized studies in the junior and senior years.[158] Changes to the later named Civilization Sequence Program over the years notwithstanding, AUB has held to the view that the first years of the collegiate experience must be devoted to a general education so that students can cover a broad range of topics and acquire the analytical skills necessary for any successful completion of the full university program.

Conclusion

The first hundred years of the school's existence took the educational process at SPC and AUB from the old unity of truth, delineated by a prescribed curriculum in Arabic and wrapped in evangelical Protestantism, to a new pedagogical orientation with the American liberal education system, taught in English and based in a Western civilizational coda. Daniel Bliss held tight to the reins of the curriculum and refused to initiate the wholesale changes implied by an acceptance of Darwin's ideas. While Bliss wielded the greatest power in this process, other professors and even the students held some degree of agency. Professors such as Edwin Lewis and Cornelius and William Van Dyck initiated their students into the new scientific methods gaining ascendancy in America. They struggled to continue to teach in Arabic so the students could integrate the new ideas into their own linguistic and societal structures. The students, for their part, took the message of American education, especially as transmitted by their favorite professors, and demanded that the administration grant them agency over their educational lives. The students did not win this battle, but they succeeded in setting a precedent for student protest in the generations to come.

3 | MAKING MEN
Religion, Education, and Character Building

At the 1904 inauguration of a statue sculpted in his likeness and commissioned by Egyptian and Sudanese graduates of Syrian Protestant College, Daniel Bliss (1866–1902) declared, "No block of marble was brought to us to be worked upon, but living boys and living men came to us from the East, from the West, from the North and from the South, to be influenced for good. They were all human and consequently imperfect; they were all human and consequently capable of perfection."[1] He continued, "As the workmen broke off from the block of marble all that surrounded this statue, so the College tries to break off from these young men, vanity and inventions and to leave standing the ideal man, made in the image of God."[2] He concluded, "We do not aim to make Maronites, or Greeks, or Catholics, or Protestants, or Jews, or Moslems, but we do aim to make perfect men, ideal men, God-like men, after the model of Jesus Christ, against whose moral character no man ever has said or can say aught."[3] Bayard Dodge (1923–1948) used much the same imagery when he wrote in 1920, "The first step in the production of leaders for the new Near East is to break down prejudice and to create a homogeneous mass out of the raw material, from all parts of the world. The second step is to train up thoughtful, healthy boys, whose minds are filled with wholesome love of sport and whose hearts are tuned to the highest emotions of Christian development."[4]

Bliss's and Dodge's use of phrases like "to be influenced for good," "to break off from these young men, vanity and inventions," "to make perfect men," and "to create a homogeneous mass out of the raw material" draws a vivid picture of the school's leaders chiseling away at the students' bad qualities while refashioning them into something new and beautiful. "Making men" was never so drastic or formulaic, but this imagery captures the dynamic elements of the program very well in that the American presidents frequently declared the necessity of breaking away the corruptions of Arab society before character reforms could be successfully made. American Protestant missionary efforts always entailed more than just liturgical teaching; acceptance of a new religion could not take place in a civilizational vacuum. An Americanism inevitably seeped into Protestant preaching in Syria, for it was in America that Protestantism had been reformed and rejuvenated as a "city on a hill," its people mandated to accept "an errand into the wilderness."[5] Until approximately the early 1950s, the leaders of SPC and AUB enunciated a conversion project that combined together liberal education, the late nineteenth and early twentieth centuries' American Social Gospel and Progressive movements, and the changing goals of American Protestant missionary efforts. This "making men" program challenged students to acquire a character modeled simultaneously on Jesus Christ and an American man able to negotiate the vicissitudes of modern society. He would be the "A.U.B. man" defined year after year in the student handbook; his comportment would include

1. Habits of personal cleanliness, regular exercise, etc., which are essential to good health.
2. The chivalrous ways of a courteous gentleman which make him acceptable in polite society.
3. A background of general knowledge about man and the world in which he lives.
4. The spirit and method of science, with its love of truth and freedom from prejudice.
5. A high degree of proficiency in his chosen line of work.
6. An appreciation of the beautiful which enables him to enjoy good literature, music, or drama, etc.—some one of the fine arts.
7. A genuine disinterested love of his own people which shows itself in some form of constructive citizenship, which is real patriotism.

8. A spirit of tolerance and magnanimity which enables him to live happily and work harmoniously with his fellows, even though he may hold opinions different from theirs.

9. An ability to think for himself and to stand loyally by his convictions, while at the same time graciously granting the same privilege to others.

10. A philosophy of life which is built around a staunch faith in a supreme importance of spiritual values.[6]

At no time in the school's history did any member of the student body have to accept Protestantism as a prerequisite for matriculation or graduation, but Protestantism permeated campus life and provided a whole way of interacting in the public and private spheres.[7]

Students embraced this framework, as seen in a study of over sixteen hundred articles published in forty-five English, Arabic, and French student magazines between 1899 and 1935.[8] In them, student writers of SPC and AUB sought to enlist their fellow students in this same quest for modern transformation; by so doing, they wrote their own "making men" program in conjunction with the mandates laid out by the school and the Arab nahda movement flourishing at the same time. In the pages of these papers, writers speak to "you," the student at SPC and AUB; you must understand who you need to become in order to modernize yourself, your nation, and your community. Many student articles of this era end with the command to "awaken" or to "work," words meant to catalyze student action; Arab society had fallen far behind the West, and students needed to go out into the world and work toward progress. These SPC and AUB student writers, like Arab nahda writers all over the region, portrayed themselves as the "apostles of the self-made man," providing their colleagues with blueprints for the successful modern character.[9] The school's presidents and students initiated a conversion to modernity project (to paraphrase the title of Peter van der Veer's book) that translated into a comprehensive guide for the Arab hoping to become a modern man.[10]

Proselytizing for Religious Modernity

Daniel Bliss opened and ran his missionary college hoping to show the light of salvation to his students, using Jesus Christ as his unchanging model of masculinity. In "What I Must Do to Be Saved" (1888), Bliss asked of his students, "And what must you believe? In the willingness and the power of the Lord Jesus Christ to save you, for He is able to save to the uttermost, all those that put their trust in Him."[11] The Bible and specifically the actions of Jesus Christ explained history, morality, and even the future; students needed to model themselves on Jesus to consciously improve their conduct and to find the proper means for aiding their society. In "The Thrones of Service" (1895), Bliss told the story of the Last Supper and said, "The twelve thrones the disciples were to sit upon in His Kingdom *are thrones of service.*"[12] As Bliss explained, "Washing the feet and visiting the fatherless involve the same principle, teach the same duty; and that principle and duty may be expressed in these words: —*wherever help is needed, give a helping hand.*"[13] The corollary, Bliss stressed, was the precept that "if any man would not work, neither shall he eat."[14] The ultimate goal of this service was not permanent aid but proud self-sufficiency for the recipients. In Bliss's iteration of "making men," only through a forceful transformation of the students' character could they come to understand the light of this Protestant message. As Bliss preached, "If we follow the principles laid down in the Bible, our lives will be harmonious, useful and spiritual."[15] Toward this goal, students had to study the Bible regularly and attend daily chapel sessions, while simultaneously following complex in loco parentis rules set out and regulated by the faculty.

An examination of Bliss's in loco parentis system illustrates how he melded together a self-regulated honor system with a strict list of injunctions to be used when the students did not take responsibility for their conduct. As he explained, "The discipline enforced here aims to develop sentiments of honor and manliness, where this fails, a prompt warning follows, for a graver offence, temporary suspension and finally, expulsion."[16] The regulations bound the students to be on time, be honest, be obedient, and, most importantly, be morally upright. During Bliss's presidency, the administration and the faculty were one and the same; the general faculty meetings took on as one of their many tasks the regulation of student transgression.[17] A large percentage of the faculty sessions address student crime, indicating that this was an ongoing issue for the professors because students continually found ways to break the many rules and also that control of student actions was as important to the faculty as determining curricular directions for the school. As early as April 22, 1868, the faculty minutes report that a student "has been pursuing a course of conduct throwing suspicion on his moral character."[18] This student was expelled. Over the next decades of Bliss's presidency, several students followed this first one; all were expelled for issues related to "moral character," while others faced the same punishment for violence against other students.[19] When two students engaged in an unspecific act of violence in May 1878, not only were they expelled "with disgrace," but "all students and servants [were to] be warned against having any intercourse with them under pain of expulsion or dismissal."[20] Punishments served as a cautionary lesson for any other student who might transgress the rules.

Incidents of moral transgressions and violence remained relatively infrequent; more common were absenteeism from class and prayers, staying out beyond curfew hours, and smoking and drinking while on campus. A typical punishment for these minor infractions involved writing out pages of texts. For example, for disorderly conduct in French class, the faculty voted on February 21, 1899, that a student "be required accurately to copy twenty pages from the French of Jules Verne, and hand the same to the Faculty within one week."[21] Regulations involved not only the many punishments to be meted out for transgressions, but also control over every aspect of the student day. For example, in 1877, the faculty voted that "students will always leave the Chapel in the following order. First the Medical students beginning with the seniors, then the Literary in the order of their classes, then the Electic [sic] & finally the Prof. classes."[22] The faculty also set up a process whereby students could apologize for their crimes and be allowed to return to campus in good standing. In March 1883, the faculty voted that "four students having presented an apology for drinking beer and speaking disrespectfully to Mr. [Faris] Nimr, the President was directed to give them a private admonition."[23] In the same meeting, one student "having gone on horseback to the Pasha's Gardens contrary to the order of the President and having presented an apology for the same, the President was directed to give him a private admonition also."[24] As these examples show, understanding the significance of Protestantism could only come when students consciously reformed their everyday actions. In the meantime, in loco parentis regulations worked to whittle away the students' poor qualities while helping to explain why "making men" required such transformations in conduct. In undergoing this transformation, students were supposed to find a way to fully embrace the message of Jesus Christ even if they did not take the next step and convert to Protestantism.

Both Bliss's academic classicism and his continuing emphasis on evangelical Protestantism went against the prevailing trends both in America and in the mission station. Religion was becoming more societally based, with less emphasis on individual salvation. Denominational and liturgical

Protestantism was giving way to a more liberal Protestantism that looked for similarities rather than differences between religious sects. On campuses, elective courses were offering students more independent decision-making power over their educational experiences, and in loco parentis regulations were easing as students took on the responsibilities attendant to the new educational program. Education was becoming a holistic experience, geared to transforming the character of its students. When Woodrow Wilson served as president of Princeton University (1902–1910), he expressed the opinion that "the most pleasant thing to me about university life is that men are licked into something like the same shape in respect of the principles with which they go out into the world; the ideals of conduct, the ideal of truthful comradeship, the ideals of loyalty, the ideals of co-operation, the sense of *esprit de corps*, the feeling that they are men of a common country and put into it for a common service."[25] If character meant good citizenship and respect for others, then the universities had to devise ways that taught their students to acquire just such a character.

On the university campus, these processes could not begin until the school's leaders broke religion's dominance as the base of knowledge in the old unity of truth; only after that momentous step had been taken could the openness required to validate new pieces of knowledge function within the classroom. Removing religion as the cornerstone of morality and ethics meant that university leaders had to find new ways to teach these elements as part of their character building programs. By the early twentieth century, as Julie Reuben reports of religious practices at American Protestant universities, religious obligations may have remained on the books, but "the emphasis on conduct over creed submerged religion into daily activity," and the chapel services grew shorter and emphasized songs and simple prayers.[26] George Marsden adds, "By the early decades of the century, exclusivist elements of the heritage had been abandoned, and Christianity was defined more or less as a moral outlook. It promoted good character and democratic principles, aspects of the old Whig ideals that were potentially palatable to all Americans."[27] The bulk of religious exercises shifted out of university control and became increasingly ensconced in voluntary institutions like the Young Men's Christian Association (YMCA). The YMCA had been founded in London in 1844 to address social problems arising from industrialization. By 1851, branches had opened throughout America and soon thereafter proliferated on university campuses; the YMCA came to serve as a nondenominational Christian place where young men could study the Bible and learn lessons in how to resist the temptations of the *voluntary venue of religion*

community service

modern world. As long as students received religious guidance in voluntary venues, in the view of university leaders, "disestablishment could be seen as a plausible trade-off, in which the locus of religious activity had moved from the center to the voluntary periphery."[28] In this new liberal Protestantism, as it came to be called, religion represented an umbrella over shared civilizational attributes, both societal and individual.

The liberal education program also began concentrating on character transformation as a vital goal, in particular calling on students to see success as achievable only if they used their educational knowledge to aid their societies. The most famous enunciation of the integration of university education and societal improvement came in Woodrow Wilson's 1896 speech at Princeton, titled "Princeton in the Nation's Service."[29] He disdained the belief that universities should remain aloof from the everyday concerns of the world:

> Of course, when all is said, it is not learning but the spirit of service that will give a college place in the public annals of the nation. It is indispensable, it seems to me, if it is to do its right service, that the air of affairs should be admitted to all its class rooms. I do not mean the air of party politics but the air of the world's transactions, the consciousness of the solidarity of the race, the sense of the duty of man towards man, of the presence of men in every problem, of the significance of truth for guidance as well as for knowledge, of the potency of ideas, of the promise and the hope that shine in the face of all knowledge."[30]

William Rainey Harper, president of the University of Chicago (1891–1906), formulated a yet more activist connection between the work of the university and public life in America.[31] Because of the educational processes flourishing on American campuses, Harper felt that "the university . . . is the prophetic interpreter of democracy; the prophet of her past, in all its vicissitudes; the prophet of her present, in all its complexity; the prophet of her future, in all its possibilities."[32] Echoing Woodrow Wilson, Harper declared, "The true university, the university of the future, is one the motto of which will be: Service for mankind wherever mankind is, whether within scholastic walls or without those walls and in the world at large."[33] Because students stood in the vanguard of the fight against parochialism and prejudice, they served as a vital instrument in constructively uplifting communities and nations. The value of education lay in students taking responsibility for their own educational experience while also remaining cognizant of using their newly earned skills to aid their communities after graduation. In essence, as Laurence Veysey states, university leaders wanted to "make each of its graduates into a force for civic virtue" and to "train a group of political leaders who would take a knightly plunge into 'real life' and clean it up."[34]

Outside campus gates, parallel developments within the Social Gospel and Progressive movements accelerated the synthesis between religion and society. Richard Hofstadter notes, "The key words of Progressivism were terms like *patriotism, citizen, democracy, law, character, conscience, soul, morals, service, duty, shame, disgrace, sin,* and *selfishness*—terms redolent of the sturdy Protestant Anglo-Saxon moral and intellectual roots of the Progressive uprising."[35] Progressives sought to enact major national and social reforms, from anti-trust laws to the establishment of urban settlement houses to, as founder Jane Addams explained, "aid in the solutions of life in a great city, to help our neighbors build responsible, self-sufficient lives for themselves and their families."[36] Charles Hopkins describes much the same framework for the Social Gospel movement of the era, which was "defined by one of its leaders as 'the application of the teaching of Jesus and the total message of the Christian salvation to society, the economic life, and social institutions . . . as well as to individuals.'"[37] In forming the Kingdom of God on earth, proponents of the Social Gospel sought to bring Jesus' message out of the esoteric isolation of the church so that its followers could solve the real-life problems emerging from American industrialization, urbanization, and immigration. As SPC president Howard Bliss (1902–1920) described it, the Kingdom of God "is concerned with the whole of a normal man's activities" and, importantly, "it seeks primarily to set men in their true relationship to God and their fellow men."[38] The lines between morality and service to the nation, on the one hand, and religion and democracy, on the other, became blurred. All served interconnected goals for activists of the Social Gospel and Progressive movements.

James Barton, corresponding secretary for the American Board of Commissioners of Foreign Missions (ABCFM; 1894–1927) and founder of Near East Relief, the American program for aiding Armenians in the Ottoman Empire during World War I, exemplifies the ideological transition that was simultaneously taking place in missionary programs. In "Modern Missionary" (1915), he explains that the missionaries of the past focused mostly on an "individualistic conception of Christianity" and that they relied too heavily on statistics to measure their success.[39] "At the present time, the missionary preaches salvation no less than before, but it is salvation for the life that now is—salvation to oneself and for himself, and to society and for society—salvation for the sake of the world in which he lives."[40] John Mott, a frequent visitor to SPC and a longtime contact of Howard Bliss, served as a leader of the student and international YMCA, leader of the Student Volunteer Movement, and general secretary of the World's Student Christian Federation. For him and his colleagues, "the earlier missionary motivation based on snatching sinners from hell's fires was slowly yielding to that oriented more toward the reform and improvement of all life, present and future."[41] Speaking at Carnegie Hall in 1900, Mott said, "We do not minimize the importance of any missionary work which has been and is being used by the Spirit of God. We rather add emphasis to all the regular forms of missionary work, such as education, medical, literary, and evangelistic."[42] The Social Gospel and an increased interest in social welfare projects was thus influencing missionary practice at the same time that liberal Protestantism was affecting campus life and work. Missionaries like Barton and Mott pledged to reform whole societies, not just the individuals standing before them; scriptural Protestantism lost ground to an inclusive, civilizationally defined Christianity.

Daniel Bliss's primary focus on individual enlightenment had few adherents by the time his son took over as president in 1902. Howard Bliss found no more converts than his father, but his civilizationally based Protestantism resonated more successfully with the students as they struggled to determine who they ought to become as a result of their SPC educational experience. From the beginning, Howard Bliss staked out a more liberal religious position than his father. He wrote in a letter to Daniel on February 3, 1902, that he would never sign the Declaration of Principles imposed after the Darwin Affair.[43] As he explained to his father, "I expressly and distinctly stated [to the board of trustees] that I belonged to the Liberal branch of our Congregational Body and that I could accept the Presidency only upon condition that I was not called upon to give any [assent] to this Declaration."[44] The trustees agreed to his demand, and over the next few months voted to remove the declaration from the school's statutes. Once Howard Bliss was in office, his iteration of "making men" emphasized, more than anything else, the inculcation within his students of an inclusive and tolerant religion that would inevitably catalyze them to think not just of their own reformation but that of their society as well. In his first annual report, in 1903, Bliss envisioned religion as an activist pursuit:

> We are bound by our very name to set so high, so noble, so broad, so ecumenical a type of Christianity before our students and through

them before the world as to enable them, as fearless students of science, as ardent lovers of literature, as eager investigators of history, as wise disciples of philosophy to hold to all that is fine and chivalrous and noble and true in all religions and to discover the secret of the universe in Christ's attitude towards God and man and life.[45]

In his last published article, in 1920, Bliss applauded the changes taking place all around him, seeing new men arising because of the positive influences modeled by SPC. Of the SPC student, he wrote,

He is not, indeed, always aware of the changes in himself. With perfect sincerity he would probably deny that he is being affected so powerfully by his environment. The fruitage of this seed may not come till long after he has left the College campus. But a change is being wrought, and he is daily learning, not merely, not chiefly, from his books, lessons in fairness, in honesty, in purity, in respect for labor and learning and culture, in reverence, in modesty, in courage, in self-control, in regard for women, in the many forces which make for civilization. And wherever this man goes, he makes it easier to foster education, to overturn tyranny, to soften fanaticism, to promote freedom in state and church.[46]

Throughout his tenure as president, Howard Bliss always affirmed the school's missionary character but also emphasized that he did not seek to convert anyone to his Christian faith. Liberal Protestantism meant for him that many religions could potentially live under its umbrella, for he stressed the civilizational and social aspects of religion over the denominational and liturgical. In a speech given on campus in May 1909, Bliss declared that the students did not have to become homogenized by their SPC experience. Instead,

the unity comes through the common search for perfection, the diversity comes as the study produces different expressions of personality. So in religion: while we have different ways of expressing our religious experiences, we must find an underlying principle, —belief in God, obedience to God; a purpose, as Bishop Wilson says, to make Reason and the will of God prevail; and you will remain a Moslem, you a Jew, you a Christian and you a representative of one of a dozen religions, but we shall be bound together by the underlying desire, to be true to Almighty God. We shall be diverse, but our college will develop unity as it seeks to do God's will.[47]

In this inclusive faith, Protestantism remained the primary pillar because only it could supply the proper guidance for the other faiths. Bliss reiterated in many letters to David Stuart Dodge, president of the board of trustees (1907–1922) during his tenure, "It is our aim to permeate recitation room, dormitory and campus with the spirit of Christ"; only then would the students truly understand the holistic lessons to be learned from Christianity.[48] In a report to the 1910 World Missionary Conference, Bliss declared his belief that "the missionary enterprise can be best advanced through the establishment of a Christian missionary system of education. The success of such missionary work cannot be tabulated in figures but its influence, although not subject to measurement by numbers, is powerful and all-pervasive."[49] He noted, "While very few converts can be said to be made within College walls, it is yet my thorough conviction that no student leaves one of these institutions without being powerfully affected and influenced in the direction of a more intelligent apprehension of the Christian ideal."[50] Protestantism grew stronger when it recognized and respected the faith of others; it now sought to teach those who still held to chauvinistic sectarian beliefs. In Bliss's vision, the college campus stood as the only stronghold in the region where all the faiths could constructively interact inside the chapel and classroom together.

While Bliss retained the obligatory religious requirements during most of his years as president, he, like his father before him, also used voluntary religious organizations on campus as venues for further dissemination of the religious and service elements of his "making men" message. This voluntary realm, in particular, opened a space for extended discussions about the tenets of liberal Protestantism, the Social Gospel, and Progressivism. In November 1886, SPC students organized a YMCA and immediately attracted sixty-two members and twelve associates; the organization existed for most of the remaining years of SPC's existence.[51] The stated goal of the school's YMCA branch by 1904–1905 was "to unite the students who desire to promote the spiritual life of the institution, to lead them to feel their responsibility in the religious work of the College, to deepen their spiritual life, to guard them from temptation, to lead other students to Christ, and to promote the advancement of the Kingdom of God throughout the world, and especially in those lands represented in the membership of the Association."[52] Furthermore, "The purpose of a College training is to equip men for effective service to their fellow men. To this end, no less than the trained and cultured mind, is needed the strength of a will that chooses the good, the guidance of a conscience that discerns good from evil, and the impelling force of a heart filled with love."[53] As these words indicate, the YMCA stressed, as did its sister institutions in America and around the world, taking religion out of the church and into the streets. "Believing that college students as a favored class have peculiar responsibility to the less privileged, the Association provides opportunity for its members to work for the mental and moral welfare of the college neighborhood."[54] The longest project undertaken by the students of this era was the funding and staffing of the Ras Beirut Boys' School.

Howard Bliss worked with the YMCA to run annual prayer week sessions so that students could find more opportunities for using God's message to reform their characters. Every December or January, faculty members and guest speakers gave sermons each night for a week, often on coordinated topics. After the sermon ended, faculty members broke up the assembled students into small groups so they could discuss the evening's sermon. While always voluntary, the sermons typically attracted one to two hundred students each night, with a slightly smaller number opting for the discussion sessions. The topics illustrate how Howard Bliss melded religion, character, and social service into his "making men" program, equating this project with his definition of liberal Protestantism. He preferred this voluntary venue over his father's strict in loco parentis regulations.

The sermons given most frequently spoke of how the students could integrate Jesus' message into their everyday life and, by so doing, build up characters that seek to help those around them to follow in the same path. Bliss noted in a letter to board of trustees president David S. Dodge that he prepared for the 1903 series by speaking to the students on the following subjects: "Man's need of God," "Man's search after God," "God's care for man"; the sermons for the week called on students to affirm, "I ought," "I can," "I will."[55] After the sermons finished, Bliss wrote to Dodge, one of the seniors stood up and said, "I must be perfectly honest in this matter. I said 'I will' but I am not sure that though I said it, as my mind is not fully made up. I want to say it and I hope to say it but I cannot just now.'"[56] Bliss described this as "a noble brave declaration. It brought a note of reality and genuineness to the service."[57] Since Bliss did not mention it, it is safe to assume this student did not convert to Protestantism as a result of these sermons. Instead, Bliss applauded him for declaring his desire to follow God's precepts to live his life in a moral way. Later in the week, Bliss again wrote to Dodge, describing a conversation a faculty member had recently held with a student. "He told me of one student who told him that since the meetings week before last he had given up masturbation."[58] The SPC man had to control his baser urges and suppress all unhealthy desires in order to be properly transformed.

In 1908, the sermons focused on Peter's life and message: "What Peter Saw in Himself"; "Peter Leaving His Nets"; "What Peter Saw in Christ"; "Peter's Fall"; "The Restoration of Peter"; "The Fulfillment of Christ's Prophesy for Peter"; and "Peter's Losses and Gains in Becoming a Follower of Christ."[59] Bliss reported in his weekly letter to Dodge that the sessions had been particularly successful, with the light shining brightly from the students' eyes. About a discussion meeting Bliss ran, he wrote, "I asked all those who had stood at any time to rise and it was a stirring sight to see the immediate response, scores of students standing up with smiling faces and remaining standing during the prayer of special consecration."[60] These reports to Dodge suggest what Bliss was trying to achieve with these prayer weeks. He wanted a student to stand up to pledge himself to live as Jesus had done, believing that Christ bequeathed the best model for character building. This student must also recognize that he had a duty not just to himself but to his whole community; he must light the way for those less fortunate. Bliss constantly let this student know that the task ahead was a difficult one since it involved a wholesale transformation of his relationship with God, himself, and his society. In all, 125 students stood up in 1908; few, if any, converted to Protestantism.

Making the American Man

Bayard Dodge's (1923–1948) "making men" narrative evoked a much more specifically American model for modernity than anything his predecessors had articulated. The Blisses had drawn an image of a sober man working hard to earn the respect of his God and community; Dodge exhibited to his students an exciting future for the man transformed by the AUB experience. If the Blisses saw Protestantism as providing character lessons, Dodge extolled what he called "America, a Light to the Nations."[61] In a 1924 article of the same name, he wrote, "The grandeur of Rome was in her legions; the power of Spain was in her galleons; the pride of Italy was Cavour. But may our glory be our learning, enchanted by our American idealism,—freely given to the nations, unselfish in name and purpose,— that health may replace disease; that cruelty may give way to chivalry, and bigotry to love."[62] In Dodge's imagery, the American man could build skyscrapers, fly across the Atlantic, and build cars at rates never imagined before; American education brought this spirit to Beirut.

In 1923, as Dodge took over the reins of AUB leadership, he detailed the most important attributes he felt the students needed to learn from the Americans:

> The idea of the Brotherhood of Man.
> The great content of modern, scientific learning, which fits men for active life and professional service.
> A broad culture, which produces liberality of thought and a well balanced judgment.
> A manly attitude towards work and play, which overcomes laziness, creates clean sport, and develops a well rounded type of manhood.
> The fact that religion is not a matter of rites and names alone, but a matter of the spirit, which expresses itself in a practical way by noble character and good living.
> A devotion to the great moral principles of God, and a consecration to the service of mankind, such as Jesus had.[63]

In the romantic American world depicted in this speech, brotherhood united immigrants, the wealthy protected the poor, and educators spread their benevolent spirit. The American man worked hard to embody the qualities of integrity, ingenuity, and inquisitiveness; he dared to take chances and ventured into the unknown with unflinching energy; and he harnessed the religious spirit for communal and social improvement.

Dodge told many a story of boys arriving at SPC or AUB, filled with intolerance for those outside their religious sects and, just as often, never having worked in their lives; American education made them broad-minded enough to overcome their innate prejudices against others while also pushing them to work with their hands so that they could come to understand the value of individual toil. In one such tale, he wrote of boys from all different religious backgrounds, studying and playing together on campus, even though their parents would not have been able to interact without suspicion of each other. In an article for the *Presbyterian Banner* in 1920, Dodge wrote, "If you should learn to know the boys of high school age in any part of the Near East, you would find them to be disappointing in many ways. They are either ignorant peasants, dirty, illiterate and without ambition, or else they are 'gentlemen' and 'above' the more practical things in life. Members of this latter group consider any kind of bodily exertion or hard work to be beneath them."[64] After their American educational experience, and with "the great ideals of our Christian America" imbuing them with new ideas, these students are transformed. "The person of Jesus is the hero of their growth. They learn to honor women, to take morality for granted; they appreciate clean, powerful bodies; they become accustomed to decent entertainment and they strive to be like their teachers, all of whom are picked men. Service of their country is held before them as the reason for education and service of their God as the reason for life itself."[65]

Dodge always clarified such stories by telling the students they must follow the maxim that "social evolution and the progress of mankind as a whole can only take place as individual men and women cause it to take place." One section of his 1934 baccalaureate sermon was entitled "Ideals Must Have Exponents or Interpreters."[66] One section was entitled "What Causes World Progress?" In listing individuals who had changed the world, he asked, "What unified the Arab world and freed it from idolatry? A camel driver summoned by God to become a prophet . . . What gave the world the godsend of modern nursing? Florence Nightingale . . . What freed the world from slavery? The efforts of William Wilberforce, a wealthy London politician, and Abraham Lincoln, reared in a log cabin of the American wilderness."[67] According to Dodge, if the Americans at AUB could successfully impart to their students the importance of this human agency, the Arabs would be able to advance as the Americans had done. Dodge pointed out, "As Americans we are in a peculiar position to teach cooperation and majority rule. Not only are our forty-eight states cooperating together, but the millions of immigrants in our country are living together with a harmony, which is far from perfect but still a remarkable lesson in team-work."[68]

The American democratic structure, for Dodge, was the perfect merger of the American style of education and religion; for him, "Democracy, fraternity, and individual growth are the very foundation stones of both Christianity and American idealism."[69] He felt that America could show the peoples of the East how to construct a democracy that would truly aid the citizenry of the region. Elections and legislative forms of government are important, but only if people choose to resist the temptations that come with such responsibility and freedom:

> We must help the people of the East to realize these dangers and to try to meet them by efforts of a constructive nature. We can teach them that national prosperity can only come if citizens will sacrifice their per-

sonal interests and sect prejudices, so as to have unity. We must emphasize that reforms and progress will only come as a result of private effort and philanthropy. Most important of all, we must show that our own prosperity in America has been produced by labor and work in connection with economic affairs, rather than by agitation and political strife.[70]

Dodge explained to the board of trustees in his 1929–1930 annual report that when a new student arrived on campus and met up with the "freedom of European life" for the first time, it was the duty of the older students and teachers to "help him to understand what is good and what is bad in western civilization."[71] To succeed at this task, "he is kept under strict discipline, while his character is forming and his understanding maturing. At the same time courses on sociology, talks on the practical relationships of life, and contact with what is best in western culture, enable him to gain a constructive interpretation of modern things, which saves him from the license and fits him for citizenship."[72] Individuals uphold democracy, freedom, and tolerance when they learn how to responsibly participate in the institutions modeled on these concepts.

Even though the American University of Beirut had by 1920 eschewed SPC's missionary goals, religion remained essential to the man Dodge hoped to mold. In the shift to the new and expanded university framework, students had the right to choose whether to attend chapel or an alternative religious exercise. Assembly and baccalaureate speeches, however, still came wrapped in religious precepts. Instead of being enclosed within Howard Bliss's liberal Protestantism, Dodge presented religion as a peculiarly American brand, identified by its reliance on the concepts of patriotism, citizenship, conscience, and freedom, which Dodge felt exemplified American success. In Dodge's words, "The greatest service that the University can render is to kindle a flame of enthusiasm and a desire for service in the hearts of the students. Muslims, Christians, and Jews alike need to have a spiritual awakening, that selfish nationalism will be changed into team work, corruption into public service, and indifference into a new faith."[73] Unbelief could only lead to materialism and fanaticism; religion, properly understood, inevitably activated public service and a constructive nationalism. Overall, Dodge believed, "religion seems to be a consciousness of God; a life of the spirit, manifesting itself in the conduct of each day, and it is when we wish to make this fact intelligible to our students that we hold before them an ideal personality, whose actions were so supremely guided by submission to the divine will and whose sacrifice blazed forth as a beacon to mankind."[74] Dodge believed AUB had established a perfect relationship between religion and knowledge. "The professors are men who have received scientific training. As they take turns in speaking at chapel, the students realize that science is not an enemy of religion, but rather an argument for faith. Religion is not taught as a matter of ritual or sect"; rather, "there is a consciousness of brotherhood and a desire to worship by means of serving others."[75]

In the new atmosphere of AUB, the YMCA gave way to the nondenominational West Hall Brotherhood in the 1920s. Its first director, Professor Laurens Seelye, reported that its founding charter called on all students, regardless of religion, to come together in religious fellowship. "It is believed that a thoughtful, sincere man, whether Moslem, Bahai, Jew or Christian can join this Brotherhood without feeling that he has compromised his standing in relation to his own religion. In becoming a member, no one, whether Christian or non-Christian, is asked to give up anything which he considers important in his religious beliefs or practices."[76] In summary, "The practical aim of all these meetings is to emphasize the fact that the supreme need today is for men of character; and that the time is ripe for men of all races and religions to cooperate in the use of everything—thought, energy, possession, and social relationships—in the construction, under God's blessing, of a world of righteousness and human brotherhood."[77] As the brotherhood motto read, "The realm in which we share is vastly greater than that in which we differ."[78] On March 28, 1927, Professor James Stewart Crawford gave a morning chapel address entitled "The Religious Policy of the A.U.B." In it, he set forth the school's official religious policy.

> I. We believe that the first great essential for our experiment is Freedom. We grant the fullest freedom for the mind, for the conscience, and for individual growth. This means that there is genuine freedom to think differently from one another, on religion, and to develop on different lines . . .
>
> II. The second essential for our new missionary experiment is that we all—teachers and students together—cultivate co-operation in religious fellowship and activity. This cooperation must be made possible inspite of the differences in our beliefs. Half of our students, at least, will always be non-Christian. We insist on promoting a genuine unity of spirit amid our outward diversity of creed . . .
>
> III. But there is a third essential to the great religious experiment of

the A.U.B. and that is the unquestioned fact that our University has a distinctive Christian contribution to make to our mutual experience of religious freedom and cooperation."[79]

Freedom of inquiry, as the basic source of liberal education, carried over into faith, as the administration enjoined the students to maintain their beliefs while freely asking questions of those around them. As Dodge reported, "The students and young teachers have found that they could express their religious ideas in simple devotional gatherings and also by the gospel of the Good Samaritan. Night classes in the city, work in backward schools, recreation for the children, relief for the unemployed, public health work, adult education, village welfare among the farmers and other forms of work have bound together the members of many sects in the service of God and man."[80] In the interwar period, these ideas translated into the social work done by the West Hall Brotherhood, as well as the Village Welfare League (VWL). Modern man incorporated these lessons into his lifestyle and actively sought to spread them in his community.

Thus Bayard Dodge's AUB man sought to acquire a complex set of individual characteristics so he could improve his own actions and then improve his society. This man eschewed his natural laziness by rolling up his sleeves, taking personal responsibility for his actions, and doing the hard work he once relegated to servants. Within the parameters of the new liberal educational curriculum, he had a breadth of knowledge in the humanities and social sciences, and followed the precepts of freedom of inquiry and tolerance of difference in all interactions with colleagues. He recognized that spirituality did not mean blind recitation of elaborate religious rituals, but an acknowledgment that morality and ethics translate into good business tactics, better societal relations, and national strength. He accepted that religious tolerance alone would not be sufficient; it needed to be actively directed toward societal and national cooperation and brotherhood. Personal energies should be siphoned only into productive, collective projects. Intertwined in this description of the successful man was the concept of self-discipline, dovetailing perfectly with the elements underpinning liberal education. Freedom of speech, worship, or action could not be exercised except by those who had proven themselves worthy of its responsibilities; only careful supervision and guidance could teach the students how to exercise that restraint. The Americans at SPC and AUB told their Arab students that this "making men" project was the only viable route to a "*good* society."[81]

Students and the "Making Men" Project

Nejib Yakub wrote a story for the May 18, 1906, edition of the *Commercial Triumvirate* describing the problematic trajectory many a student of Syrian Protestant College faced after matriculation at the school.[82] The star of the article was a fictional student from a mountain village family; growing up, he accepted without question the simplicity of life hewed to by his ancestors. Upon his arrival at SPC, "he is not yet in contact with that fierce tiger—Luxury—which is the herald and guard of what we call present civilization. He is not yet a prey to the wolf of vanity and the viper of empty showiness. He is not yet a slave of the almighty and omnipresent fashion."[83] By his second month, however, he has made new friends, a number of whom are lazy and contemptuous of hard work. To keep up with the lifestyle of his new, far wealthier friends, he takes merely a month to empty his wallet of his yearly allowance. Upon the first request, his father readily sends money, assuming that school life is costlier than he anticipated; he hesitates, however, after the second request, choosing instead to visit his son to better understand the problem. Upon his arrival, his father discovers that "the son no more wears the Kumbaz, but looks as though he were a millionaire's son in his fashioned suit and boots, and he meanly, and ungratefully, and vainly walks with his father with his feelings not at all free from shame which he should better have of his own self."[84] Almost thirty years later, K.S.J. wrote an *al-Kulliyah Review* article entitled "And Who Is This?"[85] The author portrays what he sees as a common type of student enrolled at AUB. This student arrives from "one of the most backward villages of the country, where he used to wear the native dress of the Arabs, and almost never heard a foreign language, and certainly never knew the scientific method."[86] When the student returns home, he "goes about with his hands deep in his trouser pockets, and with the most expensive tie he can find in the town, with a coloured silk handkerchief peeping out of his pocket and perhaps a tennis racquet under his arm. Whenever he sees any one he greets him with a loud, thick, and drawling 'Hallow' keeping his hands still in his pockets, and scarcely condescending to move his head."[87] His favorite phrase is, "Scientifically speaking, such and such a thing is thus"; and for those who reject his newly found modern world, he frequently retorts, "This fellow is extremely old fashioned in his ideas."[88]

In these articles, the authors fault the two students for choosing flash over substance, for acquiring the affectations of Western civilization and modernity rather than the character traits befitting a graduate of the school. Yakub even goes so far as to say that his fictional student should never have ventured out from his mountain village at all because he is "an ignorant vain fellow" and does not understand the transformative process of American higher education.[89] K.S.J. addresses the same type; the readership would readily have recognized him. In both pieces, the fellow originates from a simple but dignified rural background in which respect for tradition dominates. Upon his introduction to life on campus, he becomes alienated from the values of his home and bedazzled by the superficial appearance of wealth and modernity. As yet he is unable to recognize the true character of modernity, which involves broad-mindedness, hard work, and service to community. Both authors also equate backwardness with flawed character traits; these cannot be automatically corrected even through education at SPC and AUB. Students may graduate with the look of educated men, but they remain backward if they fail to actively transform their characters. "His dignity, his nobility of mind and heart, his real advancement in life," writes Yakub, "do not come by the kind of suit or boots or hat or any other article of dress that he puts on, but by the character that he builds up day after day, founded on true virtues, and by the right career that he chooses in this perilous life."[90]

To forestall the fashioning of the wrong kind of student at SPC or AUB, given the pivotal role graduates should play in serving their society, the students used their campus publications to lay out a transformative program for their colleagues. At the beginning of the twentieth century, student writings focus on self-help; almost half are devoted to issues of character, civilization, religion, science, history, and models for individual success. Within this general rubric, there are some variations. The English-language papers, for example, extol Western great men more than the papers in Arabic, but even in the latter, men such as Voltaire, George Washington, and Herbert Spencer appear regularly as reference points. Arabic-language papers, on the other hand, tend to devote more pages to historical and literary studies of the Arab world than anything published in papers in other languages. The English-language papers focus more attention on the "making men" project, while those in Arabic far more frequently stress the backwardness of Arab history and society. Taken together, these minor differences fail to outweigh the striking similarities in theme, subject matter, style, and tone found across all the papers. Articles in the 1935 al-Kulliyah Review cover the same themes as the first papers published in 1899.

The influence of the American presidents and professors can be seen in these papers; at the same time, they are largely invisible because the students want to present only themselves as authority figures for their peers.

The students summarize the many speeches and sermons given by the American leaders of the school, and they present moving eulogies for men who died after serving long tenures on campus. Their exhortations to manhood cover much the same territory as the evolving "making men" project of the Americans. Furthermore, many of the pieces read like classroom essay assignments. However, the students clearly position themselves as autonomous voices of authority for the masculine template they are presenting. Americans in general should be emulated, but the student writers do not cede power to them. The students present their work as coming from their pens alone, presented to their colleagues as guidelines for who they ought to become as a result of their educational experience at SPC and AUB.

At the same time, the themes of individual and societal regeneration parallel much the same quest for identity as that expressed in writings all over the Arab world in this period of the late nineteenth- and early twentieth-century nahda. In their narratives, the students invariably present a chronology of history that posits the Arabs leading the world's civilizations in the past, only to be thrown into ignorance in recent centuries. The student writers see Western dynamism as the solution to Arab stagnation; they call on their fellow students to become modern men who strive to lead in every country of the world. In this worldview, the French Revolution begat democracy, the American emancipation of slaves demonstrated the true meaning of freedom, and Western scientific inventions improved life for everyone. The progressive and civilizational norm was the West because it had successfully harnessed the power of character, will, and ingenuity. Student articles place the center of innovation and action in the West and accredit Western models as the most worthy of emulation. Success can come only when progressive leaders, like the students at the school, find ways to accept the mantle of constructive activism taught as part of "making men." The gestalt of these papers is action—action to obliterate the individual and societal weaknesses plaguing the Arab world and action to build up the right kind of masculine character traits.

Selim Haddad, in "Syrian Youth or an Appeal to Syrian Youngmen," published in the *Commercial Triumvirate* in 1906, states that "the progress of a community depends mainly and entirely upon the utility and productiveness of an individual."[91] Haddad takes as a given that for any student attending SPC, "Ambition and love of achievement are lit up in his heart the moment he enters the College and he becomes the endeared suckling nursed at the breast of his Alma Mater."[92] The lessons he learns at that breast should convince him to "cast aside all evil customs, timidities and limitations, and to be in his place a free and helpful man, reformer, and a benefactor. He must not be content to slip along through the world like a footman or a spy, but a brave and upright man, who must find or cut a straight road to every thing excellent in this earth."[93] The "civilized nations of the old world were thickly spread all over the coasts of Syria and Palestine"; "looking now at the present world, we find that the metamorphosing agents have wrought out wonderful changes in its atmosphere, which are only manifested on European soil and under an American sky, but not on a Syrian land. Thus the American and European nations are the people whose standard we should follow."[94] Because of this marked Syrian failure, "we should but look down on our conditions and place in the scale of human society with pity and sorrow; with eyes burst in torrential tears and faces blushed with shame."[95] The circumstances in Syria are improving but primarily because foreigners, mostly missionaries, have opened schools in the region in order to teach the skills they find most useful back at home. As with so many of the student articles, the author ends with a call for action: "Let us regain what Syria has lost with lapse of years, and let us restore to our country her eras of prosperity and epochs of advancement, and let the honor of our forefathers and ancestors rest again on our heads. Let us march to the front. Let us run our race and be ahead."[96]

To make that move, student writers consistently stressed that the first step toward becoming this man was to activate change within himself. A 1914 article in *al-Thamarah* explains that young people of the day can no longer live the simple life of their ancestors, but must actively seek out education and knowledge so they can help reform their societies.[97] The *Students' Union Gazette* declares in 1913 that "education is the training of the entire man, body, mind and character, and the first of all education is physical education"; "persistent, intelligent effort will win."[98] The article ends with the command, "DO NOT WORRY, WORK!"[99] An article in a 1900 *Thamarat al-Adhan* explains that "effort is the mother of good fortune" and that "happiness assuredly comes to those who are able."[100] Abdus Sattar El-Khairi concurs in a 1906 edition of *Light*: "The master-key, by which all the doors of success can be opened, is Determination."[101] El-Khairi clarifies this point in a later issue of *Light*: "To determine to do a thing is to do that thing earnestly and enthusiastically; and to do a thing earnestly and enthusiastically means faith in himself and the thing. But faith in oneself and the thing means Success."[102] *Anchor* warns in "Plain Talk" in 1924 that "if you are not earning your living, altho [*sic*] perfectly capable of doing so, you are on somebody's back, and you will never be the man or woman you want to be until you get off." Further, "you will never develop self-reliance, the studious qualities of manhood or womanhood, until you have learned to stand alone."[103] An author writes in a 1902 issue of *al-Hadiqa* that man must not accept that "his fate is what he has become accustomed to"; rather, he should look to his teachers for direction so he can learn to eschew haughtiness and arrogance.[104] *al-Manara* declares to its readers in 1906, "To you oh cultured types of the College today who will be the sage and the doctor and the merchant and the producer. A great part of the future is dependent upon you. If you are a doctor be a nationalist in all the work you do. You should direct your eyes to the saying 'service of the nation is the happiness of man, the innermost spirit.'"[105]

Tales of the great men of history prove that these maxims lead a man to success; the *Students' Union Gazette* explains, "One of the best ways to educate ourselves is to acquire the ideas wrought by the minds of great men. It will not be of any benefit to us if we only acquire these ideas, for there is no knowledge good for any one unless he makes it a part of his own wisdom."[106] The modern man must take action, but not just any action; he must be willing to work on behalf of his community. Just about every issue of every magazine contains articles detailing the lives and works of successful men of literature, politics, and war. For example, students repeatedly exalt English writers like William Shakespeare, John Milton, and Samuel Taylor Coleridge for their eloquence; American politicians such as Abraham Lincoln for their fairness and national sacrifice; and successful military men for adherence to the concepts of freedom and liberty. These great men, however, do not appear as three-dimensional figures, with realistic strengths and weaknesses, so much as stereotypes of masculine strength and virtue. They are not unique individuals, for the students do not appear to know much about their lives besides the boilerplate "self-made man" typology. They are the hagiographies that appeared in American venues such as the *Saturday Evening Post* and the Horatio Alger stories. They are generic holders of proper character traits; birth and vocation might change, but the men achieved success because they held the same truths to be self-evident. In this narrative, the men typically came from a poor but honest family, used a combination of ingenuity and action to achieve success in their chosen fields, and then recognized that aid to others was an integral part of their life's work. In so highlighting the lives of great men, the students articulated a world where they stood as the natural successors to those they profiled, even though the men hailed from entirely different historical, geographical, and cultural milieus. The passport of SPC and AUB education granted the holder the right to determine who his intellectual, scientific, and literary ancestors were; the particular citizenship of the great man accounted for little in this equation. Modernity was equated with universalist human characteristics; any man who seeks to become modern will have to acquire these characteristics in order to succeed.

Leland Stanford, the founder of Stanford University, serves as an example of how the students framed biographies to fit the typology of the great men they sought to emulate, regardless of whether or not the men truly exhibited the qualities they prized. According to a 1906 *Commercial Review* article, he and other businessmen always sought to "use their power and their influence and their riches for the cause of the great mass. Most of them serve their nations in many ways: as philanthropists, statesmen and inventors."[107] Stanford showed his business acumen even as a young boy, when he came up with the idea of selling horseradish his father required him to dig out of the ground. Another time, he and his brothers took advantage of an abundance of chestnuts and put them up for sale. However, "This money did not go into the same pocket where does go the money that boys of his age can lay hand upon. Every cent he earned by the sweat of his brow, was dear to him, for it came from work and was intended to make him a 'better man.'"[108] Later, after making his fortune and moving to California, he and a small group of colleagues decided that obstacles to building a transcontinental railroad were not as insurmountable as others had claimed. "Courage, faith and force of character" helped them to get the initial land grant from the United States Congress.[109] For Stanford, in particular, "his iron-will never yielded, he never lost faith in himself. His success did not only make his fortune, but it did a great deal for the future of America."[110] With his great fortune, Stanford donated money to good causes, while also endowing a great university. "The biography of Leland Stanford cannot fail to stir the right man, the youth that is doomed to succeed. The key-note to success is a strong will supplemented by work. SET TO WORK NOW!!!"[111]

Of the American politicians put forward as great men to emulate, the students' favorite topic was Abraham Lincoln because he embodied all the characteristics of modern masculinity. Abraham Lincoln, according to a 1908 article in the *University Times*, was born into poverty and, through hard work, became a leader of men. "Abr. Lincoln could not trace his descent from some great man, or woman of history. His mother and his grand mother were illegitimate children. His father descended from poor laborers, who strugled [*sic*] hard for existence."[112] Lincoln became "the ruler of millions and millions of men; and the deliverer of slaves" precisely because he "fought his way to fame by his own abilities and with no one's help. Genius opens herself the doors of fame."[113] A 1927 *University* article praises Lincoln because "this man left many everlasting traces and sayings that will never die in so far as they stand for the principles of liberty and the rights of man."[114] According to an article in the *Review Organ of the Freshman School* that same year, Lincoln "longed to better his country"; "his ambition was good, a blessing to him and to his country."[115] The author calls on his colleagues to follow the path of Lincoln, for "the ambition we need is one actuated by a noble sentiment whose aim is the ultimate good of the country. Let us then covet for our country that ambition which springs from true patriotism so that we may be freed not from the yoke of a tyrant, nor from the incubus of slavery, but from the stony fetters of ignorance."[116]

In terms of military prowess, students endlessly debated the role of Napoleon Bonaparte, finding him either a charismatic leader or an oppressive despot, depending on the aspects of character they chose to ascribe to him. The *Commercial Triumvirate*, quoting Napoleon, declared in 1906, "Success depends upon three things, . . . energy, system, perseverance. The 'man of stone and iron, capable of sitting on horseback sixteen or seventeen hours a day, of going many days together without rest or food, except by snatches, and with the speed and spring of a tiger in action,' gave new possibilities to the meaning of the word 'energy'."[117] The author feels that "probably no other man lived who equaled him in this remarkable quality, not even Ceasar [*sic*]."[118] In the majority of articles, however, Napoleon provides a cautionary tale for the students trying to find the proper character for themselves. For example, ambition is a necessary trait for success, but it must be the right kind of ambition. According to the *Review Organ of the Freshman School* in 1927, Napoleon Bonaparte's ambition was merely "a result of his selfish desire for ephemeral glory."[119] In contrast to Napoleon, Demosthenes never sought a military reputation or aspired to public office; rather, "he longed to deliver his country from the yoke of Philip, oppressor of Greece."[120] A 1905 article in *Happy Days* questions whether Napoleon was a truly great man because he did not leave behind anything constructive. In all his many battles, "It came to no result. All passed away like the smoke of his artillery and left no trace; except the millions of faithful soldiers who lay dead on the battlefields of Marengo, Leipsig, Waterloo, etc."[121] Furthermore, "All the ideas of liberty and equality were crushed down under his despotic government, while, [*sic*] religion got a lever [*sic*] blow in the imprisonment of the pope. There are many other harms which Napoleon did to Europe, but now Europe which at times had supported Napoleon with more than half a million soldiers could not yield more than 100,000. And the cry 'Enough of Napoleon' is universal."[122] A 1926 article in the *Sub-Freshman Star* declares that while Napoleon and Alexander the Great certainly conquered great swaths of land, they failed as contributors to world advancement. James Watt, who revolutionized the steam engine, was the greatest man in the world because "his contributions are the basis of the present success and culture of all the civilized nations. Had it not been for these inventions, the world would not have reached this present state of civilization, but it would have remained as it was. Factories and machines would not have existed, but the old impliments would have remained in use up to the present day."[123]

Men living outside the West could also be declared great, on condition that they successfully persevered in their vocation and granted those who followed them a liberal dose of freedom. One student characterizes Genghis Khan as a hero in large part because "he granted equal rights to every religion whatever their creed was."[124] General Nogi [Maresuke] of Japan succeeded because his "courage and his resolve never to give up . . . saved him from defeat."[125] Nineteenth-century reformer Muhammad Ali of Egypt is cited as an example of someone who succeeded because of steady endeavor. "He was not satisfied until he took Egypt as an independent territory for himself and his descendants, and so on. A man who has a powerful will is always ambitious so that he should work for his goal patiently and with higher aims. He should never rest until his good is better and his better is best."[126] A 1931 article praises Gandhi:

Ghandi [*sic*] is an advocate of toleration, of enlightenment, and above all of LOVE. His pure heart knows no slights, no hatred—absolutely none of the kind. His challenge is against the rule of capital and matter. In our days, the most acute and painful diseases of the world, are born of blind and ignorant submission to such a merciless rule. Men have unconciously put on their necks the yoke of the worst tyrants that humanity has ever known. And Ghandi is doing his utmost to perpetuate the denunciation of this sordid and pagan allegiance. Ghandi defies greed and selfishness, defies the exploitation of the weak, defies the unnatural distinctions in the society, defies ignorance and darkness—all the progenies of the crazy rule of capital and matter.[127]

As these few articles indicate, through sheer repetition of themes, delivered in declaratory fashion, student authors used their magazines to write their own "making men" project for SPC and AUB. These writers wanted to make sure their readers did not take the path of Yakub's fictional student, choosing the superficial affectations of modernity over the more weighty success the school's man and the Arab nahda necessitated. Hundreds of articles gave students the proper guidelines; a 1916 issue of the *Students' Union Gazette* provides a good summary of the student version of the SPC man. Yusuf Abs defines his ideal character, in line with that set out by the school's presidents. "In the first place, he is polite and kind," and has a "love of work."[128] For this latter trait, this gentleman recognizes that "he does not depend upon others to do his work. He is not ashamed to carry his valise from the train to his house—an act which many think is disgracing. A gentleman is not ashamed to do any kind of honest work because he knows that work is an object of life."[129] Furthermore, "With many things around him to interest him and occupy his time he is never lonely or lazy. He is always in good spirits, no matter where he is or what he is doing."[130] Abs also distinguishes modern man's duty to his nation, fulfilled through service. For Abs,

> Service, or, in other words, the good, useful work one accomplishes for his community, is the measure of his worth. The man whose services are necessary to his community is the person who is the true Gentleman of the S.P.C. because we come to this college to learn how to serve our community, country and the world but the Gentlemen of the S.P.C. are those who serve for the sake of humanity, for the sake of the welfare of their community. Therefore the Gentleman of this college is the man whose motto is, "I serve."[131]

In conclusion, Abs writes, "I believe that the true Gentleman of the S.P.C. is a warm, sincere friend; a hard working man; an efficient member of his community; and an embodiment of all that is noble and true in manhood."[132]

The Muslim Controversy of 1909

The themes of these student newspapers indicate that the primary elements of the Arab nahda and the school's "making men" programs usually complemented each other; however, given the dual influence the school and the Arab world always had over the students, a shift in focus by one side could potentially put into question the authority of the other. The one moment of sustained conflict in this early period occurred in the spring 1909 semester, when Muslim and Jewish students walked out of Bible class and chapel services, accusing the college of denying their religious freedom. Individual students had frequently complained about the religious requirements on campus over the years, but never before had anyone waged concerted action against them. The new Ottoman government, which had come into power in 1908, brought with it an intellectual atmosphere that was permeated with passionate discussions of liberty and democracy. Students were prompted to question why Americans exalted these themes but did not put them into practice on campus.

The westernizing reforms of the nineteenth-century Ottoman Tanzimat program generated rising yet unfulfilled expectations among the very groups who had been produced by the reforms. By the end of the century, the new bureaucratic bourgeoisie had joined forces with army officers and students clamoring for the Ottoman government to make the reforms more effective in stemming European military and economic intrusion into the region. A rallying point for these new groups was the 1876 Ottoman constitution, which limited the power of the sultan and called for government by parliamentary rule; students and young military officers and professionals supported this kind of government because it had the potential to distribute power more equally. However, almost immediately after the constitution was established, the new sultan, Abdulhamid II, ascended the throne and suspended the constitution and the recently elected parliament. Over the next decades, his government grew increasingly despotic as it fell into debt to European banks, ceded territory to European colonial control, and failed to stop nationalist revolts throughout the Balkans. In reaction, the new strata established oppositional political organizations. By the early twentieth century, the most powerful of these organizations was the Committee of Union and Progress (CUP), more colloquially known as the Young Turks; they comprised young officers, civil servants, and students demanding that the constitution be reinstated. As Erik Zürcher explains, "Abdülhamit's major weakness was his failure to instil loyalty in the new generations of bureaucrats and officers, the Ottoman intelligentsia, which his own expanded educational institutions were producing."[133] These young officers, bureaucrats, and students embraced Ottoman patriotism and "the liberal and constitutional ideas" that would become the mantra of the Turkish political opposition movement.[134] In 1908, the Young Turks successfully captured control of the government, leaving Abdulhamid II and his successors to serve merely as political figureheads.[135]

For the first year, the Young Turks exuded excitement and confidence about the future; they represented the dynamic strata emerging throughout the empire, which struggled to find the perfect balance between Eastern heritage and Western modernity. They spoke extensively of the freedoms a constitutional government protected; they backed up those promises by reconvening parliament and allowing the press to flourish with unprecedented freedom. Howard Bliss vividly describes the new atmosphere in 1908 and 1909 in his annual report to the board of trustees: "We are still rubbing our eyes in wonder" at the new constitution and parliament.[136]

> Where a Government has not only ceased to proscribe and hunt down
> men for the use of the words Liberty, Equality, Fraternity, but pro-
> claims these words as watchwords of its policy, it means that a new era
> has dawned, however imperfect and distorted the popular conceptions
> may be as to the meaning of these great words. With an Empire thus
> pulsating with new and strange forces, with confused and extravagant
> notions as to the well-nigh limitless rights of personal liberty; with
> a Constitution proclaiming Islam as the religion of the State and at
> the same time pronouncing that there was to be everywhere liberty
> in religious belief; with the further declaration that all schools would
> be under the surveillance of the State; with all this seething ferment
> of feeling suddenly released after generations of unnatural and cruel
> confinement, it is small occasion for wonder that the spirit of eager
> restlessness has entered the educational institutions of the Empire, and
> that for many of them it has been a difficult and anxious though a most
> stimulating year.[137]

The Young Turks could not maintain their passion and enthusiasm much beyond the first year; an increasing emphasis on their Turkish identity and a descent into authoritarianism in the face of continuing nationalist revolts alienated the many groups, such as the Arabs, who were articulating their own national identities at the same time. For the students at SPC, however, 1909 proved to be the perfect moment when the discourse emanating from Istanbul brought into stark relief what they considered the hypocrisies present within the school's educational and religious policies.

As early as summer 1908, articles began appearing in newspapers published in Beirut and Cairo criticizing the compulsory religious requirements at SPC.[138] When the semester began, the school received letters from Muslim parents asking that their children be exempt from these obligations. At this point, Muslims and Jews comprised a minority on campus, while the majority claimed loyalty to one of many Christian sects resident in the Ottoman Empire. In the 1908–1909 academic year, of the 876 students enrolled, 128 were Muslim and 88 were Jews.[139] At the start of the semester, the administration immediately posted on the bulletin board a clear statement of the school's right and desire to maintain intact its religious policy, regardless of the pleas it had received. The announcement stressed "the impossibility of divorcing character-training from the inspiration of religion, and the belief of the College that the Christian religion best developed character, with the assurance that we were impelled to include a study of the Christian religion in our curriculum and to require uniform chapel attendance."[140] As the fall semester progressed, students organized around this issue, first asking for the right to establish a Muslim union; the college rejected the request on the grounds that the school would not allow a religious-affiliated organization to exist besides the YMCA. Students then requested permission to attend mosque for prayers each day; the college agreed. Students suggested that a representative hold regular meetings with the faculty in order to discuss ongoing issues of concern; "the Faculty voted to take no cognizance of this request, seeing that to recognize a representative was tantamount to organizing for them a society, a matter already declined."[141] Students again tried to form an organization, stating that it would be a literary society, open to Christians, but would focus on the literature of Islam; "this was smothered in committee."[142]

The return to campus in January 1909 brought the students and the administration into open conflict, sparked by a sermon given during the prayer week held during the second week of the semester. Edward Nickoley, who was serving as acting president while Howard Bliss was visiting the United States, reported that one evening that week, the Reverend Mr. James H. Nicol of Tripoli gave a sermon on the text "Put ye on the Whole Armor of God." Nickoley wrote that the Muslim students claimed Nicol said during his sermon: "We the Christians are surrounded with great walls of enemies, the Moslems and others. They prevent us from spreading the true call and await the opportunity to devour us. It is our business then, our sacred duty to break down these walls and tread upon them."[143] When students and local newspaper editors expressed outrage at these alleged statements, the school's leaders vociferously denied that Nicol had said or implied any of them. Regardless of the truth, this speech lit the flame that led to a protest by the majority of the Muslim and Jewish students on campus. To begin their fight, the Muslim students circulated a petition, signed by ninety-eight of their colleagues, asking that they be excused from all religious obligations. By the following week, city newspapers were publishing articles attacking the school and supporting the students' action. The conflict escalated when about seventy of the Muslim students swore an oath on the Qur'an that they would not attend prayers as long as attendance remained compulsory, that all would leave campus if any of their group was expelled, and that if they were asked to leave the school, they would do so only by force. They also decided that they would scrupulously follow all the rules of the campus that did not involve Christian study or worship; they wanted to prove to the school's leaders that they were mature men embarking on a legitimate act of protest. The strike officially commenced on Sunday, January 17, with about seventy-five Jewish students participating as well.[144] Students immediately sent telegrams to the minister of the interior, the grand vizier, the "Sultan as Caliph," and the American ambassador in Istanbul, asking for legal clarification concerning the Young Turks' support of religious freedom.[145] The students and their allies in Beirut called on the government to issue a decree rejecting SPC's right to impose compulsory religious requirements.

After this burst of activity, the situation devolved into a stalemate; the administration chose not to expel the students for fear of the repercussions, but also held to its belief that SPC could not do its work without Christianity serving as its ideological bedrock. In the end, the administration and the board of trustees in New York decided that the students would not be required to attend any of the Christian religious services during the course of the spring 1909 semester, provided they presented themselves at an alternative religious service, went back to Bible classes, caused no disturbance on campus, and accepted the fact that all the rules would be fully reinstated at the beginning of the fall 1909 semester. Any student who did not want to comply with the religious rules of the school at that time would be free to withdraw, as the school was a private institution and could impose rules it believed to be necessary to its proper functioning.

Through faculty reports, local newspaper articles, and a small number of student statements that have been preserved, it is possible to determine the arguments the students made for rejecting compulsory religious exercises.[146] Taking up the cause of freedom lit by the Young Turks and SPC's educational program, the students demanded that they receive the right to worship as they pleased, as modern society had dictated, and as the school had promised. Of the students' perspective, Professor William Hall said:

1. That the College is in honor bound by the law of humanity to receive any student who applies providing such student posseses [sic] the necessary moral and intellectual qualifications. This College being the only one in Syria which offers such an education it is bound to open its doors to all worthy applicants. 'Freely ye have received. Freely give', they quote.

2. The College does not have the right to require students against their will and conscience, to receive religious instruction and to attend worship which is not only distasteful but which violates their consciences.[147]

Professor Franklin Moore added, "Their contention that we have no right to expel for disobedience of the regulation in dispute they base upon the announced program of the new party in government which they confidently expect to see promulgated as law."[148] An article in *Lewa* reported that "A. of the Syrian College" said,

Now it is passing strange that our faculty have undertaken in forcing us to attend church and teaching us Christian doctrine inspite of us, in view of their pretense of religious liberty. It is contrary to reason and at variance with the regulation of all the schools of the world, among them those of America universally. Moreover the college has no right to make a regulation by itself and put it into execution without getting the sanction of the Ottoman government which is in possession of the legal power in the country. Has the government sanctioned this regulation?[149]

In addition, the students believed that the new government in Istanbul was obligated to legitimate its claim to religious tolerance. They sought out local government officials who could issue a decree declaring inviolate the Syrian Protestant College policy of requiring students to worship in an institution outside their faith. Rumors swirled throughout the spring that the Young Turk government had issued such a decree, but in fact no such law had passed. Ottoman government officials spoke informally to the American consulate in Istanbul, voicing their opinion that the school could not compel non-Christians to attend Christian services, but no formal decree or law backed up their statements.[150] Only in September 1915 did the Ottoman government finally issue educational decrees prohibiting the school from imposing religious requirements on non-Christians. In order to remain open during World War I, the school administration temporarily organized alternative religious exercises. The substitute courses "consisted of various readings—biographical, historical, philosophical, educational" and "in place of the required Sunday afternoon Bible School, there have been given courses of instruction of ethical benefit to the students."[151]

This crisis illustrates how the students integrated the new political atmosphere of the Ottoman Empire into their identities as students. They took the discussions of liberty and tolerance emanating out of Istanbul and used those arguments to try to alter the relationship between themselves and the school's administration. They attempted to establish societies to research their literary and religious ideas, issued petitions stating their desires, and organized a united effort to show that they were not recalcitrant students, but respectful, mature adults seeking redress of valid grievances. They also worked closely with the community's leaders in an effort to gain more leverage against the school. Their complaints certainly addressed specific religious requirements for the school, but their arguments also engaged the American educational system, as their predecessors had done in 1882. The students disputed the school leaders' sole right to define the parameters of their educational experience by delimiting the borders of freedom in what they felt was a discriminatory manner. Student protestors recognized the inherent contradiction between a "making men" program based in liberal education and a missionary school that denied religious freedom. However inclusive or tolerant SPC's liberal Protestantism may have been, Christianity's existence at the center of the character building program automatically rejected a similar role for other religions. The juxtaposition between a progressive Protestantism and intolerant Arab Eastern religions allowed no room, at this point, for a wider discussion of Middle Eastern contributions to the school's religious policy. For the school's leaders, their Christian identity trumped the freedom inherent in liberal education; for the students, freedom negated religious compulsion. Howard Bliss's Protestantism was more inclusive than his father's had been, but students still had to be just as obedient to it, and to the religious obligations imposed on campus. Inspired by the Young Turks, the students took action.

Conclusion

The first leaders of SPC and AUB sold to their students an idealistic image of a Protestantism and an Americanism that had no social, religious, economic, or political problems; as such, it had the most constructive answers to the problems faced by modern society. The school's leaders transmitted what they defined as that Protestant American character into their framework for "making men." They saw American education transforming the whole man and seeding the region with modern missionaries for their program. They constructed a man who would actively seek out enlightenment, knowledge, and personal and societal improvement. He could not, however, find these traits in his own Arab society, for only America and Protestantism had the tools for this progressive future. In this paradigm, a mythologized good and dynamic America stood juxtaposed to an equally mythologized failed and stagnant Arab world: the workers versus the lazy, and the honest versus the dishonest.

Liberal education calls for active participation by students; in a very literal sense, the students fulfilled this requirement by writing their own character building program and disseminating it to their colleagues. Writers of this first generation of student papers accepted the Western civilizational parameters of the program and followed many of the same prescriptions put forward in Arab newspapers of the day. The fact that the students chose to publish them for an audience of their peers shows that they wanted to display for their colleagues the attributes of modern civilization and masculinity; even more, they wanted to exhort their colleagues to become the men that the school and their own society modeled. The Muslim Controversy of 1909 shows that the students did not blindly follow their American professors, but sought to find a balance between the often complementary, but sometimes contradictory, forces influencing them. In this era, the students acted as constant negotiators in regard to their own educational experience.

MAKING WOMEN
The Goals of Coeducation

Coeducation began at the American University of Beirut in the fall 1921 semester, but as late as the 1950s, administrators and students on campus continued to question the validity and purpose of it. A reporter for *Outlook* could still see the need to ask of her fellow students in 1957, "Do you think women should be kept outside the campus?"[1] The answers reflect strong support for coeducation, with slight differences of opinion as to its purpose. One male student answered, "Besides offering her an opportunity for finding a valuable profession, a university education better equips a woman for her role in marriage. In dealing with many kinds of people she acquires the social assurance to make a gracious hostess. She learns much that will be invaluable to her in the upbringing and education of her children, and she prepares herself to be an intelligent companion to her husband. AUB is a pioneer for the modern way of life in the Middle East."[2] Another male student offered, "University women are badly needed to participate in social activities through which they can serve their country and destroy the ignorance deeply rooted in a majority of people. However, I object to the presence of married women in the university because these could serve society best not by leaving their homes and seeking education, but by devoting

their lives to a more important mission, namely the development of a new young generation strong in mind and body, high in courage and spirit."[3] A third man said, "The same chance must be given to both sexes. Women and men complement each other and their cooperative work is needed every where and in every age."[4] A woman student responded, "University education helps the women to enter in [to] social life. On the other hand, the presence of women in a University creates in men the ability to sustain platonic friendships. They will learn to be respectful to girl students, and they will realize that women can be their real companions."[5] Another woman stated, "I believe that coeducation in a university is helpful because it teaches women to understand men. They will get to know them better, their ideas, likes and dislikes, and this will create a more friendly atmosphere between men and women, but this competition will help both sexes to achieve perfection."[6]

American administrators, faculty members, and male and female students discussed the role of women on campus and in the society at large from the moment women could first enroll as graduate students in the Schools of Medicine, Pharmacy, and Dentistry in 1921. Women were then admitted (for a brief time) as members of the sophomore class in 1924, as members of the junior and senior classes in the School of Arts and Sciences in 1927, and as members of the freshman and sophomore classes in 1952. Without a doubt, AUB stood in the vanguard of coeducation in the Middle East in the 1920s, for only a small number of schools in the region had initiated higher education at any level for women.[7] Nonetheless, AUB's coeducational program did not immediately flourish as an equal opportunity educational provider just because the faculty voted for it and just because women walked through the Main Gate. Women attended in increasing numbers after the administration made the initial decisions in the 1920s, but the curriculum and the educational goals remained designed and geared for men; AUB's leaders set no guidelines for what the women were supposed to become as a result of their educational experience. Women had arrived, but "making men" still ruled supreme; women students were coeds in the sense that Barbara Solomon found in America until well into the twentieth century. "The 'coed' often remained a second-class citizen, for male attitudes depended on the mores of the particular institution."[8] At least through the 1939–1940 academic year, the school handbook still included a section entitled "An A.U.B. Man." No comparable list of characteristics for making women appeared in any of the handbooks for this era, regardless of the increasing numbers of women enrolling.

The five respondents quoted above encapsulate the key themes enunciated about women's higher education for almost forty years. As these students explained, women in the first stage of AUB's coeducational history, from 1921 until well into the 1950s, positioned higher education as training for scientific motherhood and companionate marriage with educated men. In this program, women and men, functioning in their separate spheres, worked together to uplift their families, societies, and nations. Coeducation did not, in this era, openly challenge the dominant "making men" ethos on campus. In this atmosphere, the pioneering women students began the process of clarifying why they deserved to receive higher education at AUB.

AUB's Coeducational Program

A key element in how coeducation came to AUB resides in the difference between women's education and coeducation. Long before 1921, American missionaries and the leaders of SPC had come to accept and encourage girls' and women's education. SPC opened a nurses' training school in 1905. In 1917, the faculty took another step when it placed into record a desire to admit qualified women for graduate work. According to the faculty minutes of December 11, 1917, the faculty "voted, that in view of an application for opportunity for advanced study by a young woman of Beirut, the Faculty approve in principle the admitting of young women who hold the B.A. degree from an approved institution to work leading to the M.A. degree."[9] As it turned out, the Turkish woman who asked to be admitted could not take up her position because she left Beirut during World War I.[10] This vote thus amounted to a statement of principle rather than a change in policy. In 1921 the administration allowed women to enter the graduate programs of the Schools of Medicine, Pharmacy, and Dentistry, provided they had received proper preparation.

While supporting women's education in general, and allowing women to study as nurses and professionals at SPC and AUB, the school's leaders struggled against having to supply coeducation at the university level.[11] On February 1, 1920, acting president Edward Nickoley (1920–1923) wrote to Howard Bliss (1902–1920) that the Jerusalem and East Mission, the United Free Church of Scotland, the Church Missionary Society, the London Jews Society, and the British Syria Mission in Jerusalem had debated opening up a women's college and "a men's college of rather ambitious range and scope" in Jerusalem.[12] In his letter, Nickoley is far more concerned about the possibility of a new men's college. As he wrote to Bliss, "Personally I should very much regret having Palestine cut off from us as a field from which we draw students and to which we send our alumni."[13] This letter indicates that women's education could continue apace in Jerusalem, with little comment from AUB's acting president; Nickoley saw a problem arising only if the male college siphoned off students from AUB.[14] In March 1967, Emma Nickoley, the first dean of women students (1934–1937) at AUB and the wife of Edward Nickoley, penned a short memoir about the beginnings of coeducation at the university. In her recollection, "One evening Mr. Nickoley came home from a long drawn out meeting to tell me that the Administration had voted to accept women students to the junior and senior classes the following year. I was stunned! No hint of such a venture had been spoken of by any member of the faculty. How it had been brought to book was not revealed. It had simply been proposed and after long discussion, voted upon."[15]

After this inauspicious beginning, the dominant theme in the documents is the recognition of the inevitability of women's higher education coming to Lebanon; the debate was over what institution would actually supply it. As the documents all attest, AUB's faculty and administrators gradually accepted their leadership role. By 1920, sufficient numbers of women had graduated from the various secondary schools in the area and were putting pressure on institutions like AUB to expand their offerings. Given these conditions, AUB passed stop-gap measures to help the women they accepted into their professional schools, but they refrained from moving to the full coeducational model, continuing to hope that another institution would accept the call. For example, women could enter the special sophomore class in the School of Arts and Sciences when coeducation began in 1921, but could only receive special training for their future graduate programs, not a BA. The school moved toward a fuller acceptance of coeducation only when it became clear that neither the American School for Girls (ASG) nor any of the neighboring schools would be able to prepare such a program quickly enough in the 1920s. In the breach, in 1924 AUB's leaders temporarily allowed women to enter the sophomore, junior, and senior classes to pursue a BA, and then, in 1927, when the newly established American Junior College for Women (AJCW) opened a sophomore-level class, AUB restricted coeducation to the junior and senior classes and above.[16] In going forward with coeducation, AUB was acceding to demands raised within the context of Beirut and the surrounding area;

Emma Nickoley's recollections indicate how little discussion actually took place at AUB concerning coeducation before it came into being. The exigencies of the moment demanded it. On the other hand, no SPC or AUB president used the argument that women were not qualified for higher education, as so many of their colleagues were saying in America. This decision put AUB on a different path from its educational models. Harvard, Amherst, and Princeton did not accept women for decades.

While making these decisions, AUB's leaders struggled with how to define the purpose of coeducation. Pressure had built, the concept itself had been accepted, but AUB's leaders did not know how to fully institute the program. When AUB's leaders allowed women to temporarily enter the sophomore class in 1924, the faculty minutes stated, "This vote was passed reluctantly, as the Faculty feared that Muslim girls would not be able to enter the University and [the school] had therefore spent over three years in trying to persuade other organizations to develop a college for girls alone."[17] When the administration took the next step, allowing women to enter the junior and senior classes in 1927, Edward Nickoley, by then dean of the Faculty of Arts and Sciences (1924–1937), summarized for the alumni the basic rationale for coeducation. Nickoley reports, "Some years ago the authorities of the American University of Beirut sensed a demand on the part of its constituency for women's education of a higher grade than that provided by the high schools for girls conducted by various agencies carrying on educational work in the country. The University expected that one of these high schools would develop its curriculum to provide facilities for higher studies for women."[18] In permanently extending coeducation to the junior and senior years, Nickoley assured his readers that the change would not alter the school's program or men's status.

> The criticism at the present time most frequently advanced against
> the plan in operation is not that it is co-educational, but the fact that
> women are being educated in such a manner that they will and must
> compete with the men in those vocations which have in the past been
> monopolized by the latter. This criticism, of course, grows out of the
> fundamental error that a college or university education is primarily or
> exclusively a means for making a living. With the recognition that a
> higher education is a means for enriching the life of the individual and
> the community rather than a device for improving the economic condi-
> tion of the person educated, this criticism falls to the ground.[19]

Nickoley did not envision women graduates competing with men for scarce professional jobs; rather, the American liberal education system aimed to teach students how to acquire the character necessary for living a fruitful life in the modern era, regardless of the students' actual postgraduate pursuits. In essence, Nickoley did not articulate a coeducational program challenging the male-dominated framework at the school; in his definition of the program, AUB would remain intact. Nothing would change, he assured the alumni.

In keeping with this minimalist effort, AUB never followed the example of many coeducational and women's institutions by offering courses in home economics. For example, over one hundred universities in the United States offered the new program to women students by 1910; in Lebanon, the Sidon Girls' School and AJCW established related courses in the 1920s and 1930s.[20] In asking for donations for the program at Sidon, the school's leaders equated home economics with "practical education," seeing a more academic curriculum as antithetical to the proper aims of girls' education.[21] Nadya Sbaiti reports that in the 1920s students at Mary Kassab's Syrian National School, or the al-Ahliah, "learned that citizenship and national duty included actions that ranged from cooking 'national' dishes to maintaining public cleanliness and hygiene."[22] In Margaret Lowe's descriptions of similar programs in American universities, "Home economics faculty expected students to understand sophisticated nutritional principles, memorize specific food properties and calorie counts, and then apply those standards to themselves and others. The new food scientists advocated a rational, businesslike approach to eating rather than the untrained, unpredictable, 'messy' dictates of the appetite."[23]

The home economics program at Cornell University, a prototype of such programs, represented both new opportunities and the institutional separation of the women from the larger (male) campus arena. Charlotte Conable notes several positive aspects of the Cornell home economics program: "Here highly selected, able women from diverse backgrounds were able to obtain a state-subsidized education which had both a domestic and a professional orientation. In fact, this college emphasized vocational preparation and provided career guidance for its students at a time when the assumption was made in most other academic units that undergraduate women were destined only for marriage."[24] This type of program also provided an arena for female academic advancement, it was reasoned, since faculty and students in these programs did not face competition from men in the classroom. On the other hand, home economics departments and courses ghettoized women into their own, specialized zones, taking them out of the biology, chemistry, and physics courses designed for men and solidifying the educational maxim that women's higher education should not challenge men in the public sphere. The result: "Strict segregation of the sexes was maintained; only women were admitted to home economics and only men were permitted to prepare themselves in such fields as engineering and law."[25] Home economics glorified domesticity, undergirded with a scientific rationale, rather than economic independence and social and political equality for women.

None of the administrative written documents preserved at AUB discuss home economics in any form; no debate about its values or problems appears to have taken place among the faculty or the administration. Nickoley suggests that AUB could not afford to finance such a program: "For obvious reasons the University could not duplicate its equipment for the accommodation of women students and, in the absence of a practicable alternative, co-education was introduced."[26] An examination of the financial and ideological context for the decision, or the lack thereof, shines some light on the issue. AUB entered the 1920s and its new existence as a university in deep financial trouble. Syrian Protestant College had remained open throughout World War I but succeeded in doing so only because of dramatic cost-cutting measures. By 1920, the school needed to raise $80,000 for that academic year and $320,000 to replenish the endowment and wipe out the deficit.[27] In determining what projects to fund, the trustees in 1920, for example, "sanctioned the expenditure of enough money to replenish the laboratories and recitation rooms, as well as to repair the buildings and set in order the dining halls, so that some of the ill effects of neglect during the war time will be overcome before next autumn."[28] Through the aegis of the Near East Colleges Association during the 1920s, AUB's trustees succeeded in raising millions of dollars in donations, eliminating the debt, and allowing for an expansion of the campus and its programs.

In the many discussions taking place about how to distribute these new funds, no mention was made of courses specific to women. The priority lay with making the transition from a college to a university, opening new fields of study, improving the laboratories, expanding the campus infrastructure, and hiring new professors and staff. The university as a whole interested AUB's leaders; women were not considered a special category of student when this new money and the school's future came up for discussion. This situation had both positive and negative ramifications for the women who came to attend AUB. By choosing not to establish home economics courses at AUB, the administration forced women students to join the men in all their classes. This allowed for integration in the classroom setting, while also avoiding the conflicts that might have arisen when pressures mounted to end such separate courses for women. When women proved that they could excel at their academic pursuits, they did so within the male-dominated domain, not in courses specifically designed for them.

The segregation occurred outside class, as the school's administration catered to concerns the Beiruti public had about the mingling of women and men in unchaperoned arenas. As Nickoley declared when he first announced the 1927 decision, new institutions, such as a women's dormitory, would give women a designated living space on campus, while also "giving them a more normal field for their own distinctive extra curriculum activities than is at present possible. In such a residence they would have their own Dean of Women under whose direction certain lines of instruction would be offered exclusively for women students, such subjects as are especially suited to meet their peculiar needs in preparing them for a fuller and a larger participation in the life of their communities."[29] In fact, AUB did not provide women's housing until 1958; before that, women students lived at home, at the AJCW, or in women's hostels near campus, while allowed access during the day to special rooms in College Hall. Emma Nickoley served as dean of women from 1934 to 1937, but not until 1945, when Elsa Kerr took the post, did the position become permanent.

The female population at AUB was initially small and overwhelmingly Christian. Between 1921 and 1927 there was an average of only 18 women out of a student body of 539. Between 1927 and 1952, there was an average of only 73 women out of 763.[30] Among the women students, there was a significantly greater proportion of Christians than in the school population at large. In 1927, the first year when women could enroll in the junior and senior classes, Christian women represented 83 percent of all the coeds; thirty years later, Christian women still accounted for 64 percent of all women. By contrast, the male college population was divided about evenly between Christians and non-Christians from the 1920s on.[31]

The administration, fearing that parents of potential female students would hesitate if the students could socialize outside carefully controlled venues, rejected student requests for coed activities such as co-acting and co-dancing until the 1940s. *al-Kulliyah Review* explained in 1937, "In order to safe-guard the traditions of centuries and to prevent a too sudden change in the status of women, the A.U.B. has ever been anxious to comply with public opinion and yet to increase the opportunities for women students, academically and socially."[32] Men and women students worked together in the many social welfare projects, such as those organized by the Village Welfare League (VWL), but the most contentious arenas continued to be dancing and acting. When the administration refused to budge on this issue, students occasionally bypassed the prohibition by organizing dances at hotels off campus. Only on May 12, 1942, did the administration begin to make changes to the on-campus regulations. On that day, the executive committee recommended allowing women to dance in Dale Home and the Women Students' Hostel, although still not in the student center of West Hall. It was required that the women receive their parents' permission beforehand, that proper "chaperonage" be supplied, and that "men be permitted to come only if individually invited and that a proper control be exercised over the invitations."[33] On May 9, 1944, the university senate voted to extend dancing to West Hall during summer vacations, "but with the added proviso that, in case there is dancing, it shall be restricted to those who do not wear boots with hob-nails or steel plates on them."[34] As for co-acting, before the administration allowed it in 1945, men and women produced separate performances.[35]

The Role of Coeducation in "Making Men"

That Daniel and Howard Bliss spoke little of the role of modern womanhood is not surprising; no women were on campus under the former's presidency and only a small number of nursing students attended during the latter's tenure. When Bayard Dodge took up his position as president (1923–1948), he wrote repeatedly about the status of women in the region and of the related need for women's education. He rarely, however, addressed the women students as "you," as he did so often for the men in the "making men" program; instead, he spoke of women when he reported to the donors and the trustees tasked with maintaining the school's financial foundations and when he spoke to the men students charged with becoming modern men modeled on a Western template. In the former, he applauded Americans for their vanguard role in uplifting the status of Middle Eastern women; in the latter, he challenged the male students to reform their ideas about women. Dodge said of the Americans, "We can aid orientals to understand the West, by giving them a wholesome attitude toward an emancipated womanhood and proper relations between the sexes."[36] In Dodge's view, men are the catalysts, the controllers of societies' destinies. He spoke repeatedly of the need to educate women and to grant them the respect they deserve in the modern world. However, the actors were not the women themselves but a West that had already liberated its own women and a group of Arab men who had been educated in the American educational structure.

In describing liberated women, Dodge chose to focus more often on their public appearance than on the more substantive issues concerning their lives. In particular, clothing styles represented for Dodge a key identifier of the modernity coming to womanhood in the Middle East; in taking off the veil, women achieved modernity. Dodge wrote in "The Awakening of the Near East" in 1935 that myriad changes had arrived in the area with the closing years of the Ottoman Empire. Western examples and influences had shown Muslim women how to move into the public arena, and Middle Eastern governments and societies had begun to accept the West's lead in this regard.

> In Turkey the process has been hastened by government action. In Cairo and Alexandria it has been helped by the European life of those large cities. Even in provincial districts the education of women, the throwing back of the veil, the mixing of the sexes in cinema halls, and the employment of women in commerce are becoming common place affairs.[37]

Even with these changes, Dodge still found female medievalism and modernism literally sitting side by side. In one such instance in 1930, he described a home where "several rotund ladies of the old school, with loose garments and dyed hair are sitting stolidly, smoking their water pipes and talking in Arabic. Side by side with them, thin girls with bobbed hair and [the] latest Parisian fashions are smoking cigarettes, talking French and passing cognac to their guests."[38] In Dodge's imagery, the public representation is more important than the ideology behind the process. Women take off their veils; they are emancipated. No discussion of political or educational rights exists in his stories; if women have donned the public persona of modernity, they have been liberated. If they can leave their houses unencumbered by excessive clothing, they can take their place in a modern world modeled by the West, leaving Arab ignorance and superstition behind. Women's agency is missing from this narrative; the West alone catalyzes change.

When Dodge discussed the actual women on campus, he spoke in much the same third-person style, addressing not the women themselves but the trustees and potential donors who received his reports. In such writings, Dodge distinguished between the clothing and actions of the first women students from those who followed them in the late 1930s and 1940s. In 1947, he wrote, "A quarter of a century ago there was such a demand for women teachers, that the University tried the experiment of allowing women students to enter the Upper Classes of the School of Arts and Sciences, as well as the professional schools."[39] In regard to the women pioneers, Dodge said, "Whenever they walked across the campus, the eyes of the men students followed them and they had to sit in the rear of the Chapel to avoid embarrassment."[40] The first Muslim woman "wore two veils and was chaperoned by her husband, who was also enrolled as a student. The girls swam at separate hours from the men, never thought of going on week-end trips, and played tennis at off hours, clad in long skirts. They were not allowed to act in theatricals and dancing was prohibited."[41] In contrast, at the end of his tenure as president in 1948, Dodge could report, "Men and women students are seated alphabetically in chapel and class rooms without embarrassment. Dancing has become popular and the girls take part in theatricals with men. They go on week-end excursions for skiing and picnics, swim in modern bathing suits and play tennis in shorts. They take part in welfare work, speak in public meetings and serve as officers of student societies."[42] These transformations in male-female relationships cannot be discounted; the women students of the 1950s faced few of the obstacles their predecessors had. Dramatic and deep changes had come to campus as women slowly moved away from their coed status and toward one as students. On the other hand, Bayard Dodge's writings about the change in women's status did not address the true meaning of the equality that gradually came to campus, nor did he challenge men to adopt a new image of AUB citizenship upon the arrival of the women students. To become the men modeled by AUB, the male students needed to improve their opinion about women, but neglected in this call was a mandate for addressing the women students on campus in new and progressive ways.

The few areas of the curriculum that discussed the status of women in the region reiterated the idea that only males serve as the agents of change for women's enlightenment. The social sciences curriculum, the basis for the liberal arts structure in the interwar period, confirmed the trajectory that saw women as passive actors in their educational enrichment; since no women could attend the freshman class prior to 1952, the text and the class addressed their precepts to the male students. The AUB civics text, *Social Relationships in the Near East*, states in its introduction, "It is more than a Civics course in the narrower political sense in that it deals with all the social relationships of a citizen."[43] Professor Stuart Dodd prepared the text, used throughout the 1930s; it reads like a primer for the "making men" project, as it includes almost every aspect of the program elucidated by Bayard Dodge. An entire section is titled "The Status of Women." The book specifies that the most important catalyst for the modern transformation of women is Western influence, making explicit the view that indigenous forces in the Middle East would not be able to initiate such changes. After a short history of the successful women's movement in the West, the text states, "The Near East turns its face, so to speak, to the West rather than to the East, and is therefore more susceptible to Western influences. Little wonder, therefore, that the women's movement in Europe, like many a movement that preceded it, has found its way to our countries, and that we are today faced by the question of how to meet those changes."[44] The text calls on students to adopt the "desirable changes coming in from the West," such as those encouraging the unveiling, education, and marital equality of women, but to recognize that all of these reforms should not be undertaken too rapidly for fear of destabilizing society.[45] In speaking directly to the male students attending the class, the text reads, "The progress of the women's movement depends largely upon the attitude of educated men. There is no doubt that each one of you do a great deal by your attitude and your actions."[46] The text's narrative focus does not challenge the male students sitting in the classroom to ameliorate any problems existing between themselves and the actual women on campus; they are not required to rethink their relations with them in any concrete ways. The only AUB woman student mentioned is the first to receive an MD; she comes across as a marker of AUB's vanguard position and not as a full-fledged member of the student community, particularly since her name, Edma Abu-Chedid, is never even mentioned.[47]

Reflecting the message disseminated by Dodge and the school's curricular offerings, male students wrote their own narrative of women and women's education; their writings position women into a secondary, and often demeaning, relationship to men. These male student writers largely write AUB's women students out of their stories of progress and modernity, preferring to discuss the archetype of the educated "woman," to laud "women" as unattainable symbols of desire, or, more often, to ridicule them as materialistic girlfriends and nagging wives. When AUB's women students come under scrutiny, the men express little interest in engaging positively in their activities and desires; poor treatment of the women by the male students serves instead as proof that men have not attained the marks of modern manhood laid out in "making men." As with Dodge, the men students see men—themselves or those of the West—as the actors in the process of female enlightenment. They speak to each other about the proper hallmarks of female modernity and they continually debate how to treat women; they do not address women students and their particular concerns or issues. While the male students wanted to be active participants in their educational experience, they made no effort to offer women students the same agency.

In much the same style as the male leaders of AUB, the men students articulated a narrative of modern womanhood that they hoped their peers would embrace. They called on the women of the Middle East to enter modernity so that all of society could advance civilizationally. These male writings frequently tapped into the vocabulary of women's oppression common to not only Dodge's writings but also the writings of many Western missionaries, politicians, and travelers, who had for years prognosticated on the poor status of Middle Eastern women vis-à-vis those of the West.[48] While Arab males could take pride in the accomplishments of their national past, no such satisfaction appears in the writings about Arab women. The narrative written into these documents explains that Arab society of the past so denigrated women that no element of it could be used to guide women to reform in the modern period. At no time do the male student writers, in glorifying the attributes of modern society, use the actual women students as examples of the change or progress they seek. For much of the 1930s, when these articles appeared in the largest number, Ataturk's Turkey provided a model that the men students believed Arabs should follow. In this narrative, Turkish women have their "freedom," which means that

> nowadays they choose their own husbands. They are not considered as pieces of house furniture which are at any time under the disposal of the house owner. They are not a museum of beauty, nor an ornament for amusement, but they are active and productive progressive citizens, and members of a social group. Hence, they enter universities[,] study medicine, play games, attend to social meetings, and in a word they share in most social and administrative activities. It is strange to see ladies at the courts and in the shops. It is a miracle to see these women,

once secluded in their inclosures [*sic*], appear in the markets dressed with European clothes and fashion.[49]

In the same way, Arab women need to receive freedom, as defined by Western standards, so that Arab society can enter the modern era; women must move out of the harem, take off the veil, and dress like European women in order to enter into a vaguely defined "free" world of equality with men. Women achieve freedom when they destroy the traditional bonds holding them in the home; no mention is made of who might be binding the women, who freed them in the case of Turkey, why women should receive that freedom, or what they should do with their newfound freedom once achieved. These male student writers do not enunciate a rationale for women's education; rather, they write of a vague "womanhood" that must be enlightened. Moreover, the articles on womanhood often appear side by side with postcards displaying images and jokes ridiculing the girlfriend and wife who constantly demand expensive gifts from the men in their lives.[50] All the student magazines combine together these misogynistic portrayals with sugary poems and odes to love.

Women on campus enter into the written male narrative of campus days quite rarely prior to the 1950s, but when they do it is as entities separate from or even antagonistic to the male norm. The men students make no effort to connect the positive female attributes they describe in many of their articles to those women actually undertaking the educational project alongside them. Asked by an *Outlook* reporter in 1949, "What is your opinion of the AUB girl?" a sophomore arts student responded with a quote from an unknown writer on the "Element Woman":

Symbol: Woe
Atomic Wt: 51 Kilos
Properties: Boils and freezes at will.
Great affinity for gold, silver, and carbon in the form of diamonds.
Violently reactive when left alone, it turns to a dull green color when [re]placed by a more attractive specimen.
Occurrence: Found wherever men are, but seldom in the free state.
Uses: Highly ornamental; a very efficient income-reducing agent.
Caution: Violently explosive in inexperienced hands.[51]

Other respondents remarked that women were virtually hidden on campus, hiding in their "College Hall Hareem" or watching tennis players from the security of the College Hall balcony.[52] In the 1950 commencement issue of *Outlook*, reporters asked (male) students to reminisce about their experiences at AUB. In regard to women, "Opinion ranged from: 'AUB girls are too conservative' to 'they are too modern—they interpret civilization wrongly.' Rejected suitors took the opportunity to denounce girls as being 'too proud,' while those who for some reason or another feel more strongly about the matter found expression in the outcry of one: 'Never trust a lady.'"[53]

In addition to these derogatory comments, the women students on campus enter into the male narrative as components of the "making men" program, for women matter as markers for how well the male student body has embraced modernity. In one exchange in early 1934, A.L. criticizes his male colleagues for failing to respect the privacy of women on campus. As he reports, "As soon as a girl is seen playing on the tennis court, be she a student or a visitor, several students instantly appear, form groups and begin mocking, criticizing and jeering. The remarks are made loud enough to be heard by the players, and the impression of it is not at all very pleasant."[54] A.L. questions "whether these boys ever saw a girl playing tennis before. Perhaps in their native towns it is not customary to see girls participate in sport activities. Yet by the time a student enters college he would certainly have heard that girls do play tennis. If he does not know that and if he is sensible enough, he will realize that the noise only serves to make others aware of his deficiency in being up-to-date."[55] He criticizes his colleagues for not appreciating this symbol of civilization. "Are they aware that they are acting like children and not like college students? Do they know that they are being impolite to their guests, thus breaking the rules of hospitality[?]. The nomadic Arab has gained world renown for his kindness towards his guests. Shall the Syrian student be the one to violate this long-standing tradition?"[56] A letter by X.Y. in a later issue of *al-Kulliyah Review* denied that this event had ever taken place, for in his view, AUB Syrian students could not possibly act this way. X.Y. asks a series of questions of the previous writer, including, "Do you still believe, after spending three or more years in college that the A.U.B. Syrian student resents the presence of his coeds and consequently jeers at and mimics them?" And: "Do you still believe that though time is money, Syrian students stop to watch a coeds' tennis game and criticize it?"[57] He concludes, "The A.U.B. woman has always been polite and kind to the A.U.B. Syrian students in general. Shall this article destroy this long-standing tradition?"[58]

An article in 1944 railed against the male students' attitudes toward the women students, despite the odes to modernity presented in many venues at AUB. "To-day we make public confession of our narrow and backward attitude towards women. We disclose our prejudices, and we admit that ignorance, blind conservatism, and elements of surviving barbarism, are at the back of them."[59] In contrast, the goal of the educational experience should be to modernize and truly embrace Western ideas. "Our attitude towards women may be responsible for more than strikes the eye. If we do not scrape off the rust of centuries, and if we do not introduce the latest teachings of the Western World, then we shall not succeed in purifying our minds and souls, and there will persist within our very selves an obstacle to all progress."[60] In conversations overheard at places like Faisal's Restaurant, the male students "testify to our moral guilt."[61]

> Hardly a girl we do not [sic] set eyes on that a repugnant remark escapes our lips. The amount of gossip and prying in our midst would make us close second to any School for Scandal. We see, we judge, and we condemn, without troubling to get to know. The young ladies in our community live in discomfort and consciousness of our wicked thoughts. They have come to despise the very glance we throw in their direction. In one word, our attitude towards women is uncivilized.[62]

The author points to a recent debate in West Hall to prove his argument; a sweeping majority had carried the motion that "no woman is to be trusted."[63] In the author's estimation, "That one misguided youth should have proposed such a callous notion is permissible, his condition is easy to surmise. But when a large body, which might in a sense be held to be representative of our community, agrees with frothy oratory and lends its enthusiastic support, we have a clear symptom of a deeply imbedded malady."[64] Another postmortem on this debate declares, "We are still blind—rather, we are still blinding ourselves—to the wretched condition of women in the Arab World, and when a young Arab woman stands for emancipation we are sure to expect an Arab young man [to] pop up to oppose her."[65] In these writings, men are the owners of the home, the school, and women are guests in their space. These writers place AUB women students in a secondary position; AUB students are assumed to be male. The intended audience is male; coeds, the women, are the object of discussion. Treating women well serves as proof that a man has accepted the "making men" template.

In these many venues, Dodge, his colleagues, and the male students failed to articulate a clear trajectory for women's education, since they confined their discussions to vague terms such as women's "liberation" and "enlightenment." As a result, women students served as markers of modernity rather than as individuals seeking to improve and possibly revolutionize their position in society. This definition of women's education allowed the coeducational structure to expand and survive precisely because it did not challenge men's privileged gender definitions. As Howard Bliss said in 1911, the school aimed to make men who were doctors, men who were pharmacists.[66] The liberal education mandate specified only the character traits the student should acquire, not the particular professional skills. In this paradigm, education serves to uplift the individual, not prepare him for a specific undertaking. Women and men could, presumably, undergo this character transformation equally. On the other hand, the failure to lay out a new path for educated women generated questions for decades about why women should receive a higher education at all, given that their experiences were not supposed to take them out of their traditional roles, just make them better at managing those roles. In this atmosphere, if women wanted to actively enter into the student community, they needed to individually enter male-dominated arenas. The women's stories indicate that most of them succeeded in overcoming individual obstacles; all the while, they struggled to collectively silence the questions posed about their purpose for being there.

Making Women

With the male authority figures at AUB providing scant guidance, the pioneer women on campus set out to negotiate the purpose of women's education. Whereas Dodge and the other men on campus mostly spoke of archetypal women needing to modernize their clothing and attitudes, the women's voices grounded their concerns in the real-life experiences of family, school, and nation. The women involved with AUB—students, staff, faculty members, and faculty wives—articulated what amounted to a primer for a making women program in that they outlined what the women, as students and graduates, should strive to become.[67] The women themselves took on the task of explaining why they had enrolled on campus and why women in general should follow their lead. Like their male counterparts on campus, they turned to Western models as the most potent for the image of womanhood they were writing; the discussions of scientizing motherhood and household management that became predominant on campus were familiar on American campuses as well. The women students also appropriated the individual character strengths articulated through-out the "making men" narrative, turning them into the tools necessary for a modern educated womanhood. In so doing, women accepted the core tenets of the liberal education system at AUB and agreed that their charac-ters needed to be reformed, their societies uplifted; at the same time, they almost never, in sharp contrast to Dodge, discussed the veil or clothing in general. The women directed their attention to what they saw as more substantive issues facing Arab womanhood and, as Ellen Fleischmann states, "For many of the early students, having access to higher education was a means for them to either make a living or make a difference (or both)."[68]

In terms of the women students, individual graduates assuredly broke into male-dominated professional fields. From the earliest days of coed-ucation, women graduates worked outside the home as teachers, nurses, doctors, and pharmacists; a 1962 survey conducted of 174 women who had graduated from AUB between 1927 and 1959 indicated that 65 percent were currently working, and of those, 40 percent were teachers.[69] Despite the predominance of women working, the focus of making women was never on how to prepare for these public positions but on training for a scientific motherhood. More than for any other arena, the women of AUB spoke most frequently about improving or modernizing the realm of the home, making it more fully a respected woman's domain. A woman's unique edu-cation provided her with the knowledge to improve the lives of her family and her fellow citizens; her experiences made it necessary for her to extend help wherever needed. Women students thus wrote a narrative for scientiz-ing and nationalizing their domesticity without revolutionizing their posi-tion within the society and the nation at large.

Lila Abu-Lughod's 1998 edited volume *Remaking Women* analyzes many of the voices taking part in the reconstruction of women's spheres in the Middle East at the turn of the twentieth century.[70] In particular, women's magazines, foreign missionary schools, and school textbooks glorified, as Abu-Lughod cites, a "professionalization of housewifery" and "the 'scientizing' of child rearing," both cornerstones of a gendered moder-nity in the late nineteenth century.[71] The "'new' wife and mother was now to be in charge of the scientific management of the orderly household of the modern nation, as well as the rearing and training of the children who now were seen as the future citizens of the modern nation."[72] In Beth Bar-on's estimation, activist Egyptian women struggled to expand education for girls in order to make it an effective training ground for their future domesticity. Of Egyptian schools, she says, "When the first seventeen girls sat for the primary certificate exam in 1900, they found the same questions that male candidates found, for the subjects taught to boys and girls in primary schools were almost exactly the same."[73] Under pressure from women's magazines and organizations, schools began to tailor instruction for female students. "When girls presented themselves for the primary school certificate exam in 1913, they found a new test designed specifically for them. It included a practical part in cooking, laundry, and needlework plus written questions on hygiene and housewifery."[74] Alongside their sisters in Egypt, women activists in Syria and Lebanon focused much of their work on expanding and improving education for girls and women, in laying out the parameters of modern Arab womanhood, and in lobbying for political rights. For example, Julia Dimashqiyah's writings in *al-Mar'a al-Jadida* indicate that "women could not fulfil their duties and obligations if they lacked education, morals and a strong personality for knowledge acquired without good morals was a very dangerous weapon (*silah khatir*). In essence, the future of the nation in every country was in the hands of its women (*bi-yadi nisa'ahi*)."[75]

In the early twentieth century, Syria and Lebanon had a small but vibrant women's movement that organized conferences and published magazines, with the leaders laying out guidelines for modern womanhood. Simultaneously, the participants lobbied for political rights involving suffrage and personal status issues. Julia Dimashqiyah, Mary Kassab, Mary ʿAjamy, and a number of other women established political and literary salons, girls' schools, women's magazines, and charity organizations. In 1924, these and other women formed the Women's Union in Syria and Lebanon (al-Ittihad al-nisa'i fi suriyah wa lubnan). As Elizabeth Thompson explains, "It was emphatically cross-sectarian, including both Muslims and Christians, and it was adamantly Arab nationalist, uniting both Syrians and Lebanese."[76] Containing more than forty women's groups by the early 1930s, it "directly confronted paternalism in the colonial civic order by organizing public campaigns for women's rights, especially in education, health, and labor"; "in addition, the union campaigned for the reform of paternalistic religious laws on marriage, divorce, custody, and inheritance that limited women's autonomy and civic participation."[77]

By the early 1930s, having failed to secure these political rights for women, activists focused their attention less on politics and more on what Thompson terms "patriotic motherhood."[78] As she explains, "In a sense, patriotic motherhood was an inversion of the old agenda. Whereas in the early 1920s women sought the vote in order to effect improvements in their lives, they now sought the social reforms as a prerequisite to political rights."[79] Simultaneously, women's magazines declined throughout the 1930s, and male writers took up the cause of women's modernity from their own perspective.[80] As with many women's movements conceived under colonialism, the women activists subsumed their particular feminist demands under the exigencies of the nationalist cause.

There is no record of AUB women participating in the political activism of the 1920s, even though they represented the educational strata dominating this movement. The making women program did not preclude any of the graduates from involving themselves with political issues; for that matter, the making women program did not prohibit women from engaging in any endeavor. AUB women ascribed to the "making men" motto that AUB training produced a successful, hard-working, and honest individual. In the case of a woman, that individual looked to the AUB experience as a way to improve her position in her school, her family, her job, and her nation; she did not concern herself with the political conflicts she deemed outside her realm of expertise. Any one of the pioneer women enrolled during this era could have been involved in political activities in her home country, but the narrative of making women that emerges from the written record supplies no rationale for why an AUB woman would identify this work as a priority of her educational experience. The successfully made woman in this coeducational program could move into the political realm, but her more natural arenas were the home and a professional or philanthropic position commensurate with her desire to help society. AUB's educational program transformed a woman's character so that she could understand these responsibilities.

In what are probably the most succinct and clear enunciations of AUB's making women program, Elsa Kerr, AUB dean of women (1945–1960), wrote in 1946 and 1947 about the most important lessons to be learned by the women students. Kerr wrote to the 1946 women graduates of the American University of Beirut in the commencement edition of *al-Kulliyah Review*,

> I hope that most of you will marry the man of your own choice, and will establish homes which express your best selves. I hope that you will rear children who from early childhood will learn to know what is right and to follow it. The kind of person most of us want to be, the kind we want our fellow men to be, is not produced over-night. 'You can't teach an

old dog new tricks' is a trite saying. It is just as hard to instill new ideals and to change bad habits in an adult. But you should be challenged to develop good habits in your children at birth and to teach them truthfulness, dependability, hard work, unselfishness and a keen interest and understanding of people. Neither nursemaids, nor even teachers alone, can give these qualities to your children. You, as their Mother, must pass on your own high ideals to them.[81]

In 1947, Kerr stressed self-discipline and compassionate activism.

The girls of school and college age of today will become the mothers of tomorrow. During her education a girl should acquire not only book learning and modern laboratory techniques, but self discipline, a sense of values, a better understanding of life, a sympathetic relationship to people, a deep desire to serve her community, and above all a personal responsibility for training her children. Such a girl will become the kind of mother every country and every community needs[.] What better training can such a mother have than to serve her community as a teacher; as a nurse, or as a doctor or as a social worker in her [years between] college and marriage. To serve her community, to help to improve its educational, health, or social standards, will develop purpose and personality in any girl. To serve intelligently and effectively a girl must have training.[82]

These quotes illustrate the most frequently articulated ideas about women's education at AUB; the goal of women's higher education was character building, just as it was for men. Women must also, as partners with educated men, take on the burden of modernizing their societies and solving its problems. In June 1927, at the annual ladies' luncheon, a woman graduate expressed her opinion about the education she had just received, echoing many of the ideas Kerr would later share. She "declaimed the common conception that higher education tends to make women unfeminine and undomestic, adding that it teaches a deeper sense of duty which makes any occupation a delight. She likewise pointed out that if men and women have the same mental habits and point of view, there will be a truer and deeper mutual understanding. She concluded with the idea, [sic] that education leads to true humility and that true humility leads to true progress."[83] At the 1933 ladies' reception at commencement, a graduate bemoaned the fact that very few of those present would be able to pass the examinations they once took at the university, "yet this does not mean that education for women is utterly useless. Their education has given them an attitude of mind rather than a store of facts. Education helps women to assist or resist the tendencies of the day in the light of what is highest and best. They learn to seek facts for themselves, to criticise ideas and to keep values."[84]

Even though AUB never offered a home economics program, the women of AUB clearly absorbed the concepts underlying it, either as students at the AJCW or through the many venues, magazines, and textbooks available to them throughout the Middle East. In the 1962 survey of women, a small number called for women to be able to enter the School of Engineering and Architecture, a right not granted until 1967. On the other hand, "64 respondents asked for courses normally thought of in the home economics area . . . e.g., children's literature, fashion designing, clothing construction, food preparation, nutrition, child care, home nursing, interior decoration, budget management and personal grooming or hygiene. Others wanted more in fine arts; including music, drama, and dance. Still others stressed psychology, encompassing child psychology, testing, and guidance."[85]

In a January 1936 article, Lily Hawie made an explicit plea for scientific motherhood. The dominant idea about women's higher education, she writes, holds that women inevitably became housewives and thus should "major in history, literature or such subjects which agree with her delicate nature and function as a house keeper."[86] Hawie expressed the opposite view:

> To me the best thing which harmonizes with a lady's job is "Science," because I cannot think of a better physical, chemical and biological laboratory more wide and more practical than a lady's kitchen. Nothing is mysterious to a scientific lady. She does not get paralyzed if something wrong occurs in her kitchen, because she has been trained in the laboratories to overcome such difficulties. A chemist understands the mechanism of the reaction of backing-powder [sic] on her cakes and I am sure she can control them and make them taste better than when she recites a poem to them.[87]

Hawie concludes:

> To be useful to my country I need to be SCIENTIFIC.
> To be useful to my home I need to be SCIENTIFIC.
> Are you still amazed why girls major in SCIENCES?[88]

As Asma Najjar explained in 1937, the Arab world had just begun to awaken, and with it came the recognition that a woman needed to be educated in order for society to advance.

> She graduates aware of the world around her and with complete knowledge of what she needs to know and she is familiar with her responsibilities. Today, she understands the need to be clean and to be careful with food and to prepare it and to pay attention to her health, all of which are completely important. Among the Muslims, it is not possible for an Arab woman to awaken from her situation to a higher position and be a good wife and be wise and a good friend unless it is by the route of education.[89]

Making women also required of its students that they extend their roles as educated and scientific housewives out into the communities so that they could teach their sisters how to progress, as they had done. Because of their unique and privileged position in society as educated women, they tasked themselves with going directly into homes to proselytize for modernity among those less fortunate. Women could choose to do so via paid work or as volunteers. As early as 1922, Jane E. Van Zandt, the director of the nursing school, wrote,

> I do not mean to give the impression that a nurse's training spoils a woman for the home life. If I believed that, I would never advise a young girl to enter a Training School. I feel that she should be a far better and more efficient home-maker than otherwise. She knows how to keep her house neat and clean and sanitary. She is not afraid of work. If members of her family are ill, she can care for them.[90]

On the other hand, for women who choose to or have to work, such training is invaluable because only a professionally trained nurse can be truly useful. "Suppose disease breaks out in her village, she can teach the people how to prevent it from spreading. The nurse supplements, practically, the science of the doctor. Take the nurse on private duty. The doctor has many patients to visit, and can only spare a few moments to each one. If he has a trained nurse caring for a very sick patient, he knows that the treatment ordered will be carried out."[91] Kathryn Newell Adams, president of Constantinople Women's College (1924–1931), laid out the public and private duties of an educated woman in her chapel address at AUB in 1930. As reported in *al-Kulliyah*,

In the first place, Dr. Adams stated that the world is in need of trained leaders among men and women. An educated woman can easily understand and sympathise with her educated husband. She can give him advice not only about the management of the home but also regarding business and other matters of importance outside the home. An educated woman can bring up her children better than an ignorant woman, and can prepare them well for the school and college and the battle of life. In the second place, she stated, an educated woman can notice the evils in the village, town or city and country where she lives, and can give counsel and advice about the best means needed to remedy these evils. Dr. Adams declared emphatically that the world would be poorer but for the lives and work of Jane Adams [*sic*], Florence Nightingale and other women of note. Our homes would not be to-day as bright if they lacked the benign influence of educated women.[92]

At the 1934 ladies' reception, a speaker entitled her presentation "Is Woman's Place in the Home?" Near the end of her talk, according to the report in *al-Kulliyah Review*, "She came to the conclusion that, if by 'home' is meant the narrow four walls of the house, in which a woman is to be confined, as in a prison, the answer is *No*. But if the expression is to be taken metaphorically to mean wherever there is a need for sympathy, for the care of the helpless, for the training of the ignorant, for the creation of comfort and well-being, the answer emphatically is *Yes*."[93]

The women at AUB in the 1930s and 1940s built upon this concept of woman as moral compass; an educated woman had the necessary knowledge to struggle against the deprivations present in her society. Elsa Kerr picked up this theme at commencement in 1946 when she highlighted the vital role women played in their village and city health clinics and community centers. "To give to *all* of the children of your village and your country the same opportunities that you covet for your own child—that he increase in wisdom and stature and in favor with God and man—May this be your aim."[94] In January 1940, Wadad Makdisi Cortas ('30), principal of al-Ahliah School, gave a talk at AUB on the future for women in the Middle East. She listed four occupations she felt were especially suited for them.

> *Social reform*: "Very often when men lawyers have proved interested in their profession from a psychological and intellectual viewpoint, women have brought to it their humane feelings." *Nursing*: "When we have more of our educated women engaged in nursing, we are bound to have cleaner cities, less epidemics and a more enduring health for our

future generations." *Writing for juvenals* [*sic*]: "The lives of great men and women read in early childhood have enormously contributed to character building." *Revival of national arts*: "In our remote villages some beautiful handicrafts that have existed for centuries will surely die out if our women don't realise their worth."[95]

Cortas wrote in 1947 that AUB should establish a course in social studies that would "entice women in particular and give them the chance to study profoundly the questions of child crime, juvenile law, the organization of reform schools and hundreds of acute social problems."[96] She also encouraged women to enter the AUB medical school because "I believe our salvation comes only when we can recruit a greater number of women doctors and nurses who can go out into remote villages and work conscientiously fighting child mortality and child and women's disease."[97]

From 1936 to 1954, *al-ʿUrwa al-Wuthqa*, the magazine of the student Arab society, articulated a strong and empowered Arab nationalism, shifting from an emphasis on Western modernity to a specifically Arab-based program. Given that the men students were also exploring new definitions of national identity in the 1930s, it is not surprising that women students connected to patriotism in new kinds of ways as well. In the magazine's pages in the 1930s and 1940s, the theme of patriotic motherhood comes through clearly, as women writers sought not only to define their roles within the home and society but also to equate home and society with the nation. Zahiyah Qadura and Shams al-Din Najm summed up the patriotic motherhood theme in 1938: "The first field of nationalist work" is the most important for a woman, "as a wife and as a mother and as a sister and as a daughter," as well as a trustworthy friend "to acculturate her family to be the hand of man and to help him with his ideas and work."[98] At the same time, women should not be restricted solely to the home, but should engage in social welfare work to alleviate childhood poverty and promote educational opportunities for girls. Fatima al-ʿAskari writes, "Woman is the most important partisan in social life; she is the basis of the family and following that the nation."[99] Fatima al-Husseini bemoans the ignorance that still characterizes the Arab home as it struggles with "Eastern ancient time and our Western modernity."[100] She declares, "There is no solution for this problem except with the extinction of the worthless old."[101] This attempt is failing, however, because "the Arab East today is sinking under the load of bigotry, blindly still following the wrong path."[102]

In spring 1948, Balqis ʿIwad expressed the view that men had finally come to the realization that women are half of society and vital to its entire foundation.[103] "How are buildings set up and half of the pillars destroyed?"[104] Addressing a theme common to this era of writing about women, ʿIwad declares that in the past "woman lived for long periods shackled under the full light of the slavery and oppression of man; her life was a series of sorrows from cradle to grave."[105] Just when she sought to live freely, she faced a flood of disdain for her choices. When she wanted to receive equal rights as her brother, her mother retorted automatically that he was a male and she was a female and thus not equal to him. In recent years, as ʿIwad explains, education has brought to girls a new respect, and when they arrived at universities their professors extended it to them too. This change occurred in the context of an "intellectual revolution" in the region's social life, giving Arab women opportunities they had never had before.[106]

Pioneer Women

The stories of women who enrolled after 1921 tell of struggles to succeed and also of a strong pride in their accomplishments. Edma Abu-Chedid, one of the first women to receive a BA ('26) and the first to receive an MD ('31) from AUB, reported in *Outlook* in 1952 that there was no Women Students' Organization (WSO), or balls or trips, during her tenure as a student, but "I took things naturally, and I communicated my naturalness to the men. I was wrapped up in my studies—was always a bookworm—and this helped me to weather the storm."[107] Wadad Cortas, who registered in 1927, noted that while at AUB, she held particular respect for Edma Abu-Chedid, who "inspired us with her perseverance to follow up a long and difficult career. Most of us looked upon teaching as the only accessible profession. Hers was by far a greater ambition and she had undaunted courage in the face of difficult studies. Our fear of not being able to cope with the intricate subjects, and to brave the challenge of a male atmosphere of study, dwindled when we compared our simple studies with hers. In this sense she was our academic leader."[108]

As for her own experience, Cortas reports, "The university offered no social life for the women students at that time. We had to be careful about our dress, careful about contact with the men around us, and we rarely attended social events. The only sport considered proper for us was roller-skating."[109] She reminisced that "the only societies in which we took an active part were the Brotherhood and Boys Service Club, both inspired by philanthropic motives. The Service Club was the first organized attempt to fight illiteracy" and that "the only literary society that gave us a chance to debate or do any public speaking was the Students['] Union. We had no Dramatic clubs similar to those of these times and nobody ever dreamed of co-acting or any co-operation of a purely social nature."[110] On the other hand, "Although we were not allowed to attend the historical plays or variety shows that the college men put on regularly, women could participate in public speaking, and both the Arabic and English literary societies gave us opportunities to debate such issues as the emancipation of women, compulsory education, co-education, political freedom, and imperialism."[111] Just being on campus as students, she said, "We were envied by hundreds of women who could not get the same educational privileges not because of financial conditions[,] as is the case now, but mostly because they belonged to communities that were sceptical about the advantages of higher education for women."[112] When the women students needed help in any way, they sought out President Dodge and his wife. Cortas reports, "Whenever anything went amiss it was to the Dodges that we went and from them we received inspiration and self-confidence. I know that every one agrees with me that if co-education has proved to be a success it is mostly due to their sincere efforts, their never failing understanding and help."[113]

Jamal (Karam) Harfouche entered the AUB medical school in 1937 after having completed her BA at AUB the semester before. "In Medical School, I was the only girl in my class. Women students were still a curiosity on the campus. Male students and teachers did not have much confidence in women medical students. The social adjustment was tedious."[114] She saw the experience of coeducation as a character building exercise: "In being alone with no one around to give me counsel and advice, not even a Dean of women students, or a class advisor, I learnt to depend on myself and cultivated a strong sense of determination."[115] To quell any doubts her male colleagues might have held about her, "I always came prepared to class, spoke of my failures and kept successes as my own little secrets which I shared with my family."[116] Since her family was conservative, and she did not want to besmirch their honor in any way, she said, "All through Medical School I was addressed as Miss Karam, and to maintain a proper social distance I never dared to call any one of my classmates by his first name."[117]

A March 1958 *Outlook* article describes how Salwa Nassar ('35), the first woman hired at the professorial rank at AUB (1950) and later president of the Beirut College for Women (1965–1967), found AUB in the 1930s. "The number of girls at AUB was still small enough in the 1930s for people to call co-education a 'new idea.' Few girls yet ventured into the sphere of higher learning at the University, which for such a long time had been considered by many the rightful domain of men."[118] The article continues, "AUB was different from what [Nassar] had first thought it would be like . . . She had expected to feel odd, being one of the few girls on campus, but everyone had been helpful and the feeling of strangeness soon dissolved. AUB students, she realized, were too intent on getting the most out of their studies by working all together to feel uncomfortable and self-conscious about having a girl studying with them and taking courses which they hadn't thought girls could be interested in."[119] However, "The school library, then still located in the College Hall clock tower, was not a favorite haunt of AUB co-eds. 'When we had to study there one could find all of us grouped around one table,' Miss Nassar remarked laughingly. 'As a rule, we studied up at the College [AJCW].'"[120] Angela (Jurdak) Khoury graduated from AUB with distinction in 1937 and then enrolled in the AUB graduate school in the Department of Sociology, graduating with an MA in 1938. "It was due to her effort and interest in athletics that a basket-ball team of women students was organized. Field trips for the first time were organized to include women students when they were properly chaperoned. Angela was the prime mover in making it possible for women students to participate in such trips."[121] She then served as the first woman instructor at AUB (1938), teaching in the Departments of Sociology and Psychology.[122]

The reminiscences of Wadad Bulus ('32) draw a picture of a student fully experiencing the program of liberal education the Americans designed. She said of her experience at AUB that she felt comfortable with the men students, but saw other women struggling.[123] For herself, she loved the events sponsored by al-ʿUrwa al-Wuthqa and the Students' Union, in both English and Arabic, as well as the many celebrations and parties held in West Hall. Overall, she felt that the slogan over the Main Gate—"That they may have life and live it more abundantly"—described perfectly the experience she and her colleagues had while at AUB.[124] The school "had an influence over a great many students and matured their personalities and spread wide their awakening."[125] The educational structure was particularly effective, in her estimation, because it taught her to not only understand the origins of scientific ideas but to be able to transmit them to other people. "The most important thing I learned was to be true to myself and my ability to study and produce."[126] Furthermore, "I learned the value of a vacation at the end of the week and the leisure to experience entertainment and social activities which had a greater influence over us than the numerous classes which we studied and the articles which we wrote and the exams which we took."[127]

Conclusion

President John Waterbury (1997–2008) extolled AUB's legacy in establishing coeducation in his "Women at AUB: Today and Yesterday" speech for the school's opening ceremony in 2002. Waterbury congratulated AUB on its action in 1921, for it was a "momentous step that was avoided by many illustrious universities in the United States until decades later."[128] As was customary by that point for anyone discussing AUB's coeducational history, Waterbury provided a list of women who had excelled either as students or as faculty members at AUB in the subsequent eighty years. Despite this list of impressive accomplishments, Waterbury recognized that "we have not yet empowered women to the extent that we should" and that more women should be enrolled as students, be promoted within the faculty, and be welcomed into the highest levels of the administration for this empowerment to be complete.[129] In looking at history, Waterbury recast the old adage that "behind every great man, there is a woman," saying, "Behind every great woman there is nothing but her own courage and perseverance."[130]

Waterbury is correct in identifying women as the agents of change, while criticizing the level of empowerment that AUB's coeducation program brought to them. AUB was a male-dominated educational zone and the women had to find ways to fit into the classroom and the extracurricular organizations, while simultaneously rationalizing the practical benefits they could accrue from their education. The curriculum did not completely segregate women behind the walls of home economics, but women faced many problems while on campus. The picture that emerges from the first era of coeducation is of women striving to succeed in a new arena, but most doing so without overtly challenging the male-dominated society in which they learned and lived. AUB's leadership did little to integrate the women on to campus in their first years; the women themselves, later joined by their male colleagues, did the most work to establish equality for themselves and their successors. The work did not end, however, even as women came on to campus as full members in 1952, as the quotes at the beginning of the chapter attest. While "making men" disappeared from campus discourse by the 1950s, people still worked to codify making women, and women still struggled to rationalize why they had a right to be on campus.

Fig. 1. Original Faculty, Syrian Protestant College, 1870

Fig. 2. First Graduating Class, Syrian Protestant College, 1870

Fig. 3. College Hall, Syrian Protestant College, 1872–1873

Fig. 4. Ada Dodge Hall, Syrian Protestant College, 1873

Fig. 5. Lee Observatory, Syrian Protestant College, 1874

Fig. 6. Marquand House, Syrian Protestant College, 1879–1880

Fig. 7. Bliss Street, the Main Gate, and Ada Dodge Hall, 1900s

Fig. 8. Chapel, Syrian Protestant College, 1900s

Fig. 9. *Bliss Hall, Syrian Protestant College, 1900*

Fig. 10. Medical Building, Syrian Protestant College, 1900s

Fig. 11. Pharmacy Building, Syrian Protestant College, 1900s

Fig. 12. Post Hall, Syrian Protestant College, 1900s

Fig. 13. West Hall, Syrian Protestant College, 1900s

Fig. 14. Assembly Hall, 2010

Fig. 15. College Hall, 2010

Fig. 16. Daniel Bliss Hall, 2010

Fig. 17. Athletic fields, 2001

Fig. 18. Fisk Hall, 2010

Fig. 19. Main Gate, 2010

Fig. 20. West Hall, 2010

STUDENT ACTIVISM
The Struggle for Arab Nationalism

The 1952 April Fool's Day issue of *Outlook* (called "Lookout" on that day) satirized the proliferation of student protests that had dominated campus life for the previous few years. In the paper's lead article, the author declared, "A School of Revolutionary Government, designed to equip AUB students with a wide knowledge of modern techniques of conspiracy and revolution, is to be opened during the fall semester, a communique from the President's Office announced late Friday."[1] Continuing the same theme, the article reports, "All courses will include a minimum of three lab hours to be spent in street battles with gendarmes and similar applications of theories learned in classrooms."[2] President Stephen Penrose (1948–1954), the article stated, gave a Friday morning chapel talk on the new school motto: "*That they may have strife and have it more abundantly.*"[3] In a further announcement, the paper described the day's protest.

> There will be a demonstration this afternoon at 3 in front of the Medical Gate to object against everything[.] All those interested please report there promptly five [minutes] before time. The demonstration promises to be very exciting—tear gas will be used, and the slogans are simply

delightful. If all goes well, police interference is expected. If not to join, come and watch.[4]

This, of course, was not the first era of student protest; the difference by the 1950s was the widespread and sustained nature of the conflict between the administration and the students. By the time *Lookout* published its satirical articles in 1952, students had been organizing demonstrations in support of Palestinians and Moroccans, and against any and all things imperialist, since 1947; these efforts petered out in 1955 after the administration banned the two main groups organizing them, the Student Council and the Arab society, al-ʿUrwa al-Wuthqa. Students engaged in these exercises explicitly as Arabs, proud of their past and striving toward cultural, political, and economic unity in the future. In their actions, students sought to integrate their educational experiences at AUB with the real-life events taking place outside the Main Gate, for only then did they feel they could be trained to function as the vanguard initiating the necessary changes in their society.

The transition from enthusiastic acceptance of the Western civilizational template to impassioned opposition resulted from the dramatically altered circumstances in which the Arab students found themselves. With the Arabs divided into new states and colonized by the Europeans after World War I, students were less amenable to the Western civilizational model. When the United States government became a major player in the Middle East after World War II, it also became a potent symbol of Western imperialism. Further, the local politicians working with the colonial powers in territorial states established by the Europeans, such as Lebanon, Jordan, and Syria, failed to sufficiently serve their populations. Schools, jobs, and public utilities increased in number in the interwar period, but not enough to supply the demands of the new state populations. The new citizenries found their political lives delineated by European-drawn borders and their associated governmental institutions, but territorial national allegiance grew only slowly.

Disillusioned with both the old Western and the new territorial models, students looked instead to a re-energized Arab nationalism as the answer to who they ought to become as a result of their educational experience. As Israel Gershoni points out, scholars have described Arab nationalism in the interwar period "as an outgrowth and motor of social mobility, as the product of mass education and acculturation by the new media of 'print language,' and as a function of the rapid growth of literate consumer publics for that culture."[5] Those people who had benefited from the services actually provided by the mandate governments did not return the favor by supporting the mandates; rather, they decried the poverty that plagued their societies and faulted their local governments for preferring authoritarian methods over democratic ones. These Arab nationalists turned to Arab unity as the solution, positing that fragmentation and colonialism had weakened the Arab body politic; only the erasure of the region's artificial boundaries could bring true independence to the Arabs. In their writings, they found mobilizing qualities in Arabness, positioning it as the agent that could finally move the region out of colonialism and into an independent modernity.

The trajectory from "making men" and making women to enthusiastic protesters for Arab rights can be traced most easily through a study of the writings of al-ʿUrwa al-Wuthqa, the journal of the school's Arab society of the same name. The journal was founded in 1918 to provide a forum where upper-level students could improve their speaking and writing in Arabic.[6] In the publication's first incarnation, between 1923 and 1930, writers mixed together "making men" and making women articles with examinations of the current problems the Arabs faced. In its second incarnation, starting in 1936, the journal's pages laid out a primer for the man and woman seeking to find modernity in Arab history, politics, and life. Antun Saʿadeh's Syrian Social Nationalist Party (SSNP), the Baʿth Party, the Communist Party, and others attracted adherents among the student body, but al-ʿUrwa al-Wuthqa dominated campus discourse about Arab nationalism and maintained control over the most important events and often the most important elective positions on the Student Council. As in 1882 and 1909, the world outside the Main Gate gave the students ammunition with which to question the programs proffered to them inside.

The Conundrum of Arab Identity

To reach the point where student protest could become a staple of the AUB experience, the students had to find ways to break the monopoly the Western narrative had held over their educational identities. Prior to the interwar period, student writers enthusiastically accepted the American voice of authority, constructing a modern masculinity and femininity that revered Western models over their own, just as so many contemporary Arab writers were doing at that time. As SPC gave way to AUB in 1920, the educational process continued to privilege European and American successes while marginalizing potential Arab contributions to societal improvement. Arab professors gained institutional equality during this period, but this did not translate into immediate cultural equality with the Anglo-Saxon professors. The school's Western civilizational unity of truth broke down only slowly. The curriculum did not quickly integrate Arab subjects; Arab history remained, at best, an elective. Extracurricular debates and speeches about the Arab world supplemented classroom work, but their very nature as voluntary events precluded their full incorporation as respected elements in the historical narrative of progress taught by the school's leaders. Well into the 1920s, the SPC and AUB man and woman's historical roots stood proudly in a glorious Arab past; but students were still excited about the dynamic Western world of the future.

As the interwar period dawned, the leadership of SPC and AUB continued to disseminate the view that the East had fallen behind the West on the historical continuum. The presidents of the school continually presented a time line of history that glorified Christian and Western history in stark contrast to a failed Arab civilizational model. Daniel Bliss (1866–1902) grounded his worldview in the Bible; the Arab past or present played no role in his view of history, for the most important guides for life were those found in Christian scripture. Howard Bliss (1902–1920) discussed a Christian ideal as the path from intolerance to tolerance; liberal Protestantism served as the agent of change in his narrative. Bayard Dodge (1923–1948) presented a story of Arab decadence awakened to a service-minded ethos through exposure to the American example. As he wrote in "Awakening of the Near East," "The stage, upon which the drama of civilization was first enacted, was the Near East. During the dark period, when Europe and North Africa were overrun by barbarian tribes and Rome itself was sacked, the Near East remained the centre of a highly developed culture."[7] During Abbasid rule in the medieval period, "many famous Greek and Persian books were translated. Architecture and masonry, the fine arts and ancient music, poetry and theology flourished. Mathematics, alchemy, astronomy, navigation and medicine, made important progress."[8] As a result, "many a Christian crusader was surprised to find that the despised infidel was more cultured than the people of Europe. Contact with the Saracens was one reason for the Renaissance."[9] However, "like a flower, the culture of the Near East was destined to blossom and fade away," for "wild hordes of Tartars" rode in and "swarmed over the great, intellectual centers of the Near East like clouds of locust, leaving ruin in their wake."[10] Awakening came in the closing days of the Ottoman Empire, when the peoples of the region encountered European styles of life. "Political exiles returned from enforced visits to European cities and brought back new ideas. Many foreign schools were permitted to teach modern science and Western ideals of behavior."[11] Protection by the European powers allowed the Near East to flourish: "In 1860, when Mount Lebanon was made a semi-autonomous province under the protection of the European powers, it became a centre of intellectual growth. Egypt also made rapid progress after 1884, when Sir Evelyn Baring, or Lord Cromer, was appointed Consul General at Cairo."[12] After World War I, Ataturk of Turkey, the Shah of Iran, King Faisal of Iraq, and Ibn Sa'ud of Saudi Arabia "set to work as agents of modern reform."[13] In many such writings, Dodge characterized the Arabs as unable to advance without Western aid. The West was the site of any meaningful history.

A series of national displays produced by the professors and students vividly illustrates how this time line played out on campus; in these displays, Eastern and Arab history was represented as the traditional and the ahistorical. A "Tour around the World" in the fall 1914 semester brought visitors, via "Cook" tour guides, to rooms representing the cultures of the students attending SPC.[14] For example, students in the Syria room danced the dabke; Egypt showcased workers on the Nile. In similar fashion, the West Hall Brotherhood staged an "Inter-racial Night" on December 10, 1921.[15] "It consisted of a series of acts and pageants in each of which a race or nationality presented some phase of its life."[16] The Armenian students acted out the events of King Abcarus fighting the Romans almost two thousand years earlier. The Syrian students enacted the "Spirit of Syria," highlighting the part the region had played in the origins of civilization.[17] "Last, entered a peasant who said, 'Syria was great, but for many centuries she has been more miserable.'"[18] The Egyptians offered scenes of both ancient and modern Egypt, with the former represented by the president of an ancient university demonstrating for visitors the schools of astronomy, engineering, and medicine. The modern scene depicted an Egypt where Christian and Moslem clerics cooperated together. In the final event of the performance, twelve students stood side by side at the front of the stage; each held a blank card and a candle. "The first man lighted his candle, turned the other side of the card to the front, and exhibited in large letters the name of his country."[19] The light was passed to each student, and each student promptly turned his card around. "At the completion of the ceremony there stood a line of candles held by men representing the different countries. The scene was symbolic of the spread of education through the different races and nations of the earth."[20] Two years later, the school held a "Cosmopolitan Night" that included several "Around the World" exhibits.[21] The Egyptian room replicated scenes from Pharaonic Egypt, with Egyptian and Sudanese dancers performing in "Little Egypt."[22] The Greek students forbore the typical scenes of ancient life and focused on Greek mountaineers. The Mesopotamians replicated the Tower of Babel and the Abbasid Arch. The Palestinians had "a beautiful wax lady representing 'The Spirit of Youth in Palestine' pointing steadily at an excellent drawing representing the Holy City [of Jerusalem]. Nearby was a canvas field of wheat, a threshing floor with a real ox and donkey treading out imaginary grain, and a very pretty windmill for grinding the grain."[23] The Beirut performers erected an old-style café with Arab storytelling alongside a modern one "with negro music and dancing"; the Lebanese students staged a traditional wedding scene.[24]

These university nights communicated an unsolvable conundrum for the students, for the displays evoked pride in a national heritage but one that could only fail to build a pathway to the future. The imagined past of these displays focused particularly on the pastoral life of the communities under glass and gave little indication that the entire region had seen societal, intellectual, and economic revolutions in the previous century. As a result, these displays marginalized the modern culture emerging especially in the cities of the region—in large part because of the work of the alumni graduating from places like SPC and AUB. As staged at these university nights, the Middle Eastern past provided no bridge to the modernity sought by the students because Arabness contained no active elements. No vignettes showcased Arab innovation of any kind; they all depicted Arab life as a passive and unchanging one.

Students replicated this concept of Arab backwardness in dozens of articles, starting with their first publication in 1899 and lasting well into the 1920s. In 1899, in *al-Mabda' al-Sahih*, the author writes of "our situation," finding little to praise about it. In his analysis, the method of education in the area has been depleted and become dry; art and literature have suffered.[25] The author criticizes Syrians for neglect and laziness, claiming that "armies of ignorance" have left the country a wasteland. In the process, this region, the birthplace of the world's intellectuals, has fallen into a "bed of poverty" intellectually and educationally.[26] *Sada al-Isti'dadiyah* declared the "death of the East" in 1902; al-Asayf Habib Khalil Tayigh writes that his ancestors weep for the failures of their descendants; the greatness of

Syria has fallen into the deepest darkness. Tayigh exhorts, "Rise up, oh Easterners, protect your borders, bring happiness to your people, and use knowledge to raise the standard of your nation."[27] He fears, however, that too many of the educated are straying from the path of the intellectual and literary rebirth, the nahda; they have proven too weak for the task. To turn the tide, he calls on his fellows to demand freedom, justice, peace, and equality for all.[28] In 1906, *Sada al-Isti'dadiyah* expressed the view that until thirty years earlier, the schools of the region, the madrasas, encouraged idleness and destructive philosophies.[29] Even with the recent renaissance, the nahda, life had still not improved for most people because the region's leaders had focused solely on literary elements, while the West privileged science and forged ahead. An article in the *Students' Union Gazette* asserted in 1915 that the crux of the Eastern problem lay in the homes of the people. "In the East, a man is conceived in ignorance and dies in ignorance if his financial state does not allow him to go to school"; the home is a bastion of illiteracy where no boy can learn how to be a man.[30] In a 1924 article in the *Students' Union Gazette*, an author expressed concern about "our future men," explaining that students in Italy helped win independence for their country; students in India followed Gandhi's lead in instituting boycotts against foreign goods; and students in Egypt had repeatedly shown their might. The author asks, "What have the students of Syria done?"[31]

Signs of opposition to this narrative of Eastern failure appeared as early as the first student publications, but they remained singular shots in the dark until the more concerted student effort to rethink Arabness as the interwar period progressed. A 1900 article in *al-'Asr* questioned how humanity could look to the Europeans, since they were greedy and frequently incited war; no justice could result from looking to Europe for an example.[32] In 1902, an article in *al-Hadiqa* warned that the people of the East must "repel evil imported customs" in order to "liberate the nation of its perilous circumstances"; the Arabic language must be cleansed because, as of now, "our writing occurs in a great ocean of foreign words and local and western expressions with no dictionary among us, no tongue that is Arabized and no light enlightening it."[33] E. Mirshak asked in the *Sub-Freshman Star* in 1926 what the world would lose if England had never existed; he answered, Shakespeare, the Magna Carta, and Isaac Newton. If France had never existed, the world would not have had Voltaire or Victor Hugo. "But if that small strip of land, which the world does not care for, that strip of land which contains the powerful and glorious Arabs, that Syria, was not created by the great God, what would the [world] lose?

Civilization, wealth and power and the absence of these three are enough to ruin the world. Yet Westerners think themselves of great importance."[34]

The student papers *al-Kulliyah* and *Thamarat al-Adhan* ran many pieces about talks delivered on such subjects as medieval Arabic poetry and language. Writer Mustafa Sa'ada spoke in 1902 on the unique freedoms enjoyed by the first Arab Muslims, spending most of his lecture praising the purity of language found in Arabic poetry.[35] Many prominent Arabs came to speak to al-ʿUrwa al-Wuthqa, as well as to those societies devoted to specific national groupings within the larger Arab world. In 1927, Professor "Khawri" lectured on the need for Iraqi unity and, in the following year, Professor "Khûry" spoke on the life of Omar Ibn Abdul Aziz, a caliph of the Umayyad Dynasty.[36] In the 1930–1931 academic year, Professor Anis al-Khoury Makdisi delivered a series of lectures on Arab Abbasid poets for al-ʿUrwa.[37]

In the same vein, Matta Akrawi and S. Takiyyudin, both leaders in al-ʿUrwa al-Wuthqa, sent a petition to the administration on July 1, 1923, asking that Arabic be expanded as a language of instruction.[38] The petitioners recognized that a wholesale change could not be undertaken because the school was not exclusively for Arab students and professors. Given these conditions, they requested that the curriculum be better adapted to the needs of the region by allowing the teaching of courses in Arabic in the Preparatory Department and by offering more courses on the Near East in the university as a whole. In their petition, they mentioned that Professor Philip Hitti had successfully taught Arab history courses in Arabic and saw no reason why this experiment could not be expanded.[39] They applauded the few advances recently made in the teaching of Arabic, but "a little examination of the Arabic curriculum shows that Arabic has been taught up to the present time simply as a language, and that, in a University whose students are from seventy to eighty [percent] Arabic-Speaking."[40] As a result, students graduated from the university with a poor grasp of Arabic. "The public and Alumni themselves often point out the difference between the graduates of the University before 1882 and those after 1882. While the former have been the bearers of the torch of learning up to the present time by their reviews, books and public speeches, and have been the real leaders in the revival of the Arabic language, the latter have rarely been able to transmit to their countrymen the sciences and the ideas they received as students."[41] In the past, students studied subjects like science in Arabic; those subjects taught in English required far more time to master than anything studied in a native language. "The outcome is that the University graduated its former students with a satisfactory amount of science and power to transmit it; while it graduated, and is still graduating, the later generations with better science but with little power to communicate it."[42] With schools opening at all levels throughout the Arab world, the petitioners felt AUB should have been perfectly situated to fill teaching positions as Arabic-speaking instructors. Since the language of instruction in most of these schools was Arabic, the graduates found themselves at a disadvantage compared to graduates from places like Egypt. As for the School of Commerce, "We wonder whether their present education, with very few courses pertaining to the economic conditions of the Near East and with no course given in Arabic, is not preparing them to be clerks in English [in] the American companies rather than to be independent business men."[43] The lack of integrated Arabic instruction, the students asserted, meant that "the present graduates, not being able to transmit their knowledge to their countrymen, have not proved as useful to their countries as the former ones."[44]

The students behind this petition characterized Arabic as a language of education and modernity; imposing English as the language of learning replicated the nineteenth-century SPC view that the indigenous language lacked the qualities necessary for modern success, that Arabic was woefully behind the more civilized languages. In a comparable example, Mahatma Gandhi explained that as a result of schooling in an English-language school in India, "I was fast becoming a stranger in my own home"; his English education in India had created "an impassable barrier" between him and his family, who did not speak the new language.[45] Kenyan author Ngugi wa Thiong'o believes, in speaking of his missionary education, that "it does not matter that the imported literature carried the great human-ist tradition of the best in Shakespeare, Goethe, Balzac, Tolstoy, Gorky, Brecht, Sholokhov, Dickens. The location of this great mirror of imagi-nation was necessarily Europe and its history and culture and the rest of the universe was seen from that centre."[46] Even Edward Nickoley, in his post as acting president of AUB (1920–1923), felt that under the guidance of the New York board of regents, the school had become too reliant on the American system of education. "American text books are written for American students and to meet their special, [sic] needs, they are adapted to the American type of mind. It may be seriously questioned whether the extensive use of text books, foreign text books represents the best method of instruction for the University."[47] In their petition, the leaders of al-ʿUrwa al-Wuthqa attempted to rectify the weaknesses they found plaguing the quest for an Arab identity for the students at AUB. Despite the cogency of the arguments presented, the school administration refused to alter the curriculum.

In this transitional era, students also sporadically protested in reaction to events taking place in the region. One clear act of resistance began at the start of French colonial rule over Lebanon. At a reception for French high commissioner general Henri Gouraud in January 1920, two students gave speeches of welcome. Nickoley had vetted the speeches before the event, but a student from the School of Arts and Sciences seems to have added a few sentences to the end. As Nickoley wrote to Howard Bliss, "At the close he made an appeal to the General to deal generously with this land and its people, to assist them in securing a free and united Syria and words to that effect."[48] American consul Paul Knabenshue pressured the college to expel the student, which the faculty voted to do; General Gouraud, however, asked the school to reinstate the student, and the school complied.[49] The incident was a small one but points to opposition to the European political conquests of the day. Throughout the 1920s and 1930s, the students also participated in boycotts against the prices charged by the Beirut tramway system. Bayard Dodge wrote home to his mother in 1922 that "the people of the city have been carrying on a fine boycott against the tram line, as a ticket to go half way across the city costs about ten cents. Cars have been running empty and every time one goes by the people jeer and fire bad tomatoes at the conductor and windows. Jitneys are taking the places of the cars and they are cheered lustily when they appear. Gendarmes are everywhere and the whole thing has become a sort of public sport."[50] Saʿd Nimri ('32) describes another tramway boycott in the late 1920s in which students from all the schools in Beirut participated.[51] In succeeding years, Arab activities clearly engaged student interest. Hala Sakakini, studying at the American Junior College for Women (ACJW) during World War II, describes the passion with which students in the city embraced the Arab nationalist idea.

> Discussions concerning the future form of Arab unity seemed never-ending. In clubs and societies, in private rooms and in student lounges, smaller and larger groups of students were constantly debating the merits of this system of government and that, whether a federation or a confederation would be more suitable, how to prepare for that day in the future, what our part as educated men and women should be.[52]

Sakakini reports that as she returned to the women's hostel after one such meeting on campus, she heard students singing "Nahnu shabab lana'l ghadu' (To us young people belongs the future)."[53] In many years, students staged commemorative events on November 2 in protest against the Balfour Declaration.

al-ʿUrwa al-Wuthqa's New Life

In the 1920s, *al-ʿUrwa al-Wuthqa* followed the same editorial policies as the other magazines, producing dozens of articles buttressing the "making men" program. As indicated by al-ʿUrwa's petition for more Arabic teaching, the society's members also sought other ways to establish their Arab identity. When Constantine Zurayq took over as the society's mentor in the 1930s, the magazine's editorial policy changed dramatically; from 1936 on, it served as the Arab nationalist bible for the students. The ideas expressed in the journal's pages illustrate how Arab nationalism evolved on campus from the 1930s until the 1950s. Over the years, professors such as Philip Hitti, Constantine Zurayq, Anis al-Khoury Makdisi, and Zeine Zeine, among others, earned the respect of their students when they brought Arab economic, political, and national concerns into the curriculum. They produced some of the earliest studies of Arab history and politics; they and their successors later published works on the Arab-Israeli issue, the Cold War, and the problems of Arab independence in AUB's *Middle East Forum* (1954–1967).[54] Further, AUB attracted professors from all over the world, including America, who did not have the same devotion to the Western paradigm as that of their predecessors. Students followed all these leads and wrote articles that gradually broke down the monopoly Western models of modernity had held over their intellectual lives. By the late 1940s, and the beginning of the new phase of student protest, AUB's students were activated to fight for Arab causes, just as their brethren were doing all over the region. Men such as ʿIzz al-Din al-Qassem, the fighter for Palestine in the 1930s, and Abd al-Qadir al-Husseini, the defender of Jerusalem in 1947 and 1948, served as models for Arab behavior. On campus, George Habash, who graduated from the AUB medical school in 1951 and later led the Arab Nationalist Movement (ANM) and the Popular Front for the Liberation of Palestine (PFLP), took the lead among student activists working for the cause of Arab nationalism.[55]

By the time Zurayq, who served as acting president of AUB from 1954 to 1958, dissolved al-ʿUrwa al-Wuthqa in 1955, the Arab world had transitioned from colonial control to independence. A new generation of Arab military and political leaders had begun to institute major socioeconomic revolutions in their countries, under the rubric of Arab nationalism. The students at AUB enthusiastically followed these developments, working out in the pages of al-ʿUrwa what it meant to be an Arab; in the walkways of campus in the late 1940s, they challenged the AUB administration to allow them to participate in the political causes of the region. The writings of al-ʿUrwa al-Wuthqa's self-titled journal illustrate how these discrete moments of protest and Arab pride came together on campus as a cohesive narrative of Arab nationalism and empowerment, displacing the school's Western civilizational paradigm in the process.

The purpose of al-ʿUrwa al-Wuthqa was to give students an opportunity to explore their Arab identities. In its early years, according to Anis Sayigh, its members focused on lectures, festivals, and conferences as a means of studying the strength of the Arab heritage and language.[56] Mahi al-Din al-Nusuli reports that anger at Turkish attacks against Arab activists in Damascus and the excitement wrought by Faisal's Arab Revolt prompted students to establish an Arab society at the end of World War I.[57] He applauds the fact that as of 1936, al-ʿUrwa still existed and was "suckling the sons of this Arab East" as they worked to articulate Arab nationalist tenets and to "spread in the students the spirit of wataniyah strength and qawmiyah respect."[58] Matta Akrawi writes that when he attended the school's preparatory school, he envied the older students their right to participate in al-ʿUrwa because they were so involved in the qawmiyah struggle.[59] When he joined the college and al-ʿUrwa in 1920, he saw the society strengthening qawmiyah knowledge among the students by initiating programs that honored Arab language and culture. He particularly remembers the Arabic-language plays performed on campus under al-ʿUrwa's aegis; this came at a time when English-language plays had dominated the theatrical scene for years. Akrawi channeled some of this enthusiasm into his unsuccessful bid to expand Arabic-language teaching in the school.

During the first era of al-ʿUrwa's existence, from 1923 to 1930, the students were making the transition from modeling their identity on the West to an identity based on Arab nationalism. Early on, writers penned articles such as "Perseverance," "The Idea of Moderation," and odes to Western great men—such as John Keats and Ludwig von Beethoven—as well as articles on Arab contemporary issues.[60] The "Iraqi Awakening" of January 1925 praises the democracy that has come with the country's political awakening, helped by the many Iraqis who had studied at AUB and were using their skills in Iraq after graduation.[61] In 1925's "Intellectual Homogeneity," the author extols the mixing of Syrians and Iraqis on the AUB campus, seeing their intellectual interaction as a building up of knowledge about the Arab nation, the *umma*,[62] its past and present.[63] In the same issue, an article addressing the question of the possibility of Arab unity points out the geographical, historical, religious, and cultural similarities binding the Arabs.[64] *al-ʿUrwa* also began publishing some of the first articles criticizing colonialism in this early period. In "The Motivations of Colonialism" in 1928, for example, the author details how colonialism destroys indigenous institutions because all decision-making and production power are in the hands of the colonialists.[65]

Starting in 1936, *al-ʿUrwa*'s editorial policy stressed the intellectual exploration of Arab nationalism, as Arab politics directed students' attention away from the West and toward events in their own region. The year 1936 alone saw the beginnings of the Arab Revolt in Palestine, the successful Egyptian campaign to gain more political rights via a new Anglo-Egyptian treaty, the failed attempts in Syria and Lebanon to promulgate similar treaties with France; and the first of many military coups in Iraq. At the same time, the 1920 decision to give Arab faculty equal status on campus was finally bearing fruit. Memoirs from students of the 1930s praise the Arab professors for the tutelage they provided and the atmosphere of Arab unity and activity they helped generate on campus.[66] Arab students, professors, and causes increasingly held more sway, as the Americans who had dominated the school from its inception began to lose their preeminent status. Americans still held the highest administrative posts, but Arabs increasingly held the greatest influence over the intellectual paradigm dominating the campus.

When Constantine Zurayq took over as advisor for al-ʿUrwa in the 1930s, his ideas and activities had a particularly strong influence over the intellectual path of the society's journal. Under Zurayq's tutelage, *al-ʿUrwa* became primarily a medium for formulating the concepts underlying Arab unity. Amjad Deeb Ghanma describes the shift in goals in 1936 as moving from focusing on debates and training in the Arabic language to emphasizing Arab consciousness, promoting qawmiyah feelings among the students, and studying the problems of Arab society and economics.[67] Zurayq demonstrated his interest in Arab history and culture by teaching classes in

Arabic, at least for a short period of time.[68] Zurayq also became a mentor to students because of his political work off campus, participating in these activities in spite of the administrative prohibition on professors engaging in such activity. ʿAziz al-ʿAzmah reports that Zurayq and a number of other Arab nationalist intellectuals participated in a series of meetings as early as 1929 and then congregated at the Qarnil Conference in 1933 to form the League of National Action. In 1935, some of the participants living in Lebanon formed the "Society of the Red Book," named after the color of the cover of the organization's ideological primer.[69] AUB student and al-ʿUrwa member Yusif Shadid reports that in the late 1930s seven or eight members of al-ʿUrwa al-Wuthqa joined the secret organization.[70] While it is impossible beyond statements like this to determine how many *al-ʿUrwa* writers belonged to the society or read the book itself, the gestalt of the Red Book threads its way through the themes of the journal. Members passed the book around clandestinely to those who were in sympathy with its goals. Its message was not revolutionary so much as reformist, laying out what it meant to be an Arab in historical, social, and individual terms.[71]

According to the Red Book, the Arab umma has existed continuously through the ages as a united qawmiyah, bequeathing this unity to succeeding generations; Arab qawmiyah provides spiritual nourishment and benefits to its members.[72] Arabs have a right to national status, alongside other nations, because they are united by the Arabic language and live within the Arab umma, bordered by the Taurus Mountains and the Mediterranean, the Atlantic Ocean, the Arab Sea, the mountains of Habasha, the plains of Sudan, the Great Sahara, the Mountains of Bashtko and al-Baktieria, and the Gulf of Basra. The Arab "idea" mobilizes Arabs to use their unity to "liberate themselves from colonialism, slavery, poverty, and ignorance."[73] Arabs must *jahada*,[74] or struggle, with their hands and their hearts and their tongues on behalf of their umma, especially during times of danger.[75] Leading individuals must initially struggle to repair the weaknesses in themselves, destroying any individual characteristics that hinder cooperation and trust among fellow Arabs. They must then work with others to improve the umma, for "they are the umma of the future like they were the umma of the past."[76] The umma does not seek war with anyone but will fight against the colonial powers that are hostile to its advancement. "The qawmiyah mission imposes on the whole umma the need for a military spirit," and "in this spirit is gathered the manly and wataniyah characteristics of courage, fortitude, generosity, and manliness."[77]

The themes expressed in *al-ʿUrwa al-Wuthqa* from 1936 until its final issue in 1954 reflect the themes of the Red Book and also the political circumstances of the Arab world. In the early 1950s, the reenergized Arab nationalism that had emerged in the interwar period led to a wave of military coups and governmental shifts. Young Arabs enthusiastically joined these movements in the hope that the new leaders would bring political independence, economic progress, and societal dignity to the Arabs. The Arab nationalist parties that formed from the 1930s onward all called for Arab unity to alleviate the economic problems suffered by the Arabs, to return Palestine to Arab control, and to fight off European and American imperialist designs on the Middle East. Socialism had also come to the fore by the 1950s, with Gamal Abdul Nasser's Free Officers initiating socialist programs in Egypt in 1952. In 1953 in Syria, the Baʿth Party merged with Akram Hourani's Arab Socialist Party. When members of these parties gained influence in Egypt, Syria, Jordan, and Iraq, they nationalized industries, expanded educational opportunities, opened up new technocratic positions in their governments, and slowly nationalized large industries, all under the rubric of Arab nationalism. From 1936 forward, student writers for *al-ʿUrwa al-Wuthqa* were passionate supporters of this new Arab nationalism, and their identities as Arab students changed accordingly. They were excited about the new opportunities they saw and encouraged by "the growth of the spirit of wataniyah and its acculturation among the students."[78]

al-ʿUrwa al-Wuthqa: Writing the Narrative of Arab Unity

From the first issue of the first volume of 1936, the authors of *al-ʿUrwa* explicitly direct their calls to "you," the AUB Arab student, as in the earlier magazines, and demand that you recognize your vanguard position in society, use the skills you are learning to improve your society, and work for change in the Arab world. As the journal's editor wrote in fall 1945, "Among the glorious and happy motives that the Arab students of the university have are feelings of their duties toward their umma."[79] The old SPC and AUB "making men" social modernity project transitioned to an activist nationalist vocabulary. A 1941 editorial, for example, calls Arab youth the vanguard of the umma "in its toilsome path toward the future."[80] This vanguard must take on the task of understanding the dangers ahead, whether created by foreign entities or by internal weaknesses. A man of the vanguard must remain brave throughout the journey; he will not be satisfied until he has effectively guided the umma's awakening. In the same issue, Khalil Ayntabi points out, however, that being in the vanguard is not an easy path for Arab educated youth.[81] Understanding the umma's past, Arab youth recognize that unity has fragmented, creating "passions of different contradictory cultures."[82] Idmun al-Bawi writes in 1947, "If the head of the family does not know of his responsibility toward his family, he will not advance it the clothes and food that it needs. When a soldier does not know of his responsibility to the defense of his watan, he will not undertake the task."[83] The Arab student should not just understand society's problems, but assume the responsibility of establishing a group to struggle and sacrifice for his umma. He should perform these functions because he provides "the leadership of his umma, a leadership of enlightened intelligence."[84] The Arabs can overcome the ignorance and weakness pervading their society, just as Muhammad the Prophet did in the past. "Don't wait, oh Arab student, for a child of a religious prophet today to take leadership of the Arab umma; that prophet was born 13 centuries ago. Don't wait for a child of a qawmi prophet in the present time."[85] Rather, "That prophet is you, oh Arab student."[86]

Arab students will not revolutionize society merely by overthrowing colonial control; they must undergo an *inqilab*, an upheaval, within themselves. Abd al-ʿAziz Sawwaf criticizes the Arabs for focusing all of their attention on attaining political independence from foreign powers.[87] In fact, that achievement is just a beginning, not an end. Sawwaf writes of the Arabs, "If only they would direct part of their struggle inside themselves, to the great struggle, a struggle of the self," then they would achieve true independence.[88] Furthermore, "If only they would learn that the day of freedom is not the day the colonialists are thrown out of their watans, but the day their souls and intellects are freed from obsolete and traditional positions, impervious to progress, the day when they are freed from the connections of poverty and ignorance and insignificance."[89] The author makes explicit the relationship between the Arab past, present, and future by saying that the Arabs have experienced an inqilab before, when Muhammad the Prophet brought the divided and weakened Arabs together. "The present carries the future in its soul because it carries its seeds" from the past.[90] The current Arab revolution will not take place unless the Arabs "are burning for liberation and today truly understand" the future they should be making.[91] The West has resolved many of its own problems, but it did so with solutions organic to its own societies. "There is no doubt that the education of our civilization has different problems and beliefs from the education of the West."[92]

By the late 1940s, *al-ʿUrwa* writers were criticizing Arab governmental leaders because they did not introduce democracy into their regimes once independence arrived after World War II. In a spring 1949 article, Riyad al-Azhari asserts that democracy failed to take root throughout the Arab world precisely because of the failures of the local leaders in each of the Arab states.[93] The socioeconomic problems of the interwar period carried over into independence after World War II; the independent Arab leaders quickly proved they were just as incapable of resolving their countries' economic inequalities as their predecessors under colonialism. al-Azhari writes, "There are enormous chasms between our constitutions and our realities, between our official democracy and this strange marriage of political styles," all stemming from contradictory intellectual, social, and moral understandings of political processes.[94] However, he does not believe that the Arabs are unqualified for democracy; rather, the crux of the problem lies in the poor economic situation of the peoples of the Arab world. The Arab governments failed to raise the living standards of the people, a hallmark and cornerstone of all successful democratic nations. Since democracy is by the people, economic justice must prevail for this to occur. Otherwise, the rich will rule over the poor. Democracy can come to the Arab countries, but there needs to be a rational balance of resources and an increase in production so that inequalities no longer divide people.

By the early 1950s, socialism was seen as the answer to achieving social and economic equality within Arab society; in moving to such a position, *al-ʿUrwa's* writers replicated political discussions taking place all over the Arab world at that time. An emphasis on socioeconomic justice prompted political opposition figures to assert that a new form of Arab socialism was the answer to the region's socioeconomic crises. In this political configuration, intellectuals, politicians, and military officers called for the state to nationalize large industries; only then would there be a fair distribution of resources. In the 1951–1952 academic year, a series of brief statements in *al-ʿUrwa* declare that "nationalization will rescue the workers, peasants, producers, and employees from exploitation."[95] In the same issue, the editors write that "socialism is established to eliminate the exploitation of humanity"; it can do so because it takes control over the institutions that are of public benefit.[96] The editors explain that nationalization is akin to a revolution in Arab society because "true qawmi consciousness awakens one to the importance of economics in the life of the umma."[97] Independence can be achieved only when foreign companies stop "sucking up the resources from the workers and the peasants and the producers and the employees. Independence will not be complete if the withdrawal of the soldiers is not followed by the nationalization of companies."[98] The *dawla* (state) needs to take control over those companies in order to guarantee that services, not profits, guide the decision-making process.[99] In the following issue, the editors describe nationalization as "a link in the people's struggle to build the new Arab society in the shadow of Arab socialism."[100] Nationalization succeeds at this task by prohibiting the gathering of money into the hands of the greedy, thus ending the exploitation of the rest of the citizenry.

Other writers explain the organic connection in Arab society between socialism and qawmiyah. In the editor's opinion in early 1952, socialism became appealing in Europe after the effects of the Industrial Revolution spread; when the middle class exploited the means of production, the workers needed an international route for fighting against the alliance between capitalism and nationalism.[101] The Arabs, on the other hand, stand at the beginning of this economic process, and so do not have the same kinds of class disjunctions. Instead, the Arab world must contend with three social problems—"poverty and ignorance and sickness"—that have caused social and moral anarchy and fragmentation, allowing colonialism and feudalism to take away people's personal freedoms and divide their watan.[102] "Arab socialism limits ownership and forbids exploitation, nullifies feudalism and capitalism and gives the peasant land and work" while protecting him against unexpected crises.[103] Arab socialism, furthermore, prevents war because it eschews the economic competition that frequently sparks conflicts. In short, "Arab socialism is the guarantee of the achievement of the true Arab umma and true humanity."[104]

The US government's support of the establishment of Israel in 1948 and subsequent demand that the Arabs support the US in the Cold War aroused outrage among AUB students.[105] Anger at the new US governmental role in the region found an outlet in *al-'Urwa*'s call for positive neutrality in the midst of the Cold War. In a spring 1951 article, Nihad Haykal declares, "Neutrality is necessary for nationalism," explaining that some groups of Arabs have willfully agreed to work with Western armies.[106] In the past, such pairings had drawn Arabs into engagements relevant only to the Western signees: the Jordanian agreement with the British drew the Jordanian army into fighting in World War II; the Anglo-Egyptian treaty of 1936 aided in the British occupation of Suez. In contrast, victory for the

Arabs necessitates unity, independence, and social equality; Western militaries invariably prevent the achievement of these goals. The model to follow in this regard is India, which is already treading the path of neutrality.

AUB stood in a precarious position on this issue; Stephen Penrose was the first AUB president to have held a US government position prior to taking up his post. The US government subsequently gave money for the first time in the school's history, funding Point IV scholarships for students and USAID (Agency for International Development) programs for the school.[107] This money assisted the school and individual students but tied AUB to US policies in new ways. Even with this connection, however, students could and did continue to differentiate between the US government and the AUB administration. Until the post–World War II period, the US government had not been a major player in the region. AUB had been the primary representative of America for most of the students for decades; when the US government intruded, it came in the form of President Woodrow Wilson's support for self-determination. That image fit with the one disseminated through the curriculum, with Abraham Lincoln as the prototypical American politician working on behalf of the oppressed.

When the US government supported the establishment of Israel, the AUB administration and American professors on campus distanced themselves from this position. When the events of the Arab-Israeli War of 1948 began to unfold, Stephen Penrose supported Palestinian refugee rights. To a 1951 World Council of Churches conference in Beirut, he said of the displacement of Palestinians in 1948, "It is unthinkable that the Christian world at least could accept as satisfactory any solution which created a greater problem than that which it was designed to solve. Yet this is what happened during the debacle of Palestine."[108] His predecessor, Bayard Dodge, wrote an article in *Reader's Digest* in April 1948 arguing against the war he saw arising inevitably from the United Nations decision in November 1947 to partition Palestine into a Jewish and Arab state. He pointed out that the Arab states had proposed to the United Nations that all the member states take in Jewish refugees, but this idea had been rejected by the UN General Assembly and the United States. Dodge asked, "Can we really contend that the Arabs have a duty to be more hospitable to refugees than we are?"[109] When the war did take place and close to eight hundred thousand Palestinians became refugees, Dodge served as a consultant to the director of United Nations Relief for Palestine Refugees.[110] These pro-Arab moves made it possible for the students to distinguish between the policies of the US government and AUB. At the same time, students felt free to criticize the AUB administration for its control over their political and educational lives.

al-ʿUrwa al-Wuthqa: Women and the Arab Nation

A subset of articles in *al-ʿUrwa al-Wuthqa* addressed the particular issues Arab women faced in this fast-changing society. The articles on Arab nationalism use the parameters of the umma and watan to explain the jihad that is and must take place, rarely identifying who should take the lead, except for the "vanguard." Presumably, that vanguard is made up of men; women appear in articles devoted solely to their concerns. When the students write to "you" (the students who need to reform their societies), they are addressing the men, just as the earlier publications had. Separate articles deal with how women should comport themselves in the Arab nation. In this period, women have a valued place in the Arab future, but men represent the norm, the vanguard; women's positions remain complementary. Women's parameters are bounded by the home; their oath to the Arab umma as a public entity is vague in contrast to the one men are supposed to pledge. While patriotic motherhood had begun to appear as part of the making women program in the 1930s and 1940s, this new discourse on Arab empowerment took the conversation into novel realms. In this new phase, in the long debate about the purpose of women's higher education, male and female students more explicitly took on the question of whether women should be politically active.

After establishing in a number of articles that women's public lives had improved over the last couple of decades, in large part because of the educational opportunities available to them, authors turned their attention for the first time to the political rights women should receive. For example, the first meeting of the Debating Club in the 1945–1946 academic year examined the question of whether Arab women should exercise political rights.[111] In the end, despite much disagreement during the meeting, the female proponent of the position won the debate twenty-eight to twenty-five, reversing the decision made in the debate a year earlier that no woman could be trusted to exercise such rights. *al-ʿUrwa*'s writers continued this discussion, ultimately bringing up the issue of women's political rights more extensively than in any other venue on campus. They looked particularly at both the possibility of granting women the right to vote and allowing women to take on roles as political representatives of the dawla.

The former received generally positive responses, conditional on women fulfilling their duties at home. The latter generated much more controversy; some respondents feared that taking women out of the home on a permanent basis to work as political representatives or government employees would place them outside their proper societal position. The default for women was the home, the site of women's responsibilities; any other action had to be weighed against the possibility that women might not be able to complete both functions, or they might renounce their natural role.

In response to a regional women's conference held in May 1949, Habiba Sha'aban Yakun, president of the Society of Muslim Young Women, addressed the issue of women's political rights.[112] Yakun posits that all humans have the right to equal citizenship and rights. "Is the woman human? And a citizen?"[113] She asks further, "Why do our governments demand of women taxes from their property just as they demand of man? How can you introduce constitutions and not ask her opinion?"[114] In answer, she defends women's political rights. "Half of the umma is excluded from her civilized rights even though women have demonstrated in Europe and America and in our country also that they had the intelligence and ability."[115] A primary reason for the restriction of these rights, she states, is the ignorance of men concerning such national responsibilities as participation in elections. Yakun says that Islam does not prohibit women from entering into political work; it gives "mostly equality between woman and man in civic rights."[116] In response to the common concern that women must fulfill their duties in the home, Yakun says, "The active lady of the house is able in a short amount of time to make the rounds in her house and complete her work as she knows the value of time."[117] Women should first be allowed to vote and second be allowed to participate in public works projects, such as organizing gardens for children. Addressing an issue that came up frequently in discussions about women's political participation, Yakun notes that not all women will be involved in political affairs; many will choose to be in the home taking care of husband and children. "There is no fear that all of the women of the umma will cause an upheaval in order to work in politics" and to act as government representatives and employees.[118] Some women, however, do not marry and have children; they should have the right to pursue political work. A woman representative in the government would be perfectly suited to handle issues dealing with the family because she is naturally more versed in its problems than are men.

In a long discussion held at the al-'Urwa offices in West Hall on June 3, 1950, male and female students spoke about the issue of women's political rights.[119] The debaters agreed on a few positions, particularly the vital role women played in the home as wives and mothers. All felt that women's position in the home was more important than any other activity they could pursue in the umma. The extent to which a woman could participate in politics at some level outside the home generated far more disagreement. Malik, for example, states, "As for social rights, so they are achievable no doubt if the Arab woman enters public life and aids men in their work."[120] Leila expresses the view that "when women enter into public life, it does not mean the destruction of the family" because women will specifically work for issues that are relevant to their domain.[121] Fatima, on the other hand, feels that public work takes women away from positions commensurate with their responsibilities in the home. The discussants then debated whether only single women should involve themselves in political issues on a full-time basis, or if women who had children over the age of fifteen could do so also. Fatima believes that only a single woman should involve herself with politics; Leila reminds the group that when women become involved with politics, they focus on issues frequently ignored by men but equally vital to the national community. These statements represent only a small sample of statements made at the debate, but they express the basic opinions included; no person changed his or her mind as a result of this discussion.

Activating Arab Nationalism

For its entire run, *al-ʿUrwa al-Wuthqa* was an intellectual forum for the students to debate, negotiate, and articulate their identities as Arabs; when al-ʿUrwa al-Wuthqa organized Arab political protests on campus and off, few such events appeared in the pages of *al-ʿUrwa*. This division of labor represents two sides to the student quest for identity in the late 1940s. In the words of *al-ʿUrwa*, the task of understanding Arab issues and problems became the crux of who they ought to become as a result of their educational experience. At the same time, *al-ʿUrwa* focused on action, calling to "you," the Arab student, to be the person best fitted to solve the Arab world's problems. The November 1947 UN vote to partition Palestine finally brought the intellectual and activist elements of al-ʿUrwa together. Once the spark had been lit, the students continued to fight on behalf of new Arab causes for the next eight years; in the process, they identified the French, US, and Israeli governments as the main impediments to Arab progress. As students, their primary forum was the AUB campus; their most immediate obstacle was an American administration that did not support their right to protest on behalf of political causes. While always articulating their desire to protest in terms of Arab needs, students specifically spoke as students when they criticized the school's leaders for not allowing liberal education to function as advertised. The education system called on them to be active participants in their educational experience; their Arabness dictated that they be just as involved in political causes. Primed by years of writing in *al-ʿUrwa al-Wuthqa* and energized by Arab activism all over the region, student protests erupted on campus repeatedly in the late 1940s and early 1950s as their organizers clarified the connection between the rights accrued to them as Arabs and as students at the American University of Beirut. On campus, students saw the administration as an obstacle to the achievement of both these goals.

In reaction to the UN partition decision, the *al-ʿUrwa* editors called it an "abominable crime" and a "funeral of justice."[122] In December 1947, five days of demonstrations, strikes, and speech-making disrupted campus; simultaneously, the Student Council and al-ʿUrwa al-Wuthqa organized several events, including a fast, a blood drive, and a first-aid training session.[123] Elie Salem ('50) reports that students rushed to join the Arab volunteer army of Fawzi al-Qawuqji.[124] In January 1948, Hasan Saʿb declared the partition decision a destruction of basic human rights, and the Arab struggle to retain Palestine, at its very essence, a fight to reclaim those rights.[125] On November 2, 1948, the members of al-ʿUrwa al-Wuthqa held their annual demonstration in opposition to the Balfour Declaration. Henceforth on that date, the student societies held fund-raising events to financially aid Palestinian students studying at AUB and to supply funds for Palestinian refugees living in Lebanon.

In March 1951, students from schools all over Beirut walked the streets of the city demanding that the French grant Morocco its independence.[126] As they marched, they called for the "fall of tyrannical colonialism" and the "fall of France," chanting slogans such as "Morocco is the graveyard of colonialism," "long live the struggle of the Arab people in Morocco," and "long live Arab unity."[127] Participants demanded, according to the report in *Outlook*, that the Arab governments not "treat the Moroccan situation with what they termed the shameful manner of Palestine."[128] In front of the French legation, a student stood to declare, "This Bastille is one of the great Bastilles in the Arab earth," and "France, whose sons destroyed the Bastille not long ago, has established today another Bastille in the Arab Moroccan country and has sent one of its sons to snatch from the

Arabs their freedom and their right to life."[129] The same year, al-ʿUrwa put together a festival of Moroccan history and culture so the students could better understand the problems the Moroccans faced in their quest to gain independence from the French. In an accompanying *al-ʿUrwa* article, the author expresses his anger at French attacks on Moroccans, identifying the history of the Arabs as "a history of preparing the gallows" because colonialism had eliminated Arab freedom.[130]

In December 1951, the Student Council called for compulsory military training for students in Lebanon. "Reasons given for the request," according to *Outlook*, "included the statement that the Arab Nation and its states cannot stand by with folded arms while surrounded by imperialist powers and threatened by Israel, but must arm and train for self-defense."[131] The Student Council voted unanimously a couple of weeks later to "strongly protest against recent [Lebanese] government action limiting student political freedom and attempting to suppress Arab Nationalist activities."[132] In this case, the government had arrested two students while threatening to deport two others, all of whom were Arab nationalists. In these protests, the students identified the oppressors who should be fought because they hindered Arab and student freedom, and called for solidarity among the Arabs as the best method for combating these foes.

The last major protest of the era took place on March 27, 1954, when al-ʿUrwa staged a demonstration against the Baghdad Pact, moving forward with its plans despite the Lebanese government's refusal to grant the organization a permit.[133] The Baghdad Pact united Turkey, Iraq, Iran, Pakistan, and Britain in a mutual cooperation agreement. Students opposed the pact on the grounds that it served Western imperialist causes rather than Arab ones; Israel, not the Soviet Union, was a threat to the Arabs. At noon that day, students gathered in front of College Hall and began to march toward the Medical Gate. Upon reaching the gate, the students threw stones at the Lebanese police and gendarmes waiting outside. At first, the security forces fought back with water cannons, but when the water ran dry they began shooting guns into the air and then directly into the crowd of students. A person not affiliated with AUB died during the shooting, twenty-six students were injured, and one AUB student was permanently paralyzed from a shot to the spine. After this demonstration, the administration temporarily suspended al-ʿUrwa. Members sent petitions to the university asking that the society be reinstated, but the university senate rejected the request, saying that it "regrets that the petitioners still fail to realize that the Urwa exceeded the terms of its constitution and violated

University regulations as well as the basic spirit of University authority and discipline."[134]

The two most important organizations functioning on campus during these events were the Student Council and al-ʿUrwa al-Wuthqa. In regard to the former, AUB students received the right to elect a Student Council in November 1949, and over the next few years it became increasingly embroiled in Arab politics and campus political divisions.[135] From its first year, the Student Council took on multiple governing tasks on campus. In 1949, it "elected a publications Board for *Outlook* whose funds came from the budget of the Student Council; it created a permanent committee on Palestinian affairs; and in the course of its first year, with the cooperation of Dr. Penrose, it investigated the restaurant facilities and the whole fees structure of the University."[136] Almost immediately, the Student Council came into conflict with President Penrose for trying to influence university policy on raising fees.[137] The first president of the council, A. H. Saʾadi, was suspended for "political activity" along with two others that Penrose felt had involved themselves with Communist activity.[138] The following year, Arab nationalists dominated the Student Council, with George Habash serving as chairman of the executive committee.[139] In the 1951–1952 academic year, the "moderate" council president Abi Naim came into conflict with the "left-wing Council" dominated by Arab nationalists, with the support of the Communists.[140] When the administration determined that the council had become too politicized, it suspended it in early 1952 and then dissolved it completely in 1954. The catalyst for the first decision, from the administration's point of view, was the Student Council's January 26 vote to support a student demonstration in opposition to repressive measures taken by the Syrian military against students in Syria.[141] Lebanese gendarmes and students clashed in front of the Medical Gate, and security forces then entered campus. Two days later, students entered classrooms and "students were reported to have beaten other students who refused to participate, and to have carried professors bodily from their classes."[142] In addition to closing down the Student Council, the administration also punished individual students for their participation in these events.

Between the suspension and the dissolution of the Student Council, students continued to push for its reinstatement. The most forceful student arguments supporting the Student Council appeared when the administration proposed plans in November 1952 to replace the suspended council with a student-faculty Coordinating Committee on Student Affairs. By that point, the Student Council had been joined by representatives from societies in many of the faculties on campus; when the administration tried to reconfigure student government, these representatives stepped forward to defend the Student Council. al-ʿUrwa affirmed,

> Only the students have the right to decide upon their own form of representation. The administration is not entitled to impose any sort of student government professing to represent the students . . .

> In order that the Arab students be properly represented, it is necessary to recreate an atmosphere of freedom. This can be achieved by repealing all sentences in the form of "probations" and "warnings" passed upon many Arab Students under special circumstances.

> Urwa Society, therefore, calls upon all Arab Students to insist upon their freedom and strive to achieve the above stated principles.[143]

The president of the Pharmaceutical Society stated, "He who refuses nothing, will soon have nothing to refuse."[144] The Engineering Society president declared that students should have the right to choose their own ruling body. "After all," he said, "students play an important part in running any university."[145] Students from the School of Nursing explained, "The administration is thrusting its finger in to student affairs and wants to be leader and adviser as it has always strived to be. So this will not be democracy; rather it will be the rule of the privileged few, namely the Administration."[146] John Racy, 1951–1952 Student Council speaker and editor of *Outlook*, wrote in an editorial that AUB had frequently faced up to the Turks and the French in the past. "Today," he wrote, "the Arab World is passing through another of history's decisive moments, but one no more critical than those the University has braved in the past. Yet we see our Administration reverse its course and, like an ostrich, hide its head in a mound of sand rather than face the challenge of the day."[147] Despite these arguments, the university senate officially voted to dissolve the Student Council in 1954.

al-ʿUrwa al-Wuthqa, which sometimes worked in concert with the Student Council but sometimes found itself in conflict with that body, formed the second pillar of student political activism in the post-1947 era. Having gained followers through their journal writings, the society's leaders found they could also inspire students to demonstrate for the Arab causes the society supported. The administration warned the society's leadership against demonstrations, but seemed reluctant to close it down even though the Student Council had been dissolved for similar activities. The society still produced a journal well respected by administration and faculty alike, while also retaining its credibility as a purveyor of Arab nationalist ideology. As a sign of this respect, when the Baghdad Pact demonstrations drove the administration to finally suspend the society in 1954, the administration allowed al-ʿUrwa to reconstitute itself as a cultural society in the 1954–1955 academic year. The new structure did not last long, however, for al-ʿUrwa's leaders continued to insist on political engagement as an integral part of the AUB educational experience. In the last clash between the society and the administration, al-ʿUrwa members convened a meeting on the badminton courts on January 14, 1955. A member took to the floor "and reminded members of the 'Tennis Court Oath' of the French Revolution and said: 'Let our meeting today be a new Badminton Oath—an oath to liberate and unite our nation; to fight for its independence and neutrality.'"[148] The effort ultimately failed, and AUB acting president Constantine Zurayq permanently dissolved al-ʿUrwa in January 1955, after thirty-seven years of activity.

In these conflicts, the students did not specifically target administrative policies; rather, they were impassioned by Arab causes. However, every protest took place on campus, and as a result, every protest represented at least an implicit challenge to the AUB administration. When the students insisted on political activism on campus, they always voiced their demand in the name of academic freedom. Their interpretation of liberal education's freedom of inquiry included the students' right to determine the elements making up their educational experience. To the activist Arab students, education could not be complete unless their Arab goals could be achieved on campus, unless freedom of action accompanied freedom of speech. Their rights as students necessitated their direct involvement in the educational process. To the school's leaders, the American liberal education system equaled freedom of speech and debate; only in this atmosphere of mutual tolerance and respect could intellectual discovery be pursued. The university could not support a broader definition of academic freedom if, when students exercised their freedom to act, they limited others from expressing their freedom. Students recognized an inherent conflict within the liberal education system; they did not believe that freedom could be curtailed by administrative fiat. Students interpreted the administration's prohibition against demonstrations as patronization—treating them like children who were incapable of practicing the freedom promised them by liberal education. They did not believe they should have to wait to fulfil their responsibility as Arab citizens; they felt they had earned the right to political activism and asserted that they were not being trained for the real world awaiting them outside the Main Gate. To the administration, by contrast, the introduction of political activism on campus meant that students had not learned one of the basic lessons of liberal education: inquiry and debate can flower only within a mutually respectful and nonviolent setting.

The administration reacted to student activism by hardening its prohibition on political activity and by holding to its definition of educational freedom. The policy against political activism on campus had been on the books since Daniel Bliss opened the school's doors in 1866, but only in the late 1940s did it become a serious source of friction between the administration and students. On March 15, 1952, the school issued a pledge students had to make in order to remain in good standing at the university:

> As long as I am a student I agree to obey all the University regulations as established and interpreted by the Faculty of the University. I will neither individually nor with a group take any action which will disturb the academic functioning of the University or interfere with the rights of other students to pursue without interruption their course of study. [Furthermore], if I feel that I cannot [conscientiously] obey the regulations of the University at any future time I will withdraw from the University quietly and of my own volition.[149]

While reaffirming that the life of the university community is "dependent upon its freedom—freedom of inquiry, freedom of discussion, freedom of learning and freedom of teaching," the statement of the disciplinary committee also stated, "The matriculation of a student in this University, as in any private University, is a privilege not a right."[150] The university clarified its position still further in August 1952:

> The University encourages freedom of thought and places no bar to expression and action by students in political, religious and social matters provided:
>
> 1. That such activity does not interfere with the main purpose for which it is assumed a student has entered the University, namely, to prepare himself through study for a more useful life of service to his community and country.
>
> 2. That such activity does not hamper or curtail the program of study in this University. The certificates granted by this University are recog-

nized by international University circles. It is in the interest of every
student that these certificates shall continue to be so recognized . . .
3. That such activity does not interfere with the freedom of expression
of any member of the University community nor employ force, coercion,
threats, or intimidations against any individual . . .
Any student who is considered to be detrimental to the moral welfare of
the University will be asked to withdraw.[151]

The regulations ended with the blanket statement, "Any person who uses
any form of coercion on another member of the University violates the
principle of freedom of thought, expression or action by doing so. Such
person renders himself liable to severe discipline on the part of the University authority."[152] In reaction to the many demonstrations taking place on
campus and administrative accusations against students for disseminating
Communist literature, Penrose wrote in his annual report in 1950–1951 that
"the University's regulations are intended to preserve the function of the
University as a teaching institution and are in no sense aimed at preventing
freedom of political thought on the part of the students."[153] In a complementary message, he published a statement in *Outlook* in 1953, calling on
students to

> have the courage to support your convictions, but be sure that your
> convictions are right. See that they are acquired by objective reasoning
> and not by any form of prejudice. Your convictions are not necessarily
> right just because they are yours. If you hold them only for this reason
> then you must expect and allow anyone else to be just as determined
> concerning his own personal views. This kind of rock-ribbed and
> wooden-headed individualism leads to atomism, not unity. In the stu-
> dent body of AUB unity is to be treasured especially because at times
> it has been so rare. I hope we may this year seek it seriously, for the
> greater good of all.[154]

In pronouncements such as these, the school's administration affirmed
that enrollment at AUB was a privilege; upon entering, all students signed a
contract guaranteeing that they would follow all of its rules and regulations.
Freedom could not be wielded, in the classroom or in any kind of public
arena, without the requisite understanding of the duties and responsibilities incumbent upon a person educated within the liberal educational structure. Discipline and tutelage maintained the societal structure on campus
and allowed classroom instruction, the main function of the university, to

continue. The regulations exemplify the connection between freedom and character that all the presidents had so assiduously sought to disseminate to their students. The presidents of the school frequently expressed the view that demonstrations were an attack against their definition of freedom and the very work of education they saw themselves espousing.

Students, for their part, put forward the counterclaim that conditions in the region necessitated their active engagement. The president of al-ʿUrwa in 1950, Abdul Fattah Jandali, declared that nations that are stable can afford to focus on enriching the intellectual and moral standards of the people. However, he continued,

> the Arab nation of today is characterized by a lack of civil rights, division, unequality [sic], and economic chaos, and for this reason it must concentrate the energy of its youth, with the aim of understanding the problems that face it and the possible cure for them.
>
> Legions of young men have lost the right road, and instead of preoccupying themselves with the questions of the unnatural division of the Arab world, and the forces that have for long guided it against its own interests, have busied themselves with the discussion of Archeological remains, inscriptions, and the mysterious message of buried skulls. I hope that these men may concentrate on understanding the painful truth and may contribute to the cure of the ills of our society.[155]

In so writing, Jandali perfectly encapsulated the AUB student call to arms of the 1950s: freedom of inquiry meant nothing unless accompanied by action. Arab students must use their education to productively aid their communities; they must not waste it on the kind of irrelevant academic study the American administration appeared to be offering. John Racy concurred in an editorial for *Outlook* in May 1951,

> The age when Education and Politics were completely separate things is past and gone. When this institution was founded around the middle of the last century, the United States Government was not in the least concerned about this part of the world. The motive was purely religious.
>
> Today, it is a different story. No one can afford to turn a cold shoulder toward the political affairs of the day. The Administration of AUB seems to be unaware of this.[156]

In this article, Racy specifically criticizes AUB for not fighting more effectively to improve its level of accreditation with the Lebanese government. His belief that university students, particularly in the Arab world, should not ignore the political events taking place around them had gained strong currency on campus by the time he wrote this article. Activist students did not see any validity to the administration's constant refrain that the school was merely an educational space devoid of political engagement. In a similar critique of the administration's definition of freedom, an editorial in *Outlook* in 1955 declared,

> The words democracy, responsibility and freedom are common passwords or cliches on campus. We hear about them in lectures, in chapel talks and over the coffee tables at nearby cafes. Nevertheless, students have little chance of proving what they have so far learned . . .

> It is the university's function to train us, its students and future spokesmen of our countries, to face the problems of everyday life. How can we do that when we are only here to attend lectures and take notes? How can we be the future liberators of our respective countries if we are not taught how to practice the basic important factors that lead to freedom from oppression?

> Students should have the right to voice their own opinions in matters that concern them. They should be able to give the administration their own side of all their problems, for the way the faculty members and the way the students see these same affairs could differ greatly.

> We, the student body, are not puppets. We do not like to be drawn by strings which we have no right to control or even influence in any way. We think. That is why we are here. We have our own life to shape. That is what we have come to learn how to do. We have our own voice to express. That is what we hope to do.[157]

In 1958, Najwa Khayrallah laid out the conflict between freedom of speech and freedom of action that raged between the administration and students. "We continually hear that students must not interfere in politics because they don't have experience; yet, it is also asserted, as frequently and as assuredly, that politics is not learned theoretically, but by self-education and experience. Will somebody tell us where this vicious circle begins or—perhaps—ends?"[158]

The situation was changing so rapidly in every one of the Arab countries that students did not want to delay their participation until graduation, as university policies dictated. As the articles of *al-ʿUrwa* had so vividly articulated, students saw themselves playing a vital role in these fast-moving events. Demonstrations broke out month after month between 1947 and 1955 in support of Arab actions around the region, and in opposition to imperialist powers oppressing Arabs. Students demanded that the campus be open to what they saw as their legitimate political activities; students wanted campus organizations, particularly the Student Council and al-ʿUrwa al-Wuthqa, to protect student political rights. By making these claims, students openly questioned the right of the administration to dictate the borders of their educational and political lives.

Conclusion

The era of "making men" and making women found almost unquestioned obedience to the American voice, which promised to lead students into a modernized future identity. Students opposed the administration for short periods in 1882, in 1909, and during the interwar period, but did not challenge the position of authority the Americans held. Arab nationalism gained ascendancy on campus in the interwar period, when Arab students emulated newly promoted Arab professors inside the Main Gate and when *al-ʿUrwa al-Wuthqa* defined an activist role for the students to play. When the administration hindered their activism in the late 1940s, the students began to articulate the first sustained and serious doubts about the program the Americans had established, focusing particularly on the boundaries set on their freedom to engage in political activism. Viewed from an activist Arab nationalist ideology, the American liberal educational system contradicted its own avowed embrace of freedom of speech and inquiry in its refusal to allow politics to be part of the educational structure. Students sought to define an independent political realm for themselves on campus; the administration, however, remained strong enough that the attempt did not succeed, and most political activities ended in 1955. By the time student activism exploded again in 1968, the concept of the campus as a civic space was not so easily quelled.

"GUERRILLA U"
The Contested Nature of Authority

In October 1970, *Newsweek* magazine christened the American University of Beirut "Guerrilla U," offering a vivid, if inaccurate, account of AUB student politics:

> Politics at AUB today is tied directly to the Palestine guerrilla movement. Many students belong to one of the guerrilla groups, mainly the PFLP [Popular Front for the Liberation of Palestine] and Al Fatah, and often spend their summers and weekends in commando training camps. Some students have even been accused of stealing chemicals from university laboratories to use in making explosives. Most of the recruiting for rebel organizations takes place at a student hangout called Feisal's Restaurant, which faces AUB's main gate. There, students and former students sit around arguing politics endlessly over cup after cup of Turkish coffee, while guerrilla scouts quietly scrutinize the talkers in search of future leaders.[1]

In fact, the student movement after the 1967 war was characterized by demonstrations, strikes, and student occupations of campus buildings. Its message was student empowerment as a tool for breaking the power of the establishment. "To *believe* is **nothing**/*To act* according to what you believe is **everything**"; "Any reform starts by *refusal*. Support this *refusal*."[2] These slogans appeared on posters students brandished during an eleven-day strike in January 1969; it had been called in opposition to the December 28, 1968, Israeli attack on Beirut International Airport.[3] In their chronology of the events, *Outlook* reporters identified the Israeli attack as the catalyst for the strike, but "the frustration and anger that were expressed during the strike are feelings that have accumulated over the years, and that have been at the root of the past strike wave over AUB."[4] That strike wave had begun in March 1968 when students protested the administrative decision to not renew philosophy professor Sadiq al-ʿAzm's contract; it accelerated in late spring 1968 in reaction to Lebanese and Jordanian military actions against Palestinian fedayeen groups operating in their territories. This era of student protest did not end until the outbreak of the Lebanese civil war in 1975.

Distilled down to its basic elements, the political platform dominating the student protests in these years laid out the characteristics of the groups students needed to fight against, and those they felt could initiate the comprehensive changes required to dramatically improve conditions both in the Arab world and on campus. Reactionary governments such as those in Jordan, Lebanon, and the United States came to represent, along with AUB's administration, everything the students did not want to be: lackeys of imperialism and thus obstacles to change generated from the bottom. In contrast, the students anointed the Palestinian fedayeen with all they wanted to achieve: the return of Palestine and the transformation of the Arab regimes from bottom to top. The former could only perpetuate oppression, while the latter represented freedom of action, of speech, and of political influence, all in the service of those who were disadvantaged by imperialist policies.

This worldview required students to intensify the discussion about the parameters of freedom already broached by the students' activist predecessors in the Arab nationalist era and to pose new questions about the nature of authority wielded on the AUB campus. More so than in the late 1940s and early 1950s, the student protestors demanded that the administration accept the intersection of freedom of speech, freedom of action, and educational growth as the existential element of their AUB education. The students explicitly questioned the administration's authority to demarcate and narrow their desired experiential education. In the process, students used the same actions and vocabulary to fight both governmental and AUB

authority simultaneously. Their desire to overthrow oppressive and imperialist governments matched their desire to participate in campus administrative decision making. Halim Barakat found in a survey of students
at Lebanese universities in the early 1970s that the leftist and progressive
students wanted "to change the whole network of structures and value orientations," with the demand that humanity be liberated from "domination,
exploitation, and deprivation."[5] By so articulating their vision of the future,
students described an irreparable break between the old, failed authority figures and those leading a movement of socioeconomic and political
revolution both on and off campus. These actions came to fruition in 1968,
when students initiated a movement to intervene in policies proposed by
the administration. The students no longer saw their professors or the
administrators as models they wanted to emulate; they saw them as standing in the way of a viable educational and political experience. In the act of
negotiating these positions, students reformulated the campus into a civic
space in which to forge their political identities.

1968

From the late 1960s forward, university campuses, including AUB, serve
as fascinating zones for political study because the whole conception of
the campus arena and the role of the student body changed as a result of
the movement that is usually identified with 1968. Since universities first
opened their doors, students have been protesting against their policies;
as scholars have noted, the campuses most active in 1968 were those that
had a history of student protest, such as AUB. In 1968, Columbia University's Students for a Democratic Society (SDS) occupied campus buildings to protest, among other things, the establishment of the Institute for
Defense Analyses (IDA), conditions in the gym, and disciplinary actions
taken against students. Nanterre students and French workers brought
barricades back to the streets of Paris to protest against the repressive
tactics of the university administration and the French regime. Mexican
troops killed several hundred university students demonstrating against
the national regime's closed political structure. Czech students enthusiastically embraced the "Prague Spring." University students all over the
globe loudly proclaimed their opposition to the US war in Vietnam.

In Egypt, 1968 saw university students protest against the policies
of Gamal Abdul Nasser's government. Egyptian students had not gone

out into the streets for years when this new wave began. The lull in student activity was, in fact, abnormal in the Egyptian context; as at AUB, Egyptian students had typically involved themselves with national political events. To forestall student revolts, the Nasser government channeled student activities after 1952 into government-run political organizations and nongovernmental societies geared to sports and social welfare programs.[6] The actual spark in 1968 was a strike called on February 21 by workers in Helwan, in opposition to the lenient military verdicts meted out to Egyptian Air Force leaders for failing to defend against the Israeli attack in the 1967 war.[7] Students from Cairo's universities along with many more workers quickly joined those from Helwan, and the action continued until February 27. Student demands went far beyond the initial catalyzing event, as evidenced by a statement sent out by the students in the engineering school of Cairo University. They demanded "freedom of expression and of the press"; "a truly representative parliament in a real and sound representative system"; and "the promulgation and enforcement of laws establishing political freedoms."[8] As Haggai Erlich explains, the demands of the students "constituted no challenge to Nasserite ideology but rather questioned its daily application by an increasingly corrupt, authoritarian establishment which also saw to their own political castration. Rather than trying to topple the régime, they demanded its purification and their own active participation."[9]

These 1960s events stand as such a watershed moment in student history because of the intersection of globalized political events, exploding university populations, and increasingly contentious questions from those student populations about authority and paternalism within state and university structures. For centuries, administrations and faculties held all the power because they controlled the access to knowledge; students had to obey their commands in order to acquire it. SPC and AUB's leaders had consistently relied on this social contract whenever students protested, falling back on the school's private status as the basis for its regulations and rights. Students had to accept the terms of the contract laid out by the school in order to remain in good standing in it. The liberal education system, as practiced at AUB, required that students understand the self-discipline underpinning the right to freedom of speech. The Arab nationalist era paved the way for this new phase of student protest because it opened the door to doubts about AUB authority. The 1950s saw students criticize administration attempts to censor their activities. When their successors protested on behalf of student rights in the 1960s, they joined their colleagues around the world in establishing a new relationship between themselves and their university administrations. In Robert Cohen's view, students henceforth "rejected the traditional notions of hierarchical decision making and paternalism; the student was no longer a child to be governed in his or her campus life by a benevolent administration. Students demanded instead to be treated as citizens with a voice in the governance of their university—at first on matters regarding their rights of political expression but soon, at least as voiced by the FSM's [Free Speech Movement at the University of California, Berkeley] more radical elements, in the realm of education itself."[10]

As an example of the kinds of transformations students demanded, Cohen cites a professor's realization that student groups such as the FSM in 1964 had redefined the whole nature of the campus community. Charles Muscatine, English professor and chairman of the Special Select Committee on Education (SCOE) at Berkeley, felt that the FSM had revolutionized his thinking.

> As I saw it, the center of the conflict was a revolution in the notion of what a university was. I and a lot of other people had been nurtured in the old medieval idea of the university as a special place which is purposely insulated from the rest of the world so that contemplation can go on. The idea was that society needed to provide a place that was free of political passions, controversy, and prejudice, for what was then thought of as the free pursuit of truth. It was still possible in those days to think, "You're a student; you're only temporary here. You're not even here all year. You live in Bakersfield, you live in Sacramento; go exercise your civil rights in Sacramento or Bakersfield. This is a different kind of place. We don't have ordinary civic activity by students in this place, because this place is a different place, a sacred place." That idea was under major attack

> The faculty animal is almost bred to be nonpolitical. We think, we talk, we vote, but we do not *act* . . . When the Free Speech Movement first broke out my reaction, nurtured on this medieval tradition, was "OK. But why don't they go exercise free speech in the city? That's where citizens exercise free speech. The campus is a special place. The police never come here, we don't have politics. . . . Why here, for Christ's sake? Why did you pick this little spot?" That certainly was a part of the reason that people like me and a lot of other liberal professors didn't get it at first.

> What the students achieved was a redefinition of the campus as the *polis*, or civic home, of the students . . . It took those months of turmoil for a lot of us to recognize that this was the students' civic place. They forced that idea upon us, and it turned out to be right.[11]

At AUB, the students of the 1950s generation had already begun the process of staking out the campus as a new forum for political identities. The social contract between the administration and the students changed perceptively as a result, coming to passionate fruition in 1968.

This new conception of campus space proved so contentious in part because the American educational system had never clarified the rights students hold while on campus. In 1947, the National Student Association (NSA) issued a report listing student rights that included the following: "the right of the individual to college admission without discrimination"; "the right to expect clear, precise written regulations and procedural due process in disciplinary actions"; and the right for student organizations "to have official recognition, to use campus facilities, to choose a faculty adviser, to invite speakers, and to refuse to disclose membership lists."[12] In the 1950s, the NSA added to this list, as Julie Reuben reports, by "encouraging students to challenge restrictions on their political activity, oppose institutional censorship of student-sponsored events, and lobby for greater student input into campus affairs."[13] Institutional practices did not change appreciably at the time, according to Reuben, but the report "did open up discussion about the nature of students' academic freedom."[14]

That discussion became the focal point for many of the conflicts that erupted between students and the administrations of American universities in the 1960s. Not surprisingly, students typically tried to widen the scope, while administrators sought to narrow it. Amidst these discussions, a consensus emerged among American administrators that faculty members and students hold contradictory rights while on campus. According to a report by the American Association of University Professors from the 1960s, in comparison to the faculty, "students' academic freedom seemed to involve a separate set of issues, such as due process in disciplinary procedures, censorship over publications, and confidentiality of records."[15] As one committee member explained, students "are essentially in a position of dependence, subject to the authority of the institution from which they hope to receive their degrees, subject to the authority of their teachers."[16] Academic freedom, such as that which protects professors' speech, did not enter into this conception of student rights. To address this issue more specifically, E. G.

Williamson and John L. Cowan conducted a study in the early 1960s and found that broad agreement existed between American administrators and students concerning the view that student free speech should flourish on campus.[17] However, administrators and students disagreed over students' rights to "act on their convictions," particularly in the form of pickets and sit-ins.[18] Mario Savio, leader of Berkeley's Free Speech Movement, criticized this reading of student rights because it meant that "students are permitted to talk all they want so long as their speech has no consequences."[19]

The activist American student of the 1960s rejected the authority vested in governments and university administrations; this movement, often overlapping with the "New Left," also abandoned those leading the older established leftist Communist and Socialist Parties. In their stead, these young people envisioned new kinds of political leaders constructing the world they wanted. As Edward Shils found at that time, "The 'big names' of present day student radicalism—Mao Tse-tung, Fidel Castro, Ché Guevara, Frantz Fanon are remote in space or dead; they have no commanding power over them, and they all share in the eyes of the student radicals a quasi-bohemian, free-floating, anti-institutional aroma. Even though they govern tyrannically, it is their anarchic element that appeals to the radical students."[20] Activist students tended to favor such adult leaders, often not much older than themselves, who could be molded in their mythology to be the perfect guides for the new world they saw sprouting from the revolution. At AUB, even Egyptian president Gamal Abdul Nasser, as a result of the 1967 defeat, receded from the student political radar. In the 1950s, he had captured the imagination of young people all over the Arab world because he put into place the socioeconomic reforms Arab nationalists had been calling for since the 1930s while also standing up to the Western imperialists trying to impede Arab progress. Even before 1967 and the Arab defeat to Israel, authoritarianism in Egypt, coupled with Egypt's increasing economic problems, had already generated doubts about Nasser's leadership. In 1967, these questions convinced activist students to look to other agents to restore Palestine and complete the Arab revolution. Halim Barakat found in a survey of AUB students in spring 1970 that only Lebanese Muslims (68 percent of them) saw Nasser as the most important leader in the region.[21] In contrast, almost half of all Lebanese Christians and Jordanian and Palestinian Christians and Muslims did not even mention him at all in their rankings. Barakat theorizes that students became radicalized because they were "increasingly aware that the dominant systems, structures, and cultural orientations in Lebanon and the rest of the

Arab society are essentially opposed to change. Gradually, students have found themselves involved in an ongoing confrontation between forces for change and forces for maintaining the dominant order. Though some of them joined the ranks of the latter, the majority have sided with forces for change."[22]

In rejecting the leaders who had failed them, students of this era elevated to new leadership positions all those fighting the forces of repression and imperialism. As Shils theorizes of "the moral revolution" that these students tried to generate, it "consists in a demand for a total transformation—a transformation from a totality of undifferentiated evil to a totality of undifferentiated perfection. Evil consists in the deadening of sentiment through institutions and more particularly through the exercise of and subordination to authority. Perfection consists in the freedom of feeling and the fulfillment of desires."[23] As the student protestor quoted at the beginning of this chapter declared at AUB, "Any reform starts by refusal." Much of what resonated on campuses throughout the world in this period filtered through AUB and came to be part of the discussion about the evil that needed to be opposed and the good that had to be encouraged, in a reversal of the same terminology used by Daniel Bliss (1866–1902) one hundred years earlier. Students saw the Palestinian fedayeen groups as the purveyors of revolution when Nasser and his generation failed to fully reform their societies and regain Palestine for the Arabs. AUB students no longer looked to AUB leaders as unquestioned voices of authority; they sought to take on that role themselves, granted them as full-fledged citizens of the university.

Student Government, Sock Hops, and Miss AUB

From the end of the Arab nationalist era in 1955 until the 1968 outburst in activity, students took charge of a proliferating array of activities on campus. In 1968, students leveraged the leadership experience they had gained from running the many societies on campus to demand that they have a voice in administrative and curricular decisions. The whole educational milieu of AUB required that students engage in extracurricular activities as part of their quest to become whole men. Daniel Bliss highlighted the role that physical fitness played, and for decades the school held annual and occasionally biannual field days; by the 1960s, the arts and sciences and engineering students had an ongoing football rivalry. In the first decades of the twentieth century, students established a variety of societies—for representing the national groups on campus, for studying great men such as John Milton, and for putting on theater productions, mostly of British and American stock. Social service organizations, the Village Welfare League (VWL), and later the Civic Welfare League (CWL) sponsored programs in Beirut and in rural areas of the country. The only hard-and-fast rule for these activities was the SPC and AUB prohibition on political activities; no societies advocating political action could exist on campus. al-ʿUrwa al-Wuthqa and the Student Council were dissolved in the 1950s for crossing that regulatory line.

The 1950s carried on the extracurricular tradition but in a much more extensive and more social way than in the earlier eras. Just about every faculty had a student society serving under its name, they all held annual elections for officers, and many participated in some kind of public service activity as part of their regular schedule. Starting in 1959, *Outlook* held general knowledge quizzes that brought out the students' competitive nature. The Engineering Students' Society (ESS) became famous for its ever more elaborate talent shows and balls. In May 1958, the members staged "Space, Time and AUB," with seven "ESS beauties" (male members of the school, since women had still not been admitted) dancing the can-can in women's clothing.[24] As *Outlook* reported, however, "The girls' repertory proved to be somewhat limited, as they repeated the same steps to the same music both times."[25] The Women Students' Organization (WSO) sponsored fashion shows open only to women of AUB and the city, and just about all the societies held dances or balls, frequently off campus at sites like the St. Georges Hotel. Students of the School of Agriculture introduced the first sock hop to campus on January 19, 1957, with both professors and students joining in on the fun. "Half-way through the party a wad of bubble-gum was distributed to every one. Then a funny spectacle was witnessed as each tried to outdo all others in blowing bubbles."[26] Near the end of the party, the women paraded in front of a group of faculty judges, who determined who had the nicest and most colorful socks. Students repeated this experiment a number of times throughout the next ten years. In addition, societies organized trips throughout the country so that students could enjoy, for example, a day of skiing. Iranian students staged the annual tradition of jumping over the fire before the last Wednesday of the Persian calendar year.

This new era of student leadership also saw women's voices entering the mainstream student activities at unprecedented levels. "Portrait of a

Coed" montages appeared in the annual commencement issue of *Outlook*. Questions by the "Inquiring Reporter" for *Outlook* asked men and women equally what they aspired to do in their lives, how they viewed their educational experiences, and how they saw male-female relationships developing on campus. Women students frequently headed student organizations and wrote for and edited the school newspapers; the Women Students' Organization became a dominant force on the extracurricular scene. The women excelled in their academic pursuits far out of proportion to the numbers they represented on campus. For example, in 1958, nine of the fifteen seniors on the arts and sciences honors list were female, accounting for 69 percent of the positions; in 1964, 16 percent of the women in the School of Arts and Sciences made the honor's list, while only 8 percent of men did.[27]

In 1950, the Civic Welfare League introduced a Miss AUB contest at its annual garden party fundraiser as a ploy to get more people to its event and more money for its organization; this contest continued until 1971.[28] In the garden party's heyday in the mid- to late 1950s, not only was Miss AUB crowned at the event but so, too, were the May Queen and Miss Lebanon.[29] The winners won ever more extravagant gifts from local vendors, sometimes culminating in trips to Cairo or Paris. In the same period, queen contests proliferated all over campus, with yearly votes for Miss Pharmacy, Miss New School Program, Miss College Hall and, on one occasion, "Trip Queen."[30] In the latter, students of AUB took a field trip around Lebanon; "the trip included some BCW [Beirut College for Women students] making the election of a Trip Queen quite in order."[31] The mere existence of women students along for the ride necessitated a vote for queen; beforehand, the organizers of the trip prepared a sash and a perfume bottle as gifts for the winner.

The Miss AUB contest clearly resonated on campus, even though no more than fifteen women agreed to run in any given year, with many turning down nominations from their peers.[32] It was the highlight of the garden party and begat the many other queen contests held throughout the rest of the year, in evidence of the old adage that imitation is the sincerest form of flattery. When something went wrong in the voting, outcries reverberated throughout campus, indicating a high level of enthusiasm for the event. In 1955, for example, a male engineering student dressed in drag won the title of Miss AUB. Over the next few weeks, as *Outlook*'s commencement issue declaimed, "The academic H-Bomb then mushroomed into a ghastly little war between 'Those with a Sense of Humor' and 'Those without a Sense of Humor.' The OUTLOOK letter box fairly smoked."[33] In its penchant for such contests, AUB was not unlike American universities of the same era. On college campuses all over America in the 1950s and 1960s, "queen contests, in fact, became the most popular and, in many cases, the primary source of prestige and ceremonial space afforded women students on college campuses."[34] These types of contests ranked "students on the basis of idealized versions of beauty, femininity, masculinity, desirability, respectability, poise, and aspirations," according to Karen Tice.[35]

The written record supplies little information about the attributes necessary for a woman to win the Miss AUB contest when it began in 1950; over time, the qualifications for Miss AUB typically included beauty, character, and participation in campus activities.[36] The winners, both before and after this 1961 statement of criteria, fulfilled this mandate. Miss AUB 1959 "is a very active teacher training major from Damascus."[37] In addition to having above-average grades, the winner "is or has been a member of the following organizations: Music Club, Folk, [sic] Dancing Club, WSO, AUB Choir[,] Dramatics Club, Executive Council of the Residence Halls, Bridge Club, and A&S Ball Committee."[38] In May 1960, *Outlook* published an editorial entitled "Right Girl—Wrong Title," praising the winner of the Miss AUB contest that year because "the young woman who was crowned is a fine example of all the qualities which are necessary for a coed to be the representative of young womanhood at AUB."[39] However, the writer felt that the title "Miss AUB" could be interpreted as referring to mere beauty rather than something more substantive and representative of womanhood at AUB. The writer preferred the Arabic translation of this title, "The AUB Girl," hoping it would prevail in English as well, since "this title seems more proper and fitting and has an explanatory charm about it. It encompasses much more than just physical beauty. And it even leads one to realize that the other equally important qualities of personality, scholarship, and activity-participation go along with beauty."[40] The winner in 1961, a sophomore psychology major, "is a talented and active co-ed at AUB. She has played the piano since she was five and has given several concerts in Tripoli. Her favorite composers are Mozart and Beethoven. At AUB she has joined a number of clubs and societies; she is an active member of the Music club, CWL, A&S society, WSO, A&S yearbook and has helped with International Evening."[41]

By 1962, the process had become so formalized that the faculty jury knew to rate the candidates based on beauty, sociability, overall rating, and activities.[42] In 1966, the criteria increased to include beauty, academic performance, character, activities, and elegance.[43] That year, the women candidates expressed a desire to, for example, continue graduate studies, conduct research, and go into nursing after graduation.[44] In 1971, the last year in which the contest was held, the candidates said they hoped to work in pharmacology, industrial psychology, fashion design, social work, nursing, and child psychology.[45] In the organization of these events, students negotiated and resolved questions about the purpose of women's education, the right of women to higher education, and the type of women representing AUB.

As part of the long process of changing women's status from coeds to students, women also started breaking through barriers set up by the Schools of Agriculture and Engineering. To succeed, women had to convince the deans of these schools that they could use their majors effectively after graduation. Dean Robert Nichols (1959–1967) and Assistant Dean Vernon Larson (1960–1962) of the School of Agriculture expressed support for the idea. They said, "*Girls would be gladly accepted in this school.* We have discovered that there were some applicants to this school in the past, and that all of them were told girls were not accepted. We would like to point out, however, that we would not accept only *one* girl student, for a solitary co-ed would be too much of a novelty and would tend to distract the attention of the boys."[46] The engineering dean, C. Ken Weidner (1952–1962), had strong reservations in 1961. He told *Outlook*, "In this School, we have limited enrollment, and the Middle East is in dire need of engineers. If we were to accept girls, then for every girl we admitted we would have to refuse admission to some boy who, on graduation, would practice his profession and become the head of a family. It is established from experience all over the world that most of the women who graduate from engineering schools never practice, and any energy exerted to educate a girl in this field would thus be wasted as far as the Middle East is concerned."[47] In October 1962, the first woman student joined the School of Agriculture; in 1967, women shattered the last male bastion by entering the School of Engineering. With these obstacles eliminated, women also saw more freedoms accruing to them all over campus. Clothing regulations for women started to become a thing of the past; as of the 1967–1968 academic year, women students no longer had to wear dresses at all times on campus.[48] Assuredly, men and women students still complained about the problems they faced in interacting and dating, but the doubts about women's right to higher education no longer held prominence in the campus discussion. The 1966 April Fool's Day issue of *Outlook* could even joke, "Are Girls Necessary at AUB"?[49] In the panel discussion, supposedly sponsored by the Sociology Society, this question came alongside those such as "Do girls have legs?" and "Do girls have wings?"[50] Women as a special category no longer existed at AUB; coeducation finally meant integrated and equal education.

While social events took precedence during the interim period, politics still filtered onto campus and generated responses by the students. Unlike the activist periods of the early 1950s and the post-1968 years, these responses were discrete moments, not sustained actions. During the October 1956 Suez Crisis, "A few students led cheers and made brief comments in support of Egypt's struggle. That set off a spark that saw students gather spontaneously. They organized in rows of four abreast and then marched through the campus, around the oval to Bliss hall, singing national songs and cheering President Gamal Abdul Nasser of Egypt and others dear to their hearts who are leading the defense of their fatherland."[51] Later in the day, a delegation of students reported to the Egyptian embassy to notify the officials that students intended to volunteer to support Egypt militarily. The administration expressed support for these actions. When 300 AUB students volunteered for military training and 264 other students signed up for "Civil Defense," Vice President Fuad Sarruf "contacted the appropriate authorities and supplied them with the lists of volunteers"; he is reported to have said, "It is the administration's desire to help the students fulfill their wishes and provide them with all the appropriate and required facilities."[52] In the end, 174 students participated in military training in Homs, Syria.[53] The faculty of the School of Engineering established a "civil defense program" and put together a series of lectures on the responsibilities involved in such a program.[54]

The administration was not as supportive of later student actions on behalf of the Algerian revolution against the French (1954–1962) and the union of Egypt and Syria in the United Arab Republic (UAR, 1958–1961). When one hundred students demonstrated on campus on February 21, 1959, in commemoration of the establishment of the UAR, the administration placed eleven students on special probation because "such unauthorized gatherings, whether spontaneous or premeditated, are strongly disapproved by the University authorities because the disturbance which results interrupts the planned and orderly academic program of the University."[55] In November 1960, the administration suspended thirteen students for participating in a demonstration on November 1, Algeria Day.[56] The students participated in the demonstration even though President J. Paul Leonard (1957–1961) had recommended that students donate blood instead, and had arranged to have the university hospital prepare for such a plan.[57] In February 1961, the presidents of several campus organizations (medicine, engineering, arts and science, agriculture, WSO, and CWL) met with Dean Archie Crawford, who agreed they could hold an Algeria Week program. To reaffirm the school's prohibition on political activities at such events, Dean Crawford sent a letter to all the students "defining the meaning of 'haram' (sanctuary) on campus: that the campus should be free from all political activity and that the students may join in political activities outside campus on their own responsibility."[58] In a later interview, Crawford explained that the 'haram' "is not an aggressive but a protective place."[59]

After the disbanding of both al-ʿUrwa al-Wuthqa and the Student Council in the mid-1950s, students continued to demand that the latter be reconstituted. In light of the new leadership positions students were taking in the many societies now existing on campus, the step toward a more structured student government made perfect sense. In each society, the students practiced a micro-level governmental process; they continually demanded of the administration that they be allowed to perform the same functions at the university level. As they had done in protest to the suspension of the Student Council in 1952, the students voiced their demands in the language of the rights and freedoms accorded them as students in a liberal educational framework.

At his inauguration in 1957, President Leonard invigorated the debate about student government when he stressed that "self-control and judgement in selecting their representatives are the traits which students must first exhibit before AUB can have a successful student council such as the one which functioned at San Francisco State College" (a previous administrative post for Leonard).[60] At a conference in November 1957, attended by society presidents and members of the faculty and administration, Leonard added to his call for student self-control by saying, "While on campus, students are 'citizens of the University,' where they have withdrawn from 'the heat of the street' in order to learn the rational approach to the everyday problems of life."[61] Regional politics should not intrude on this citizenship, but should be confined to the Arab Studies program, "where they get the benefit of scholarly guidance."[62] Those who choose to engage in political issues outside of scholarly political debates must do so away from AUB, and "they must remember that there is no longer anything to differentiate them from the uneducated masses."[63] Out of this conference came a committee of student society leaders from all of AUB's schools, tasked with writing a constitution for the Student Council. By March 1958, a consensus had been reached by the committee members on most aspects of the new constitution. Each school's students would elect representatives for the council, although no agreement on the number of representatives for each school had been agreed upon; all students would vote for the president. The matter stalled, however, over Leonard's demand that AUB's president retain veto power over the council's decisions.[64] Student representatives rejected this condition, saying in a statement to Leonard that "the students should have a free collective expression of their opinion" and that a presidential veto would violate this right.[65]

Despite the participation of the president, the faculty, and many of the students in the process, the school did not resurrect the Student Council in the 1958 or 1959 school year; for that matter, the issue did not come up again on campus until November 1961, when another committee of student society leaders met with new president Norman Burns (1961–1965) to discuss the possibility of reestablishing the Student Council. The students followed up this meeting by submitting to the Student Life Office on April 24, 1963, a constitution for the Student Council. On May 7, 1963, the university senate voted to reject this constitution, saying that "the Senate reaffirms its belief in an advisory student council," but "the question of a student council organization needs time for serious consideration"; no action would be taken on a proposed constitution during that academic year.[66] As a consolation, the president offered to let student representatives sit on the faculty-led Student Life Committee; they began to do so in 1964. According to Burns, "This was a definite move towards a greater degree of student participation in student campus government which is believed to have had a very wholesome effect upon student relations and student morals at AUB during the last year."[67] Burns saw this participation as preferable to a university-wide student union, which might be premature and might "lead to political consequences of the type that prevailed in the early 1950s when the old Student Union was abolished."[68]

Instead of moving closer to establishing a new council, the early to mid-1960s saw a period of quiet. Except for some Palestine Week programs, and the many events to raise money for needy causes, political activism had waned to the point where the biggest complaint on campus was about student apathy rather than student activism. This situation had become so acute by 1964 that a new student life committee was formed to investigate student apathy.[69] The perception of student apathy continued, and in April 1967, the Faculty of Arts and Sciences appointed the Ad Hoc Committee on Teaching Effectiveness to study the problem; professors felt that the problem had been exaggerated, but "all agreed on the fact that much could be done to decrease the apathy, no matter how small, [*sic*] existent at AUB."[70] The once vibrant social scene had also begun to disintegrate as student participation in the many societies dropped dramatically.

The Student Life Committee recommended the reinstatement of the Student Council, and in March 1966, yet another constitution made the rounds of the student societies on campus, but conflict arose over the percentage of representation to be accorded to each of the school's faculties. In its place, a student-faculty committee served some of the functions of a student government. President Samuel Kirkwood (1965–1976) explained his reluctance to reintroduce the Student Council: "The present policy of the University is based on the assumption that neither faculty nor students should be solely responsible for the supervision of student activities, but that through a cooperative effort the greatest good can be accomplished."[71] He helped create a joint student-faculty committee to meet this need. Only on July 1, 1969, did the Student Council return to campus, molded by a student body again embroiled in the political affairs of the region.

In the move to reconstitute the Student Council and establish new societies and activities, men and women students took control over their own extracurricular activities to an unprecedented extent. While every society, in every year of the school's existence, had a faculty advisor supervising its activities, each decade of the twentieth century saw that touch become lighter. By the 1950s and 1960s, students were truly running their own extracurricular lives. Even though the initial fervor of the Arab nationalist period had subsided by 1955 and the school saw moments of student apathy, campus life could not revert back to the pre-1947 period of relative calm; rather, the students used these years to gain more independent decision-making power over the dozens of organizations proliferating around them. Students learned valuable leadership skills as they took the reins of the student societies away from the administration. Whether silly and light-hearted, as in the case of many of the student entertainments, or serious and well thought out, as in the case of the Student Council negotiations, student participants gained experience in governance. Students debated what kind of governmental and extracurricular activities they wanted to produce, and they negotiated among themselves the compromises necessary to work together. All of this had, of course, occurred in student societies existing prior to this period, but now the interlocution of the faculty advisor was diminished, and the proliferation of societies of all types meant that this process of student leadership occurred repeatedly. The stage was now set for a redefinition of the campus as a civic space where students could act out their educational and political lives in an unfettered way.

AUB's 1968

In the aftermath of the June 1967 war, students helped professors conduct research into the living conditions of the new Palestinian refugees. In August, accompanied by twenty students, AUB sociology professors Peter Dodd and Halim Barakat conducted interviews with one hundred "case studies" in Camp Zeezya and with twenty-two randomly chosen refugees living in Amman, Jordan.[72] As the academic year commenced, professors continued to define the school's response to the Arab defeat. For example, on the twentieth anniversary of the United Nations partition decision, commemorated on November 27, over seven hundred students gathered in front of West Hall to hear speeches by the professors.[73] Professor Constantine Zurayq said that catastrophes like 1967 "can either destroy nations or motivate them to a fresh and more positive start," and he expressed the hope that "these countries will rise to the challenge and succeed in their endeavor of righting the wrong in Palestine."[74] *Outlook* quoted Professor Yusuf Ibish as saying that "it is not enough to have weapons, machinery and other such tools to overcome the opponents." He stated that "education and individual qualities are just as important if not more so. A development of positive enthusiasm and personal advancement as a form of preparation for future confrontations is therefore an essential prerequisite for success."[75] Higher education, as presented at AUB, would best train the students for the problems confronting them in the future; political players could not.

When students organized their first event in this new era, they repeated the messages coming from their professors. Sponsored by the Political Science Society of Université Saint-Joseph, students from all of the country's universities held a panel discussion in February 1968 to lay out the tasks university students should undertake in the post-1967 period.[76] The main conclusion was that university students have a special role in teaching others about the problems catalyzed by June 5, 1967, whether "to inform the west of our problem and present it in a real light," to lead as the "educated or enlightened element," or "to make people more conscientious and to awaken them."[77] The AUB delegate to the panel expressed the view that "the student should see facts as they really are and be able to criticize matters objectively and ferret out the weak points."[78] He saw the Arab defeat of 1967 as an explicit sign of the "inefficiency of the existing social super-structure, and its inability to mobilize potentialities."[79] The students' discourse at this stage was solely an academic one; the conditions in the immediate post-1967 period had failed to generate the factors necessary for the students to begin the process of formulating new roles for themselves on campus. For almost a year after the 1967 war, no member of the AUB campus body proffered any substantial alterations to this paradigm. Nothing in these speeches and programs presaged a new approach to education or to the Palestinian issue.

Change came swiftly as events in spring 1968 began to generate new kinds of questions about the role the students should play in guiding their educational and political programs. As was typical of so many student movements of this era, AUB's 1968 was ultimately catalyzed by a cause solely connected to the school: the March 1968 decision by the administration to not renew Professor Sadiq al-ʿAzm's contract. The momentum the students gained in this first major action propelled them into the next, a protest against university censorship of political events on campus; later, they opposed Jordanian and Lebanese military action against Palestinian fedayeen groups. Questions asked about the nature of authority wielded on campus and throughout the Arab region were the same as those that rallied students all over the world.

In the case of al-ʿAzm, students criticized the administration for penalizing the professor for his political views and failing to objectively assess the quality of his academic work. They also felt that their positive evaluations of Professor al-ʿAzm's teaching prowess had been willfully ignored by the administration. To articulate these complaints, a number of students organized into the Committee for Academic Freedom, announcing in March 1968 their reasons for calling a strike to protest administrative policies concerning the professor.

> The collective strike that took place today without one single action of violence and with the cooperation of all students, and faculty at times, has proved:
> 1. That students are responsible and dedicated to the principles of academic freedom;
> 2. That the actions of the administration has [sic] created much discontent among the students;
> 3. That the rigidity of certain officials has pushed all students into this collective strike;

4. That when the administration shuts off all constructive channels with the students, striking becomes justified;

5. That the students are not reluctant nor afraid to stand up for their rights.[80]

The supporters of the strike saw al-ʿAzm's case as a sign that the administration was neither willing to uphold standards of academic freedom nor supportive of students having any decision-making power. In so stating their position, the students of 1968 framed their desire for participatory rights on campus in much the same way as their predecessors had done in 1882, 1909, and the early 1950s. The administration, as it had done in these earlier instances, did not accept the students' definition of their role on campus; the al-ʿAzm decision was not rescinded.

Soon thereafter students used the same themes to criticize the administration for its actions in the Palestinian realm. On May 9, 1968, a group calling itself the Organization of Arab Students at A.U.B. reported that the administration had rejected proposed speakers for the forthcoming Palestine Week program, "claiming that they were from outside AUB and that they represent one point of view which is the Arab view—as if the administration wants us to invite Moshé Dayan and Aba [sic] Eban to give us lectures on Palestine."[81] In response, the students theorized that

those responsible of [sic] the University, headed by Kirkwood, think that if the Arabs were defeated on June 5, they (the administration) have the right to undermine and mock at their dignity and feelings. They think that they are capable of going ahead swiftly to execute the designed role of this University in the region which, in its foremost, is the serving of American and Zionist interests and the mutilation of the educated class in the Arab and Third Worlds.[82]

In the same statement, the organization declared, "The insolent decision of the administration proves what we were suspecting. It proves that AUB is against Palestine as well as it is against University Freedoms."[83] These statements indicate a new lack of respect for authority figures, rarely expressed in such a pointed way in past protests on campus.

When the Jordanian military and the Palestinian fedayeen clashed in November 1968 because of Palestinian attacks against Israel from Jordan, AUB students went out on strike on campus, while students from other universities protested in front of the Jordanian embassy in Beirut. AUB students had tried to march alongside the other students, but the school's security forces locked the gates; the students held a sit-in and strike on campus instead.[84] If they had gone, they would have joined a demonstration that turned violent as students closed streets around the embassy and five members of the Lebanese security forces were injured.[85] A spot survey by *Outlook*, conducted on the day of the strike, found that 60 percent of the student body supported the action.[86] A more comprehensive poll taken a few days later found "the large majority of those who participated in the strike did so in sympathy and in support of the fidaiyeen. A large number went on strike to protest against all parties concerned that seek the liquidation of the fadai movement. Another group could be described as those who went on strike as an expression of solidarity with the national (palestinian [*sic*]) cause."[87] From this point forward, support for the Palestinian fedayeen served as the default position among activist students; from that starting line, all other ideologies flowed and any group, including the AUB administration, who opposed the Palestinian revolution came under attack.

The December 1968 Israeli attack on the Beirut airport accelerated this burgeoning student movement, for it firmly placed the focus on a military solution to the Palestine crisis. In January the students instigated a twelve-day strike, including a hunger strike of fifty students. As it had occasionally done in the past, the administration accepted the validity of the strike. Kirkwood announced to the students, faculty, and staff on January 14, 1969, that "because of the extremely serious situation facing Lebanon the University has accepted during these past days the interruption of its academic program and its work in the hope that a conscientious resolution of the student actions would result within a reasonable time."[88]

In the course of the strike, the students issued a list of four demands they wanted Lebanese premier Abdallah Yafi's government to accept: "the judging of those responsible for the Beirut Airport incident; compulsory military conscription; stressing the legality of the work of the Fedayeen in Lebanon; and fortifying the frontier villages."[89] A student pamphlet issued during the strike declared the goal of the action: "We are for the creation of a new awareness in a nation that has long been in a state of stagnation."[90] As a student editorial reiterated, the strike was not called solely in reaction to the specific events; rather, "The Israeli strike on Beirut Airport was only the igniting spark to an already ripe social situation. As the situation exploded, the different religious and political groups at AUB, [*sic*] presented a united front for the first time. They united to call for a comprehensive social revolution that would overhaul an incapacitated social system."[91] Overall, the student movement "aims at a comprehensive upheaval of the present social system that is incapable of meeting the demands of a modern world with modern ways."[92] At all times, this new system must protect and advance the interests of the Palestinian revolution. "First and foremost, a strong Lebanon means a country that is not only capable of defending itself against any aggressive Israeli enemy, but also one that is wholeheartedly capable of supporting the Palestine cause."[93] The attack, and the failure of the Lebanese government to protect the country or the Palestinians within it, led the students to call for training for all university students so that they could join the force protecting the revolution.[94] The Medical Students' Society launched "a campaign for the collection of funds aimed at financing a project through which medical kits will be prepared by the medical students and sent to the villagers of the South of Lebanon in case they are needed in any future Israeli raid."[95]

When clashes erupted between the Palestinian fedayeen and the Lebanese government in April 1969, protests broke out all over Beirut, forcing the Lebanese government to declare a citywide curfew; at AUB, student activities disrupted the academic schedule for most of the subsequent eleven days. The Student Council, in calling for a sit-in and then a strike, declared,

1. The Palestinian nation should not be denied the right to self-determination which has been granted to all nations in the Universal Declaration of Human Rights.
2. The Palestinian resistance movement has been the force that brought about the resurrection of the Palestinian nation and as such it is the legitimate representative of the Palestinian masses.
3. Even though the Arab-Israeli conflict involves all the Arab countries surrounding Israel, any decisions affecting this issue should be decided upon by the Palestinian nation itself.[96]

As clashes continued into fall 1969, the students, led by the Student Council, focused particularly on the demand that the Palestinian forces be allowed to function freely within the country, without Lebanese government interference. The Lebanese government signed the Cairo agreement with PLO chairman Yasir Arafat on November 8, 1969, which recognized "the armed fida'iyin's right to be present on and move around Lebanese territory, especially to and from the 'Arqub region" and which "provided a form of extra-territoriality for the Palestinian camps." AUB students, however, continued to criticize the government for not fully protecting the Palestinians living in Lebanon.[97]

Throughout this process, the students grew gradually more militant and more strongly supportive of all things connected to the Palestinian revolution. Halim Barakat's survey of students at AUB, Université Saint-Joseph, and Lebanese University in 1970 and 1971 indicated that differences existed based on nationality and religion, but increasingly the students favored a military solution to the region's problems. For example, "The Palestinian students showed the highest inclination toward political alienation and leftist radicalism. While 86 percent indicated that they were dissatisfied with the dominant political conditions, only 71 percent of other Arabs did so."[98] While the disparity between the views of the Palestinians and their fellow students is substantial, the latter's numbers certainly indicate a high level of enthusiasm for the leftist position. At AUB, allegiance to the Palestinian commandos was particularly high. Barakat found that 78 percent of those surveyed in spring 1970 showed "strong support" or "support" for the commandos.[99] Broken down by nationality, 87 percent of polled Palestinian students gave "strong support" and 7 percent "support" for the commandos; Jordanian students polled a similar total number but with a different breakdown: 52 percent with "strong support" and 45 percent expressing "support."[100] Nationality seemed less important than religion. Almost half the Muslims polled at AUB supported "armed struggle" as the preferred solution to the Arab-Israeli conflict, while only 22 percent of Christians did.[101]

A 1969 visit to London's Hyde Park inspired a student to establish AUB's own Speakers' Corner; the primary goal was to provide a space where students felt free to express their ideas and opinions.[102] The statements made at the many Speakers' Corner sessions illustrate how at least the activist students articulated the goals they hoped to achieve, and simultaneously the identity they were trying to forge for this generation of students. Underlying almost every statement they made was diminished respect for authority, be it of the administrative or governmental variety; students defined opposition to the administration as a duty they had to take on as students and as Arabs.

The Speakers' Corner sessions of the 1970–1971 academic year were dominated by the death of Nasser on September 28 and military collisions between the Palestinian fedayeen and the Jordanian government throughout the same month. In commemoration of the former, Arabs all over the region had flown black flags in mourning; Nasser's political capital had been diminished by the loss in 1967, but his death reminded people of his past successes. In the so-called Black September events, King Hussein of Jordan successfully fought against the Palestinian fedayeen, who had established a virtual state-within-a-state inside Jordanian territory so they could attack Israel at will. When the Jordanian government chose to confront the fedayeen, thousands of Palestinians died and the fedayeen moved their operations to southern Lebanon.[103] As the events of the month unfolded, the key pillars of the student movement already stood in place. The students wanted to overthrow what they saw as the censorship, oppression, and imperialism they felt maintained the AUB administration and the reactionary Arab regimes in power. They wanted those aspects of power destroyed so that they could join the decision-making bodies on campus and, in the same calculation, the Palestinian revolution could move forward unimpeded. Student Council president Maher Masri opened the first Speakers' Corner of the year by asking for a moment of silence in commemoration of the "deaths of President Nasser and the thousands of innocent victims in Jordan."[104] A Student Council member continued on this topic:

> "I cannot remember," [he] said, "in the history of the world, a ruler killing 10,000 of his people. We cannot, therefore, but condemn the Jordanian government. We all know about the Rogers' plan. For this plan to succeed the obstacle in its path—the commandos—had to be weakened. They had to weaken this organization for the great powers to go on with their plan and this is exactly what happened."[105]

Another student connected the events of September to the larger fight of the poor against the imperialist rich. "We want to appeal to everybody—the lower classes, the fighters in Vietnam. Those upper classes who left Jordan before the fighting signed a blank check for King Hussein to do what he wanted with the lower classes, the people in the camps."[106] In summary, he stated, "We are fighting those who have been exploiting America, people who have been exploiting the black people, the poor white people, the Vietnamese and others."[107]

At the following Speakers' Corner, on October 29, Leila Khaled, a student at AUB in the 1962–1963 academic year, visited campus after having become famous as a hijacker for the Popular Front for the Liberation of Palestine (PFLP). The *Daily Star* reported that "hero-worshipping students" clapped for five minutes, chanting "we want Leila" once they heard she was in the audience.[108] They stopped clamoring only when she stepped up to the microphone. During Khaled's speech, she described the events of September 1970 as "the massacres carried out by the hirelings with the intention of wiping out both the revolution and the Palestinian people."[109] She continued:

> We have always said and will continue to say that the reactionary authorities in this area are an added advantage on the side of the enemy. These last events prove the validity of our strategy which is to overcome reactionary governments in order to overcome zionism [sic] and world imperialism led by the United States.[110]

She went on to say the massacres in Amman, in Wahadat Camp, "can only be compared to what is now going on in Israel and to the barbarism of Genghis Khan."[111]

For the next couple of years, the themes brought up at these Speakers' Corner sessions set the parameters for the debate about Jordan's actions in September, and thereafter as the government hunted down the remaining fedayeen fighters. Jordan served the interests of the larger imperialist program by attacking those poorest and least able to defend themselves.[112] The battle for the Palestinians represented not only a local fight to regain lost rights, but a larger struggle against imperialism all over the world. Just as the Vietnamese defended against the American invasion, so too could the Arabs and Palestinians effectively defeat the Jordanians who opposed their struggle against the Israelis.

Another common theme of the year surfaced in the Speakers' Corner, namely the role the Rogers Plan was playing in obstructing Palestinian aims. Even though the Arab-Israeli peace plan named after US secretary of state William Rogers remained viable in Washington for only a short period of time after its issuance in 1969, the students at AUB spoke repeatedly of the damage the plan was doing and would do if fully implemented.[113] Palestinian leaders speaking on campus perpetuated this view and the students reiterated it during their own Speakers' Corner sessions and in their other political statements. For example, Abu al-Hasan of Fatah spoke on campus in January 1971 in a program sponsored by the Student Council and the General Union of Palestine Students, an affiliate of Fatah.[114] In introducing the speaker, Maher Masri asked for a moment of silence "in memory of all those who have fallen on the path of liberation."[115] An AUB representative of the Lebanese Front Supporting Fatah attacked "liquidation schemes such as the Rogers Plan" and said that the "Lebanese masses are threatened by two enemies—the alliance between feudalism and capitalism on the internal front and Israel from across the borders. The Lebanese masses," he went on, "see in the Palestinian Revolution, and in Fateh in particular, a natural ally."[116] In his speech, Abu al-Hasan pointed out that the Rogers Plan had not been put forth when the Arab regimes were at their weakest, right after the defeat of 1967; the plan "was rather brought to light in 1970—as soon as the Palestinian Revolution was able 'to create and [*sic*] armed population enjoying political freedom,' as soon as it succeeded in resurrecting the Arab fighter and shortly after Israeli Defense Minister Moshe Dayan declared that Zionists should prepare themselves for widening their graves."[117]

At almost the same moment that Abu al-Hasan was giving his speech, new clashes broke out between the Jordanian army and the Palestinian fedayeen. AUB students went into crisis mode, with the Student Council organizing an emergency meeting to determine the students' response. They also placed loudspeakers all over campus and began broadcasting daily updates about the clashes in Jordan.[118] The "Voice of the Student" broadcasts aired commando communiqués and reports from Jordan, messages of support to the Palestinian revolution, and revolutionary songs and music.[119] Student speakers at a hastily planned conference in West Hall "denounced repeated attempts by the Jordanian regime to liquidate the Palestinian Revolution and urged students and progressive forces to shoulder their responsibilities in helping thwart the new conspiracy."[120] On January 12, the Student Council organized what they declared was a "100 percent successful walkout from classes . . . to join a nation-wide student protest against the attempt to liquidate Palestinian revolutionary forces in Jordan."[121] The approximately five hundred AUB students who joined in a country-wide demonstration of about four thousand students in the Hursh area held up placards, proclaiming:

1. The massacres in Jordan constitute a national crime and a direct assistance to the Israeli enemy.
2. They receive the blessings from London, the arms from America and the military assistance from Tel Aviv.
3. We shall crush the enemies of life with the boots of the revolutionaries.[122]

Speaking at the rally, Abu Youssef, chairman of the PLO Higher Committee of the Palestinians in Lebanon, called on the Palestinian and Arab masses to transform the present battle into a popular liberation movement against "this conspiring regime." He urged the Arab leaders to adopt a firm stand which would genuinely express the will of the masses.[123]

As verbal attacks increased against the Jordanian regime, the students also intensified their complaints against an AUB administration they saw leading the university in the same reactionary fashion. In one such move, the students established a "free university" to offer courses they thought would be truly useful for their educational experience. As reported in *Outlook* in January 1971,

> The basic assumption upon which the free University is founded is that something is wrong, or at least lacking, in the present AUB curriculum
> . . .
>
> It is also a kind of challenge to the regular university, for in effect we are saying that our interests and priorities are vastly different from the university's as decided by administrators and department heads, and therefore we will study what we deem important in spite of the program they set for us.[124]

Namir Cortas explained further in an editorial on November 16, 1971. "In the physical and social sciences, the curricula are not only completely imported and unadapted [*sic*] to the conditions and needs of the area, but are in disastrous, desolate conditions."[125]

The first course, "Revolutionary Change," had sessions entitled "September Events in Jordan" and "Che Guevara and the Third-World Revolution."[126] The free university also sought to address the "strategic needs of the Palestinian Revolution including everything from Hebrew to military strategy"; courses marked by "Progressive and Marxist social thought [were] to be offered in the Philosophy, Political Science, and Education Departments." Other proposed courses were "Revolutionary Philosophy," "Politics and Economics of Israel," "History of Palestine," "The Guitar—A Counterculture Workshop," and "Analysis and Critique of AUB and the [F]orms of Education Present."[127]

In establishing the free university, AUB students were following the lead of their compatriots all over the world. At its 1965 national convention, the American Students for a Democratic Society (SDS) proposed "free universities" to be parallel to the curriculum offered by traditional universities and to serve as models for future university reform.[128] The goal of the many new free universities established by students around the world was "to use pedagogical techniques that promoted active learning and relied on students' experience."[129] The AUB "Strike Document" of November 30, 1971, summed up the free university's goals: "One of the fundamental values of human life is freedom—freedom to formulate convictions and moral principles; freedom to live by those convictions and principles; and of course, freedom from coersion [sic]."[130] The document ridiculed the rights that students actually held while on campus.

> Last May, the majority of A.U.B. students discovered that their university allowed only certain 'freedoms' to be expressed on campus namely:
> 1. freedom to be herded into irrelevant classes;
> 2. freedom to absorb information that would soon be forgotten, since it had no use in daily life;
> 3. freedom to agree to University rules and regulations, formed and enforced without the students [sic] prior knowledge.
>
> In short, freedom to be silent.[131]

These views had been prompted by the first major attempt by the students to take control over the space of the university in May 1971. In that month, students went on strike and then occupied administrative buildings in protest against the 10 percent tuition increase announced by the president. In describing the solidarity expressed by the student body, Kirkwood reported,

> In this case student power was used to force a confrontation with University authority. This was done through extensive use of the loud speaker, domination of the public media by student reporters, and the suppression of ideas thought to be contrary to the strike. Access to the campus itself was severely limited with students in control of the gates, and thus for a time a near-perfect insular community was created, fed on its own information system of rumors and half-truths.[132]

The students' complaints certainly centered on the difficulties they faced in raising more money for tuition, but they also railed against the abuse of authority they felt came along with the unilateral administrative decision. The AUB Student Council stated that it would remain on strike until Kirkwood

1. Declares the cancellation of the 10% increase in tuition fees.
2. Announces his readiness to negotiate with the Student Council the possibility of reasonable decreases in the current tuition fees.
3. Declares his acceptance of the Student Council demands to investigate the books of the University at the Comptroller's Office to see whether there are reasonable grounds for decrease in current tuition fees.[133]

After twelve strike days and a "creeping occupation" of the buildings, Kirkwood declared the 1970–1971 academic year suspended.[134] Council president Masri responded by saying, "This is just what we expected. From now on this is our university, not Kirkwood's university."[135] Masri went on to declare, "Tomorrow there will be new occupations until the whole university is under our control."[136]

At no time in the history of AUB had students ever taken control of buildings and declared that the university was now theirs. The administration was no longer the sole power broker, making all decisions on campus; the students now felt they had the right to take this responsibility for themselves. Even Kirkwood acknowledged the uniqueness of the situation. In his annual report for the 1970–1971 academic year, he gave his account.

> While there have been other disruptions of AUB's academic life since it was founded 105 years ago, none has been as well organized, as long in duration or as effective in bringing to a halt the normal educational process as was the strike of May 13th to June 4th. Unlike other disruptions, this strike will have a profound effect on University life in the months and years ahead.[137]

The occupation ended on June 4, when Professor Constantine Zurayq worked out an agreement that convinced the students to leave the buildings. The Faculty of Arts and Sciences accepted the motion on May 31, 1971, which said, "We express the faith that a university is a locus of rational discussion. We regret that students have occupied University buildings and appeal to them to vacate them. We believe that a university is for students, and we as a Faculty will do all that we possibly can for them. We realize that all points at issue (tuition increase, student participation, examination, etc.) need lengthy, rational discussion, and we will do everything to bring about a fair solution to these issues."[138] The Student Council accepted the motion and the participating students peacefully vacated the buildings, having inflicted almost no damage on any of the equipment during the course of the strike.

Despite this agreement, Kirkwood dissolved the Student Council, suspended twenty-one students, and warned a large number of others of potential punishments; the school also instituted the 10 percent tuition increase as of the fall 1971 semester.[139] In announcing the suspension of the Student Council, Kirkwood wrote, "The University has attempted through a Student Council Constitution to bring about proper student participation in University Affairs. However, the experience of the past three years has demonstrated that the Student Council, as presently established, does not provide adequate avenues for student representation dialogue."[140] Kirkwood reiterated his position at the beginning of the new academic year, saying, "Dissent is highly prized in an association of scholars and scientists such as we have at AUB and must be preserved. But dissent without mutual respect for differing opinions is not acceptable in a university community."[141] As Kirkwood wrote in his annual report for 1970–1971, "Freedom is only valid within a system of law."[142] After a brief student strike in October 1971, accompanied by pressure from the Lebanese president, the administration readmitted the suspended students. The administration also reconstituted the Student Council in February 1972.

The punishments by Kirkwood failed to chasten the students, and they kept up their activism between 1972 and the outbreak of the civil war in 1975, with particular fervor exhibited after the October 1973 war and during the forty-one-day 1974 occupation of school buildings.[143] In October 1973, the Student Council formed a medical committee to "organize medical teams to be sent to the front if need be" and a popular committee to "be in direct contact with all parties and Palestinian organizations," which would serve as the "link between them and the student body," as well as fundraising and follow-up committees.[144] Once again, students volunteered for civil defense training. After that, the largest event of the era occurred between March 19 and April 24, 1974, when students again occupied campus buildings to oppose another 10 percent tuition increase. Mohammad Matar, then Student Council president, declared in a note to the faculty that the students "reject the assumption that AUB is here to serve the interests of the region and its people; the AUB is here to serve other interests."[145] As proof, he pointed out that "AUB is run by a Board of Trustees made up of business men who also happen to be U.S. foreign-office politicians. It clearly exposes the role of AUB as an American profit-maximizing institution. (The profit [is] surely not accrued to us)."[146] The *Outlook* editor added, "One thing remains clear, the 10% increase issue has to be understood within the context of cultural imperialism, implemented through the American University of Beirut."[147] The *Outlook* editor explained why any administrative efforts to make AUB a place separate from the outside world had failed: "No barriers can be erected around the campus and make it an independent entity, 'an entity apart from all this[,]' for they will be artificial. We are not just students, we also happen to be patriots, Arabs and 'social' animals."[148] After forty-one strike days, on April 24, "800 Lebanese security men stormed the campus and arrested 61 students who were occupying the University buildings"; on July 19, the AUB administration informed 103 students they would not be able to register in the fall.[149] The administration also suspended the Student Council and *Outlook*.[150]

The period between 1972 and the end of the strike in 1974 showed that student solidarity could not be maintained over the long term. As Lebanese politics became more unstable, and as the leftist-progressive movement fragmented around the region, so too did the student movement at AUB. For example, Fatah came to dominate the Student Council, while the PFLP founded a student general union; both groups competed for supporters on campus. The Lebanese League, Rabita, had often followed policies in opposition to the leftist, progressive movement; in both of the student occupations, Rabita gave only initial support before walking out.[151] While the 1971 student occupation of buildings had ended with little damage to the buildings, the 1974 strike resulted in "considerable property damage" and political slogans painted all over the walls.[152] Long before the most fervent of students had given up the occupation, many students clamored to resume classes. This era of student activism ended with one of the expelled students, former engineering student Najm Najm, returning to campus on February 17, 1976, killing Professor Raymond Ghosn, the dean of engineering, and Robert Najemy, the dean of students, and then threatening to kill himself and nine hostages with a grenade before being taken into custody.[153]

Conclusion

When scholars try to assess the influence the 1960s international student movement had on individual countries, they point most frequently to the social changes that resulted. For example, in the United States, the sexual revolution and the establishment of academic programs in Women's and

African American Studies resulted directly from this era's protests. When scholars look to the movement's influence on the American political system, they frequently write about the backlash that occurred by at least the Reagan years of the 1980s. Assuredly, many of the 1960s generation maintained their leftist political activism, but the country as a whole gradually and then swiftly moved to the political right. For AUB, an analysis of the legacy of this student movement is harder to calculate since no similar social revolution took place. Furthermore, in Lebanon, the outbreak of the civil war diverted the students' attention away from the civic space they had fought so hard to create on campus. As of 1975, the administration and the students had to work together to keep the campus functioning throughout the fighting, as new fissures emerged along the lines established throughout Lebanon. The war makes it impossible to determine what direction student politics might have more naturally taken after 1975.

Nonetheless, the late 1960s ushered in a moment where student passions did hold sway for a time at AUB, regardless of how hard the administration sought to keep them down. The students made the administration take into account their political views and it had to listen to them, as they blared out their ideas over loudspeakers at the Speakers' Corner or as they occupied buildings to assert their demands. As Muhammad Dajani Daoudi, president of the Student Council in 1972–1973, declared, "The simple fact is that this movement stems from our conviction that students have a legitimate right to express their opinion on ALL university matters. Students, we believe, should participate in such university bodies as the curriculum, admissions, disciplinary, and scholarship committees."[154] Only in 1971 and 1974 did the students physically take over the campus, but throughout the period between 1968 and 1975, student voices dominated the campus as they redefined the rights they held. The messages the students disseminated, particularly about the oppressive nature of authority and the demand for a new kind of student freedom, resonated on campuses all across the globe in the post-1968 era. The AUB movement had waned by 1974, as the activist students no longer worked together but for increasingly more fragmented political positions. The earlier moments of student activism had garnered at least passive support from a majority of the student population, but by the dawn of the civil war, political divisions, rather than solidarity, marked the movement. Halim Barakat theorizes that the student movements fragmented due to "a lack of cooperation of students across universities and colleges in Lebanon and consequent failure to establish a general union." Furthermore, "Student politics reflect the existing authoritarian tendencies in the society. This is vividly exhibited in the behavior of the student leaders." Instead of cooperating together, "the student leadership has been fighting its own battle to improve its position in the power structure."[155] The era ended ignominiously with the killings of Ghosn and Najemy.

REBUILDING AUB
Reaffirming Liberal Education

In 2004, AUB gained accreditation with the Middle States Commission on Higher Education, a voluntary, nongovernmental membership association. "Middle States accreditation instills public confidence in institutional mission, goals, performance, and resources through its rigorous accreditation standards and their enforcement"; the commission has accepted that AUB and the other accredited institutions in its roster "are fulfilling their stated purposes and addressing the publics' expectations."[1] To achieve this status, AUB's administration and faculty undertook a three-year evaluation of the school's strengths and future goals. The authors of the study recognized student pressure to abandon the American liberal educational structure in favor of one more specifically focused on professional training. They wrote,

> The commitment of AUB to liberal education may indeed place the University against prevailing currents in the culture. However, this commitment contributes to the uniqueness of AUB among the institutions of higher education in Lebanon and the Middle East region. It is also possible that its unwavering adherence to liberal education is a

key reason why the University has come to be so valued in the region it serves. The liberal education element in AUB's conception of itself and of its mission should, therefore, be preserved, strengthened and effectively communicated.[2]

Today, the mission statement proclaims, "Graduates will be individuals committed to creative and critical thinking, life-long learning, personal integrity and civic responsibility, and leadership."[3] The mission statement published just prior to this, written in the 2000–2001 academic year, declares, "The university emphasizes scholarship that enables students to think for themselves, stresses academic excellence, and promotes high principles of character. It aims to produce men and women who are not only technically competent in their professional fields but also lifelong learners who have breadth of vision, a sense of civic and moral responsibility, and devotion to the fundamental values of human life."[4]

In an interview in 2004, President John Waterbury (1997–2008) concurred, stating, "At AUB, we are unique and we have to make that clear. Other universities use [the] same books as the ones we use but we are different in that we help students to challenge ideas: *'it's not what you know, it's how you think.'* We try to emphasize mental flexibility and shape the value systems."[5] In his inaugural address on May 4, 2009, Peter Dorman explained that despite sometimes strong pressure to abandon it, the school continues to offer a liberal arts curriculum. "The simplest answer," he said, "is that life is abundant" and "we cannot embrace the fullness of life with learning that is applied narrowly or offered only for a brief span of college years. In essence, the liberal arts inform us that how we choose to earn a living is not the same thing as how we choose to live life."[6]

These affirmations of the school's educational pedagogy came amidst the rebuilding process AUB has been undergoing since the 1990s. During the Lebanese civil war (1975–1989), the school's administrators, faculty, staff, and students struggled to keep the school functioning, with few resources available for building anything new or expanding any of the programs.[7] When the war started, AUB was already on a precarious financial footing, and the situation did not improve over the following years. Even before the war destabilized life on campus, donors had been wary of giving funds to a school disrupted by student protests, and the US government threatened in 1975 to end its annual USAID (Agency for International Development) grant after three years.[8] The school remained open because the Lebanese government stepped in with loans, the US government continued to proffer aid despite its threat, and efforts at fund-raising kept revenues flowing in, however sporadic and unpredictable. The administration instituted cost-cutting measures by eliminating doctoral-level programs, canceling plans for curricular expansion, and reducing staff levels as enrollment numbers declined. For a brief period, AUB opened a campus in East Beirut to accommodate the professors, staff, and students who could not travel to the main campus in West Beirut. Those professors who stayed found themselves teaching their normal courses, filling in for those professors who had left, and cooperating with the remaining staff to make sure administration tasks were covered. The school also aided in outreach programs in the city. Professor Huda Zurayq reports, "We as a faculty got involved in the public health situation of Beirut city and we were working with NGOs [nongovernmental organizations] to try to document some of the infectious diseases that were happening, to participate in cleaning up the city. I mean, we were very much engaged with the forces that were in Beirut at the time[,] be they NGO [or] even some of the political parties because everybody came together in trying to keep Beirut alive and [we were] doing our bit as a School of Public Health."[9] When in 1987 the US government prohibited US nationals from traveling to and working in Lebanon, American AUB presidents served in New York, and a series of deputy presidents maintained the school's programs in Beirut. Only in 1997 did John Waterbury return as president in residence in Beirut.

While these internal problems plagued the campus throughout the war years, the disturbances coming from outside proved even more destabilizing. The AUB campus could not avoid the realities of the war, although a number of sources commented on the safe realm the campus usually provided.[10] Robert Fisk describes a somewhat surreal scene he encountered one day during the Israeli bombardment in summer 1982. "One became affected by this sense of timelessness, sealed into west Beirut like a bacillus from the new Lebanon outside. Down at the American University, founded by the stern Daniel Bliss in 1866, students could still research through Ottoman newspapers or play tennis on the hard courts. Beside the main hall, the trunks of Roman columns baked in the sun beneath red and pink creepers. Only now there was an anti-aircraft gun at the bottom of the lawns."[11]

AUB was located in the midst of the cross-fire of events taking place throughout West Beirut. Just as AUB was thoroughly of Beirut in times of peace, so too was it of Beirut during the war. Professors report that militias tried to threaten them to post higher grades or to give favors to their students.[12] John Munro relates that in 1975, "From time to time there was indiscriminate shelling of residential areas, which resulted in the death of one student and severe injuries to others when two rockets hit the Penrose Men's Dormitory. Fortunately, though stray bullets and small caliber shells fell on the campus, there were no other serious casualties nor serious property damage" in 1975 or early 1976.[13] The summer 1982 Israeli invasion of Lebanon epitomized the scene Fisk had described; the campus was safe compared to many other parts of the city but still came under threat as Israeli shells hit and as fighting intensified throughout West Beirut. Dean of the Faculty of Arts and Sciences Elie Salem (1975–1985) reports, "On 7 June 1982, as I took refuge alone in a supposedly safe corner in my faculty home on the campus of the American University of Beirut, a shell fired from an Israeli ship a few kilometres offshore hit our living room. The impact left a gaping hole in the wall and sent debris flying throughout the house."[14] Fisk tells of his visit to Professor John Ryan at AUB during the summer of 1982. "In the greenhouse, the generator pumped a mean trickle of water across the plants, turning the warmth into a clammy heat relieved only by the thin breeze that insinuated its way through a jagged hole in the roof. There were a few diamond shards of glass clustering the roots of one plant, evidence of the shell splinter that intruded from the real world outside."[15] On August 5, a car bomb exploded near the American University Hospital (AUH); almost immediately thereafter, an Israeli shell hit the roof of the hospital itself.[16] Despite coming under fire like this on a number of occasions, AUH served the whole community of Beirut throughout the course of the war.

When primarily Shi'ite groups started the practice of kidnapping Americans in 1982, AUB personnel became a particular target. Of the approximately one hundred foreign nationals kidnapped by Hezbollah or one of a number of Shi'ite and leftist groups, at least eight came directly from AUB. President David Dodge (1981–1982), son of Bayard Dodge (1923–1948), was the first, kidnapped on July 19, 1982. According to Fisk, a group of Shi'ites known as Islamic Jihad had surfaced as a new political player. "None of us knew then how important Dodge's kidnap really was. We had still not heard of Al-Jihad Al-Islami—Islamic Jihad, or Holy War—and we had no idea that the Iranian revolution had penetrated so deeply into the aspirations of the Shia population in west Beirut."[17]

David Dodge's kidnapping, as well as those that followed, was not instigated by students or by anyone affiliated with the university. Students had made the connection between the US government and the AUB administration as early as the late 1940s, when the US government offered grants to the school for the first time and it supported the establishment of Israel. In the late 1960s and early 1970s, the student battles against authoritarianism made that connection more explicit, with students accusing the AUB administration of being as reactionary as the US and Jordanian governments were. Students from all the universities in Beirut frequently protested in front of the US embassy.[18] For example, on April 18, 1970, AUB students joined with others from the city in throwing stones at the embassy in protest against US support for Israel.[19] As previously described, Leila Khaled called out the US government for its imperialist activities; Mohammad Matar had made the connection between US financial interests and AUB administrative actions; pro-Palestinian actions on campus were frequently accompanied by verbal attacks against the imperialist US government. The narrative of student identity equated the fight against oppressors in the Arab world with that of the Vietnamese against the US military. At other times, students accused the Arabs who increasingly came to dominate AUB's administrative posts of selling out to the US government.

Despite such actions and statements, the student protests of AUB's 1968 did not focus as much on the linkages between the AUB administration and the US government as much as the means by which students could make the school more relevant for themselves. To use just one student's perspective, Muhammad Dajani Daoudi said when he was Student Council president in 1972–1973, "I have met no student who wants to do harm to AUB. We are here because we respect the academic standard of this university and its achievements in this part of the world."[20] When he returned to campus in 2005 after thirty years, he described the environment he found so intoxicating as a student. In comparing the classroom and the campus civic space, Dajani Daoudi found a disjunction between the message disseminated by the administration and the dynamic role students established for themselves.

> My message then was: we would like to have a say. Why should we have encounters, why should we have wars? Let us have peace, but give us a space, and give us respect, dignity. That's very important to have dignity and if you don't teach us dignity here, how are we going to have dignity outside, and if you are not teaching us how to practice democracy here, how are we going to practice democracy outside?[21]

Even as the students accused the administration of colluding with the US government, they still wanted to be students at this American institution. No organized student movement called for the nationalization of the school at any time in its history; no student movement demanded that it stop being an American institution. Students like Dajani Daoudi criticized the school for not living up to its meta-narrative and of not adapting quickly enough to the ever-changing circumstances in the Middle East. They addressed the administration using the language of American liberal education, demanding that their voices be institutionally recognized and respected, as liberal education promised. Even as the civil war raged outside the Main Gate, students continued to protest inside whenever they thought their rights as students at this American institution were being violated.

These types of protests forced the school to evolve and adapt; they did not present a threat to AUB's existence. The larger challenge came from outside as combatants in the civil war targeted the school as a symbol of American intervention in Lebanon. The United States, through money and weaponry, had aided its allies since the beginning of the civil war in 1975, but only in late August 1982 did US troops become directly and consistently involved militarily. While entering Lebanon ostensibly as part of a multinational peacekeeping force along with French and other troops, US soldiers quickly attacked the leftist factions supported by Syria so they could help the Christian factions supported by Israel. In retaliation for these military moves, suicide bombers affiliated with Hezbollah destroyed the US and French barracks in October 1983, killing almost three hundred soldiers and convincing the United States government to pull out its troops by February 1984. These events were accompanied by a series of attacks against AUB personnel, beginning with the January 18, 1984, killing of AUB president Malcolm Kerr (1982–1984). Kerr had long been connected to AUB, having been born in the AUB hospital in 1931. His father, Stanley Kerr, had taught chemistry from 1925 to 1960, and his mother, Elsa Kerr, had served as dean of women from 1945 to 1960. As Kerr left the elevator and walked to his office in College Hall, he was shot; the perpetrator has not been definitively identified.[22] Following this attack, different organizations, primarily of Shi'ite origin, kidnapped a number of AUB employees, including electrical engineering professor Frank Regier in January 1984; librarian Peter Kilburn on December 3, 1984; AUH director David Jacobsen on May 28, 1985; dean of the Faculty of Agricultural and Food Sciences Thomas Sutherland on June 9, 1985; Professors J. Leigh Douglas and Philip Padfield in March 1986; and Joseph Cicippio on September 12, 1986. Peter Kilburn, J. Leigh

Douglas, and Philip Padfield were killed on April 17, 1986, in retaliation for the US raid on Libya two days earlier; all the others survived.

Finally, unknown attackers bombed College Hall on November 8, 1991, killing one AUB employee who was sleeping in the building and destroying much of the structure. Professor Kamal Salibi describes the event: "After the explosion, the AUB clock tower transformed into a missile and entered the main reading room of the library."[23] The bomb was so enormous that "the lifts . . . on the 3rd and 4th floors had been blown out of their places, thrown across that very, very large hallway . . . to the other side of the building," and windows all over AUB were broken.[24] After the bombing, Ussama Makdisi reports, "Its reconstruction was financed by hundreds of alumni, by various Lebanese, Arab, and American corporations, and by the tax dollars of the American people." Makdisi continues, "Today a significantly larger College Hall stands in the original building's place. The rebuilt structure was expressly designed to evoke the memory of its predecessor."[25]

With the war finally ended, AUB began its rebuilding process, starting in 1998 with work on the medical school and then extending throughout campus. In the process, new schools and centers have arisen, including the Suliman S. Olayan School of Business, the Center for American Studies and Research (CASAR), and the Issam Fares Institute for Public Policy and International Affairs. In 2007–2008, AUB began offering doctoral programs in Arabic language and literature, biology, engineering, and physics. Having ceased publication during the war, *Outlook* resumed in 1997, with the students taking charge of buying the equipment needed for the project to get started.[26] Publications like the *Main Gate* and *AUB Bulletin Today* now appear as regular alumni and campus magazines.

In the 1992–1993 academic year, student government returned in the form of the University Student Faculty Committee (USFC). Lebanese students have always accounted for at least half the student body in any given year of the school's existence, but their specific concerns never dominated the campus political stage. Arab issues typically pushed Lebanese ones to the student margins. After 1975, the realities of war meant that few non-Lebanese traveled to Beirut to attend school; everyday concerns generated by living in a war zone meant that Lebanese issues infiltrated the campus. Today, student politics are more entwined with particularly Lebanese problems than at any time in the school's history. Nevertheless, Lebanese politics fail to dominate the campus completely. Students affiliate themselves with Lebanon's political parties and alliances, but campus politics are also vibrant. Just as in the earlier periods of student political activism, campus concerns catalyze student action as fervently as those taking place outside the Main Gate. Makram Rabah, vice president of the USFC from 2004 to 2006, says of student government in the current era, "Student activism at AUB is defined by the democratic environment that AUB fosters. Our highly competitive, sometimes controversial student elections are always conducted in a civilized and democratic manner. Yes, there can be sweeping victories, but the culture is such that no group can ever deny the right of other groups and individuals to peacefully campaign and try to attract student support for their platforms."[27] In maintaining AUB's activist legacy, students have continued to protest whenever they see their rights obstructed; for example, in 2005 and 2010, students protested fee increases.

While the war created unprecedented problems for AUB, the rebuilding process reflects the adaptability the school has always displayed. As this study has shown, the school's pedagogy has changed over time; the liberal education system extolled in mission statements and speeches evolved only slowly. To establish this system and to maintain its relevancy for the students, the school's leaders had to continually revise the structure of the school's programs. An analysis of the written documents, discussed within their historical context, illuminates how the educational process progressed. The school's liturgical Protestant narrative showed cracks when it became clear that the Christian absolutes of Daniel Bliss (1866–1902) were not flexible enough to integrate the newest of scientific advances the American educational system required. After the Darwin Affair, Bliss tried to reset the strict boundaries around his unity of truth, but the American educational structure was changing too quickly to abide such an exclusionary system. Charles Darwin had to be allowed into the classroom precisely so that students could intelligently and scientifically debate the elements of all new theories, the sine qua non of the new educational pedagogy. Rather than his father's evangelicalism, Howard Bliss (1902–1920) taught liberal Protestantism as the success story in his time line of civilizational progress. His Protestantism needed to be introduced to the students of the Middle East because it gathered under its umbrella the character traits necessary for individual modernity: tolerance, honesty, hard work, and self-control. His Jesus Christ provided lessons to peoples of all faiths because he alone provided the guide for moving beyond petty sectarian strife. In so constructing his modern model, Howard Bliss addressed the changes taking place in the mission station, the YMCA, and the American university campus at the beginning of the twentieth century.

Bayard Dodge (1923–1948) made the final transition from Daniel Bliss's liturgical Protestantism to educational liberalism by declaring America, and specifically the American character, as the most successful entrant into the historical continuum. His idealistic America resolved urban problems, built soaring skyscrapers, manufactured innovative cars, reformed religion, and, even more importantly, trained human beings who actively sought to improve life for all. The missionary-classical dependence on absolute truths gave way to the liberal educational structure, which emphasized the multiplicity of paths to many truths.

The civilizational coherence of these curricular and character-building messages broke down rapidly under fire from Arab professors and the students sitting in their classrooms, starting in the 1930s and accelerating a decade later. When Arab society galvanized students to oppose imperialism of all kinds, students responded by questioning the voice of authority presented to them on campus. To make themselves fit for that world students demanded that the campus be opened to Arab politics; they wanted to act on their convictions while at school so they could go out as the vanguard that would solve the Arab world's problems when they graduated. The administration did not accede to all the students' demands, but over time, student influence did increase. The students did convince the school to acknowledge at least some aspects of the ideological and physical changes that were taking place outside the Main Gate. They worked with the Arab professors, and then, by the 1950s, professors from all countries, to facilitate a blurring of the walls between the campus and the Arab world. Curriculum changes, although never as rapid as the students wanted, did come to reflect the students' calls for more relevant courses, particularly concerning any and all topics related to Arab concerns. The students, both male and female, also played a key role in defining the role of women on the AUB campus.

Even as the "making men" program receded into the background of student life at AUB, students still sought to be transformed by their educational experience; over time, however, they wanted their education to better reflect the real issues they faced as Arabs, and not just what their American teachers taught. They wanted to be not just active participants in their own individual educational experience but also institutional voices of authority over the program being delivered at the school. This idea gained adherents in the activist period between 1947 and 1955 and then accelerated as part of AUB's 1968 moment. If an AUB institutional personality can be identified for the school throughout its history, it would be here, in this student quest for identity and empowerment. The school's programs and leaders challenged students to take on this project as a vital element of their educational experience; the student narrative shows that students accepted the call.

In July 2009, alumni and students reenacted the school's Speakers' Corner as part of the "AUB Student Politics: Past and Present" program. Fuad Bawarshi (BA '70, MBA '77), a former president of the AUB Student Council, spoke at the event, saying of his years as a student, "At that time we had no internet to chat on, or Facebook to write on its walls, so we had to resort to the podium to express ourselves freely and to fight apathy among the student body."[28] He recalled, "Here we gathered to start marching in demonstration against imperialism, Zionism, as well as the university administration . . . We were committed, we were angry, and we were involved with everything that was going on around us."[29] In a fitting summary of the activist role students have historically played on campus, Fuad Bawarshi ended his Speakers' Corner speech with a plea to the school's current students, saying, "It's not necessary to be as mischievous as we were, but please make sure your voices are heard."[30]

Notes

Chapter One

1. Daniel Bliss, *The Voice of Daniel Bliss* (Beirut: The American Press, 1956), 67.

2. Howard Bliss, "Baccalaureate Sermon," *al-Kulliyah*, vol. 2, no. 8 (June 1911), 270. American University of Beirut/Library Archives. Hereafter AUB.

3. Bayard Dodge, "Inaugural Address Delivered by President Bayard Dodge," *al-Kulliyah*, vol. 9, no. 8 (June 1923), 126. AUB.

4. Peter F. Dorman, "Inauguration of Peter Dorman," American University of Beirut, May 4, 2009, 5, http://staff.aub.edu.lb/~webinfo/public/inaug_dorman/dorman_speech.pdf, accessed September 26, 2009. Many of the presidents of SPC and AUB have been related by family or marriage. Howard Bliss was Daniel Bliss's son; Bayard Dodge married Howard Bliss's daughter, Mary. David S. Dodge (1981–1982) was the son of Bayard Dodge and thus the great-grandson of Daniel Bliss. Peter Dorman is the great-great-grandson of Daniel Bliss.

5. "Risalat al-ʿurwa," *al-ʿUrwa al-Wuthqa*, vol. 1, no. 1 (1936), 1. AUB. The name of the organization was in homage to a similarly titled journal published by Jamal al-Din al-Afghani and Muhammad Abduh in Paris in 1884. The title translates roughly as "The Indissoluble Bond" and reflects al-Afghani and Abduh's desire to bring the Muslim world together to stave off European incursions. Both men fronted the intellectual movement that came to be called Islamic Modernism.

6. Manshurat lajnat al-diʿayya wa-l-nashr, "Risalat al-ʿUrwa al-Wuthqa," *al-ʿUrwa al-Wuthqa*, vol. 16, no. 1 (December 1950), 5. AUB.

7. Ibid.

8. Ibid., 7.

9. The school initially opened in rented rooms in 1866. The current campus, in the Hamra, or Ras Beirut area of Beirut, began with the laying of the cornerstone of College Hall on December 7, 1871. Soon thereafter, the school's leaders built walls around the entire campus, with the Main Gate serving as the primary entrance. The Main Gate, an important landmark for the campus, gives its name to the current alumni magazine. The Medical Gate is along the wall toward the American University Hospital (AUH).

10. "AUB Mission Statement," American University of Beirut, http://www.aub.edu.lb/about/mission.html, accessed September 26, 2009.

11. Julie A. Reuben, *The Making of the Modern University: Intellectual Transformation and the Marginalization of Morality* (Chicago and London: University of Chicago Press, 1996), 2.

12. Bliss, *Voice*, 66.

13. Data on the number of students converting to Protestantism do not appear in the SPC written documentation. Daniel and Howard Bliss frequently wrote about the students who "saw the light" of the Protestant message, but such phrases were never clearly defined. As a result, it is impossible to determine if the school converted anyone to Protestantism. Protestants did attend the school, but the documents do not make clear how or when they became Protestants. As students, they comprised about a third of the student population in the nineteenth century, at a time when Christians of all denominations accounted for close to 90 percent of all the students. In 1899, for example, Protestants comprised 29 percent of all the students. Daniel Bliss to the Board of Managers of the Syrian Protestant College, 1899, in *Annual Reports to the Board of Managers, Syrian Protestant College, 1866–67–1901–1902*, 155. AUB. By the time the school became AUB in 1920, and the numbers of Christians and non-Christians started to equalize, Protestant attendance relative to the total student popu-

lation had decreased. By the 1957–1958 academic year, Protestants accounted for 12 percent of all students, and 21 percent of all Christian students. J. Paul Leonard, *Report of the President Covering the Years 1957–58 and 1958–59*, Appendix C. AUB.

14. *General Education in a Free Society: Report of the Harvard Committee* (Cambridge: Harvard University Press, 1945), 65. This report, commonly called the Harvard Redbook, reflected two years of intensive study of high school and college programs and proved to be the most influential document of the era, for it provided "a complete educational philosophy for American education." See Chapter 4 of Timothy P. Cross, *An Oasis of Order: The Core Curriculum*, http://www.college.columbia.edu/core/oasis/history4.php, accessed July 29, 2008.

15. *General Education in a Free Society*, 72.

16. Richard Hofstadter, *The Age of Reform: From Bryan to F.D.R.* (New York: Alfred A. Knopf, 1955), 36.

17. In the nineteenth century, Syria and Lebanon were collectively known as Syria. Only after World War I did the modern states of Syria and Lebanon emerge under colonial rule. They both achieved independence after World War II.

18. Egypt technically remained under the sovereignty of the Ottoman Empire until the outbreak of World War I, although it maintained a largely autonomous existence throughout the nineteenth century. Thus, the histories of Egypt and the Ottoman Empire are discussed separately in this text. The reforms of both governments influenced Beirut and the surrounding area because the Ottoman Empire held sovereignty over all these areas from the initial conquest in 1516 until the Ottoman defeat after World War I. Between 1831 and 1840, the Egyptian government of Muhammad Ali took over Greater Syria, including all or parts of present-day Lebanon, Syria, and Israel/Palestine.

19. For more information about the events of 1860 in Lebanon, see Ussama Makdisi, *The Culture of Sectarianism: Community, History, and Violence in Nineteenth-Century Ottoman Lebanon* (Berkeley and Los Angeles: University of California Press, 2000).

20. In two instances, in 1915 and 1965, the government in power lodged formal complaints against the school and its professors for using objectionable textbooks in their classrooms. In 1915, Azmi Bey, governor general of Beirut, and Jamal Pasha, governor of Syria and commander in chief of the Fourth Army in Syria, Palestine, and Arabia, protested against the use of *Elementary Geography*, by Ralph S. Tarr and Frank M. McMurry, in SPC's Preparatory School. The 1907 version of this text declares, "The Turkish government is the worst in Europe. The ruler, called the *Sultan*, is an absolute despot, who governs his people so badly that they are kept extremely ignorant and poor." And, unlike the rest of Europe, which was dominated by Catholics and Protestants, the empire was run by Muslims, or Mohammadans. "They are religious fanatics, and dislike Christians very much." Ralph S. Tarr and Frank M. McMurry, *Elementary Geography* (New York: Macmillan and Company, Ltd., 1907), 225. Howard Bliss, *Fiftieth Annual Report of the Syrian Protestant College, 1915–1916*, 15–16. AUB. Djemal Pasha insisted that Professor William Hall, the principal of the Preparatory School, leave the country as punishment. Hall left, but returned in 1919 after the school offered a formal apology to the government. John M. Munro, *A Mutual Concern: The Story of the American University of Beirut* (Delmar, NY: Caravan Books, 1977), 62. In 1965, the Lebanese government protested against the use of St. Thomas Aquinas's *Summa Theologica* in the required Civilization Sequence Program because it contained a paragraph disparaging the Prophet Muhammad. The text had been used for years on campus, but in 1965 became a political issue when the newspaper, *Shaab*, published an excerpt from the book. In the end, the government forced Professor John Spagnolo, the person responsible for including the text that year, to leave the country. Munro, 158–159.

21. The student newspaper, *Outlook*, published an article in 1951 reporting that a few Lebanese politicians in parliament had proposed nationalizing AUB. They "implied that the University was the instrument of the U.S. State Department" and wanted all foreign institutions

placed under the effective control of the Lebanese government. According to the article, Prime Minister Abdullah al-Yafi rejected such a reading of the situation. This particular debate did not lead to a parliamentary decision and no other record of such an effort exists. "Nationalization of AUB Threatened," *Outlook*, vol. 5, no. 1 (October 27, 1951), 1. AUB. In contrast, the Egyptian government and nationalists began pressuring foreign schools to come under different levels of government control as early as the interwar period of the twentieth century. See Heather J. Sharkey, *American Evangelicals in Egypt: Missionary Encounters in an Age of Empire* (Princeton: Princeton University Press, 2008), 116–133.

22. "Bureaucratic bourgeoisie" comes from Fatma Müge Göçek, *Rise of the Bourgeoisie, Demise of Empire: Ottoman Westernization and Social Change* (New York and Oxford: Oxford University Press, 1996), 44. For the Arab world, comparable terms are the *effendiyah* and *'isamiyyun*, translating roughly to "men of the modern educated middle class" and "self-made men," respectively. Michael Eppel, "Notes and Comments: Note about the Term *Effendiyya* in the History of the Middle East," *International Journal of Middle East Studies*, vol. 41 (2009), 537; and James L. Gelvin, "The Other Arab Nationalism: Syrian/Arab Populism in Its Historical and International Contexts," in *Rethinking Nationalism in the Arab Middle East*, edited by James Jankowski and Israel Gershoni (New York: Columbia University Press, 1997), 236.

23. Selçuk Akşin Somel, *The Modernization of Public Education in the Ottoman Empire, 1839–1908: Islamization, Autocracy and Discipline* (Leiden: Brill, 2001), 19.

24. Selim Deringil, *The Well-Protected Domains: Ideology and the Legitimation of Power in the Ottoman Empire, 1876–1909* (London: I. B. Tauris, 1998), 93.

25. Michael Provence, "Late Ottoman State Education," in *Religion, Ethnicity and Contested Nationhood in the Former Ottoman Space*, edited by Jørgen S. Nielsen (Leiden: Brill, forthcoming).

26. Somel, 52–53.

27. Provence.

28. Ibid.

29. Benjamin C. Fortna, *Imperial Classroom: Islam, the State, and Education in the Late Ottoman Empire* (Oxford: Oxford University Press, 2003), 124.

30. Philip S. Khoury, "The Paradoxical in Arab Nationalism: Interwar Syria Revisited," in *Rethinking Nationalism in the Arab Middle East*, edited by James Jankowski and Israel Gershoni (New York: Columbia University Press, 1997), 277.

31. Butrus al-Bustani is equally famous for his many Arab nationalist writings. During his lifetime, he published a dictionary of Arabic and an encyclopedia of Arab history; he wrote many newspaper pieces extolling Arab heritage and identity. Albert Hourani describes al-Bustani's writings as "contributing to the creation of modern Arabic expository prose, of a language true to its past in grammar and idiom, but made capable of expressing simply, precisely, and directly the concepts of modern thought." Albert Hourani, *Arabic Thought in the Liberal Age: 1798–1939* (Cambridge: Cambridge University Press, 1983), 100. The Maronites settled in Mt. Lebanon in the tenth and eleventh centuries because the region's isolated location gave them protection from Byzantine persecution over differences concerning the nature of Jesus Christ. During the Crusades to Jerusalem, the Maronites pledged allegiance to the Pope, although they never embraced all aspects of Roman Catholicism.

32. Provence.

33. Jens Hanssen, *Fin de Siècle Beirut: The Making of an Ottoman Provincial Capital* (Oxford: Oxford University Press, 2005), 181 and 182.

34. Nadya Sbaiti, "Lessons in History: Education and the Formation of National Society in Beirut, Lebanon, 1920–1960s," PhD diss., Georgetown University, 2008, 52.

35. Fortna, 12.

36. Ibid., 34.

37. Göçek, 44.

38. Roderic H. Davison, "Westernized Education in Ottoman Turkey," *Middle East Journal*, vol. 15, no. 3 (Summer 1961), 291.

39. See Sharkey, 149–178.

40. Albert Hourani, "Ottoman Reform and the Politics of Notables," in *The Modern Middle East: A Reader*, edited by Albert Hourani, Philip S. Khoury, and Mary C. Wilson (Berkeley and Los Angeles: University of California Press, 1993), 85.

41. For a discussion of the narrative produced in early twentieth-century Arab textbooks, see Betty S. Anderson, "Writing the Nation: Textbooks of the Hashemite Kingdom of Jordan," *Comparative Studies of South Asia, Africa and the Middle East*, vol. 21, nos. 1 and 2 (2001), 8.

42. Reinhard Schulze, "Mass Culture and Islamic Cultural Production in Nineteenth-Century Middle East," in *Mass Culture, Popular Culture, and Social Life in the Middle East*, edited by Georg Stauth and Sami Zubaida (Frankfurt: Campus Verlag, 1987), 191.

43. Stephen Sheehi, *Foundations of Modern Arab Identity* (Gainesville: University Press of Florida, 2004), 3.

44. Ibid.

45. Tom Pendergast, *Creating the Modern Man: American Magazines and Consumer Culture, 1900–1950* (Columbia: University of Missouri Press, 2000), 55.

46. Elizabeth Suzanne Kassab, *Contemporary Arab Thought: Cultural Critique in Comparative Perspective* (New York: Columbia University Press, 2010), 21.

47. Keith David Watenpaugh, *Being Modern in the Middle East: Revolution, Nationalism, Colonialism, and the Arab Middle Class* (Princeton and Oxford: Princeton University Press, 2006), 8.

48. Ibid.

49. Beth Baron, *The Women's Awakening in Egypt: Culture, Society, and the Press* (New Haven: Yale University Press, 1994), 155–156.

50. Hussein bin Ali claimed descent from the Prophet as a member of the Hashemite family and had served as the Sharif of Mecca, an Ottoman appointee, since 1908. He ruled over the Hijaz region of Mecca and Medina until defeated by the Saud family in 1924.

51. The League of Nations charged the mandatory powers with preparing the Arab regions under their control for eventual self-government.

52. On August 20, 1933, nationalists from Syria, Lebanon, Palestine, Iraq, and Transjordan convened a conference at Qarnil, Lebanon, to "set the national independence movements in the Arab territories on a firmer footing by systematically coordinating their activities." At the end of the conference, the attendees announced the formation of the League of National Action. "Its goals were Arab sovereignty, independence, and comprehensive Arab unity, and it particularly emphasized the need for economic development and integration in order to wage a successful struggle against the exploitation of foreign powers and against feudal landowners." Philip S. Khoury, *Syria and the French Mandate: The Politics of Arab Nationalism, 1920–1945* (Princeton: Princeton University Press, 1987), 400–401.

53. Gamal Abdul Nasser came to power as part of the Free Officers Revolution of July 1952. He held the presidency from 1954 until his death in September 1970. For more information about Nasser's Egypt, see John Waterbury, *The Egypt of Nasser and Sadat: The Political Economy of Two Regimes* (Princeton: Princeton University Press, 1983); and James P. Jankowski, *Nasser's Egypt, Arab Nationalism, and the United Arab Republic* (Boulder, CO: Lynne Rienner Publishers, 2002).

54. For more information about the Ba'th Party, see John F. Devlin, *The Ba'th Party: A History from Its Origins to 1966* (Stanford, CA: Hoover Institution Press, 1976).

55. Fayez A. Sayegh, *Arab Unity: Hope and Fulfillment* (New York: Devin-Adair Company, 1958), xiv–xv. This unity project was short-lived; a military coup in Syria in 1961 led to its dissolution.

56. See, for example, Robert Cohen and Reginald E. Zelnik, eds., *The Free Speech Movement: Reflections on Berkeley in the 1960s* (Berkeley and Los Angeles: University of California Press, 2002); Seymour Martin Lipset and Philip G. Altbach, eds., *Students in Revolt* (Boston: Houghton Mifflin Company, 1969); Gerard J. DeGroot, ed., *Student Protest: The Sixties and After* (London and New York: Longman, 1998); and Philip G. Altbach, ed., *Student Political Activism: An International Reference Handbook* (New York and Westport, CT: Greenwood Press, 1989). The expression *"educational* process" comes from James Axtell, *The Making of Princeton University: From Woodrow Wilson to the Present* (Princeton: Princeton University Press, 2006), xviii.

57. Philip G. Altbach, "Perspectives on Student Political Activism," in *Student Political Activism: An International Reference Handbook,* edited by Philip G. Altbach (New York and Westport, CT: Greenwood Press, 1989), 12.

58. Ibid.

59. Munif al-Razzaz, "Munif al-Razzaz Yatadhakkar: Sanawat al-Jami'ah," *Akhar Khabar* (January 3–4, 1994). Munif al-Razzaz was a longtime leader of the Ba'th Party.

60. Named after Robert H. West (served 1884–1906), professor of mathematics, principal of the preparatory school, and dean of the Collegiate Department, West Hall opened as the student center in 1914. The Milk Bar was the primary cafeteria and meeting place on campus; it no longer exists. Faisal's Restaurant stood across the street from the Main Gate for decades, catering to the AUB community and providing a space for much of the student political organizing in the 1950s, 1960s, and 1970s. It is now a McDonald's.

61. Ussama Makdisi, *Artillery of Heaven: American Missionaries and the Failed Conversion of the Middle East* (Ithaca and London: Cornell University Press, 2008), 215.

62. Ibid.

63. Howard S. Bliss, "Statement Made by President Howard S. Bliss of the Syrian Protestant College, Beirut Syria, before the Paris Peace Conference (The 'Big Ten') on Thursday Afternoon, February 13th, 1919, at the Quai D'Orsay, Paris," February 13, 1919. Bliss Family Papers, Box 2: Speeches. Amherst College Archives and Special Collections. Hereafter Amherst.

64. The exact numbers are hard to calculate prior to 1947 because until that point the administration counted Syrians and Lebanese together. Occasionally, administrative records include addenda to differentiate between the two; when that occurs, the numbers indicate the dominance of Lebanese over Syrian students. See, for example, *Thirty-Ninth Annual Report of the Syrian Protestant College 1904–1905* in *S.P.C. Annual Report: 1898–99–1913–1914,* 31; *Fifty-Fifth Annual Report to the Board of Trustees of the American University of Beirut, 1920–1921,* 13; and *President's Annual Report 1956–1957,* 30–31. AUB.

65. *Thirty-Ninth Annual Report of the Syrian Protestant College 1904–1905,* 34. AUB.

66. Egyptian University opened as a private institution in 1908 and then as a state institution in 1925. After the July Revolution of 1952, it became Cairo University. See Donald Malcolm Reid, *Cairo University and the Making of Modern Egypt* (Cambridge: Cambridge University Press, 1990), 1.

67. The school did not designate how many of the Jordanian students were Jordanian or Palestinian, but given the demographic imbalance favoring Palestinians in Jordan after 1948, the majority of the so-called Jordanian students had to have been Palestinian.

68. Makram Rabah, *A Campus at War: Student Politics at the American University of Beirut, 1967–1975* (Beirut: Dar Nelson, 2009), 38.

69. Scholars have typically designated April 13, 1975, as the specific moment when the civil war started. Fawwaz Traboulsi writes that on that day, "a car fired shots at a congregation of Phalange partisans in front of a church in ʿAyn al-Rummaneh, wounding a number of people, to which Phalangist militiamen reacted a few hours later by machine-gunning a bus heading for the Tall al-Zaʾtar refugee camp, killing 21 Palestinians." Fawwaz Traboulsi, *A*

History of Modern Lebanon (London: Pluto Press, 2007), 183. Pierre Gemayel, a Maronite Christian, founded the Phalanges Libanaises in 1935; it is often known as the Kataeb, its Arabic equivalent. Tabitha Petran, *The Struggle over Lebanon* (New York: Monthly Review Press, 1987), 42. "The Ta'if Agreement, signed on 22 October 1989 in Saudi Arabia by the Lebanese parliamentarians, inaugurated a process that put an end to the Lebanese civil war and set the country on the path to peace and reconstruction." Traboulsi, 240.

70. Author interview with Elie Salam, Balamand University, Lebanon, July 25, 2005. AUB.

71. SPC and AUB have a long history of administrative-faculty conflicts, starting with the 1882 Darwin Affair and continuing through the 1960s and 1970s, when Sadiq al-ʿAzm (1968) and Halim Barakat (1972) lost their positions on campus. This book addresses some of these conflicts, but does so from the perspectives of the administration and the students.

72. *al-Kulliyah* appeared as an alumni magazine from 1910 to 1915, 1920 to 1935, and 1947 to 1974. During its existence, the editors used many transliterations of the Arabic word *al-Kulliyah*. The spelling appearing throughout this text was the most common.

73. All issues of the *Students' Union Gazette* can be found at http://ddc.aub.edu.lb/projects/jafet/gazette/index.html. AUB.

74. Taufic Daud, "The Students' Union of the A.U.B.," *al-Kulliyah*, vol. 8, no. 2 (December 1921), 22. AUB.

75. Daniel Bliss to the Board of Managers of the Syrian Protestant College, 1899, in *Annual Reports to the Board of Managers, Syrian Protestant College, 1866–67–1901–1902*, 155. AUB. In that year, the total number of students in all sections of the school equaled 381, with "337 nominal Christians, and 44 non-Christians." Bayard Dodge, *Report of the President of the American University of Beirut for the Sixty-Ninth Year, 1934–1935*, 20. AUB. In 1934–1935, the total number of students in all sections of the school equaled 1,406, with 762 Christians. Greek Orthodox Christians made up the largest group of Christians on campus during this time period.

76. "14 Ancestors of Outlook Resurrected," *Outlook*, vol. 19, no, 6 (March 14, 1964), 1. AUB. Daud reports that students typically produced only a library copy of each issue of the *Students' Union Gazette* (23).

77. Rawda Najjar, "Li-hunna wa-l-ʿurwa mad tariq," *al-ʿUrwa al-Wuthqa*, vol. 13, no. 3 (April 1948), 16. AUB. Najjar claims that *al-ʿUrwa al-Wuthqa* was published between 1934 and 1935 under the presidency of Kazim al-Khalidi, and that she was the paper's first female editor, but no copies from those years currently exist in the AUB archives. "ʿUrwat ul-Wuthka Comes Back to Life," *al-Kulliyah*, vol. 20, no. 5 (May 15, 1934), 146, confirms that the organization resumed activities in 1934, after a one-year hiatus. AUB.

78. The motto is from John 10:10.

79. Dorman, 5.

Chapter Two

1. "Prospects and Programme of the Syrian Protestant Collegiate Institute," Daniel Bliss, *A Few Reminiscences [connected with the beginnings of the Syrian Protestant College (now called the American University of Beirut), 1861–1863]*. Series ABC76. Personal Papers. No date. Houghton Library/Harvard University. Hereafter Houghton. *Kitab al-madrassa al-kulliyah al-suriyah al-injiliyah* 1871 [Catalogue of the Syrian Protestant College 1871], 1. AUB.

2. See Stephen B. L. Penrose, Jr., *That They May Have Life: The Story of the American University of Beirut, 1866–1941* (Beirut: American University of Beirut, 1970), Appendix B, 309.

3. Ibid., 9.

4. "The New Name," *al-Kulliyah*, vol. 7, no. 4 (February 1921), 51. AUB.

5. Daniel Bliss to W. S. Tyler, February 25, 1862. Bliss Family Papers, Box 6, Folder 6, Series 1: Daniel Bliss additions 2. Amherst.

6. *Catalogue of the Officers and Students of Amherst College for the Academical Year 1851–52*, 16. Amherst.

7. "Reports on the Course of Instruction in Yale College; by a Committee of the Corporation, and the Academical Faculty, 1828," http://collegiateway.org/reading/yale-report-1828/, 7, accessed January 20, 2010. Hereafter Yale Report. Julie A. Reuben, *The Making of the Modern University: Intellectual Transformation and the Marginalization of Morality* (Chicago and London: University of Chicago Press, 1996), 26, describes the report as "the most influential educational statement of the antebellum period."

8. Yale Report, 35.

9. Laurence R. Veysey, *The Emergence of the American University* (Chicago and London: University of Chicago Press, 1965), 37.

10. George H. Callcott, *History in the United States, 1800–1860: Its Practice and Purpose* (Baltimore: Johns Hopkins Press, 1970), 62.

11. Roger Geiger, "Introduction: New Themes in the History of Nineteenth-Century Colleges," in *The American College in the Nineteenth Century*, edited by Roger Geiger (Nashville: Vanderbilt University Press, 2000), 4–5.

12. Carl J. Richard, *The Golden Age of the Classics in America: Greece, Rome, and the Antebellum United States* (Cambridge: Harvard University Press, 2009), xi.

13. Ibid., 15.

14. Veysey, 2.

15. Jon H. Roberts and James Turner, *The Sacred and the Secular University* (Princeton: Princeton University Press, 2000), 70 and 71.

16. Jon H. Roberts, *Darwinism and the Divine in America: Protestant Intellectuals and Organic Evolution, 1859–1900* (Madison: University of Wisconsin Press, 1988), 87.

17. Roberts and Turner, 35.

18. Thomas Le Duc, *Piety and Intellect at Amherst College: 1865–1912* (New York: Arno Press and The New York Times, 1969), 80.

19. Reuben, *Making of the Modern University*, 20.

20. Julius Seelye's grandson, Laurens Hickok Seelye, taught at SPC and AUB between 1918 and 1935 before becoming president of St. Lawrence University. Most of the dates of service provided in this book come from "Directory of Faculty, Staff, and Officers, 1880–," American University of Beirut, http://www.aub.edu.lb/cgi-bin/asc-directory.pl?.

21. Le Duc, 84, n. 13. Le Duc reports that Seelye wrote it for Johnson's *Natural History*, but printed it separately.

22. Claude Moore Fuess, *Amherst: The Story of a New England College* (Boston: Little, Brown, and Company, 1935), 237.

23. From *The Student*, vol. 28 (November 3, 1894), 51, as quoted in Le Duc, 86. The article further explains, "Professor Tyler intends, however, to lay particular emphasis upon the development of man, and instead of making the course an end in itself he proposes to make the study an introduction to the study of History, Ethics and Political Economy" (86).

24. Ibid., 79.

25. Ibid., 111.

26. Julius Seelye, "Progressive Apprehension of Divine Truth," *American Presbyterian and Theological Review*, vol. 5, no. 20 (October 1867), 592.

27. Ibid., 593.

28. Ibid.

29. Le Duc, 112.

30. Ibid., 89–90.

31. Ibid., 89.

32. Charles William Eliot, "Charles William Eliot, Inaugural Address as President of Harvard, 1869," in *American Higher Education: A Documentary History*, vol. 2, edited by Richard Hofstadter and Wilson Smith (Chicago: University of Chicago Press, 1961), 606.

33. Ibid.

34. Cited in David A. Hollinger, "Inquiry and Uplift: Late Nineteenth-Century American Academics and the Moral Efficacy of Scientific Practice," in *The Authority of Experts: Studies in History and Theory*, edited by Thomas L. Haskell (Bloomington: Indiana University Press, 1984), 142.

35. Ibid., 150.

36. Charles William Eliot, *Academic Freedom: An Address Delivered before the New York Theta Chapter of the Phi Beta Kappa Society at Cornell University, May 29, 1907* (Ithaca, NY: Press of Ithaca and Church, 1907), 17.

37. Ibid., 18.

38. While many universities initially followed Harvard's lead in establishing a large array of elective courses, by the early twentieth century, a backlash had set in and many schools, including Harvard, reversed this policy and moved to a system that mixed together fixed and elective courses.

39. Charles William Eliot, "Charles William Eliot Expounds the Elective System as 'Liberty in Education,' 1885," in *American Higher Education: A Documentary History*, vol. 2, edited by Richard Hofstadter and Wilson Smith (Chicago: University of Chicago Press, 1961), 713.

40. Lacey Baldwin Smith, "A Study of Textbooks on European History during the Last Fifty Years," *Journal of Modern History*, vol. 23, no. 3 (September 1951), 251.

41. James Harvey Robinson, *An Introduction to the History of Western Europe*, vol. 2 (Boston: Ginn and Company, 1904), 18, 125, 185, 198, and 216.

42. Cited in chapter 1 of Timothy P. Cross, *An Oasis of Order: The Core Curriculum*, http://www.college.columbia.edu/core/oasis/history1.php, accessed March 29, 2008.

43. Chapter 1 of Cross, accessed July 29, 2008.

44. "The President's Commission on Higher Education for Democracy, 1947," in *American Higher Education: A Documentary History*, vol. 2, edited by Richard Hofstadter and Wilson Smith (Chicago: University of Chicago Press, 1961), 989.

45. For more information about the historical context of the American missionary project in Lebanon, see Ussama Makdisi, *Artillery of Heaven: American Missionaries and the Failed Conversion of the Middle East* (Ithaca and London: Cornell University Press, 2008); William R. Hutchison, *Errand to the World: American Protestant Thought and Foreign Missions* (Chicago: University of Chicago Press, 1987); and Eleanor H. Tejirian and Reeva Spector Simon, eds., *Altruism and Imperialism: Western Cultural and Religious Missions in the Middle East*, Occasional Papers no. 4 (New York: Middle East Institute, Columbia University, 2002).

46. Rufus Anderson, *Report to the Prudential Committee of a Visit to the Missions in the Levant* (Boston: American Board of Commissioners for Foreign Missions, Printed for T. R. Marvin, 1844), 32.

47. Rao Humpherys Lindsay, *Nineteenth Century American Schools in the Levant: A Study of Purposes*, University of Michigan Comparative Education Dissertation Series, no. 5 (Ann Arbor: University of Michigan School of Education, 1965), 148.

48. Rufus Anderson, *Foreign Missions: Their Relations and Claims* (New York: Charles Scribner and Company, 1869), 99.

49. The commonly accepted number is sixteen, although eighteen students actually enrolled over the course of the first year (two students did not complete the year). Daniel Bliss provides different numbers in his own writings. In Bliss, *Reminiscences*, 187, Bliss writes, "The College was opened on December 3, 1866, with a service of prayer"; "There were present sixteen students." In Daniel Bliss to the Board of Managers of the Syrian Protestant College, June 24, 1868. In *Annual Reports to the Board of Managers, Syrian Protestant College, 1866–67–1901–1902*, 2, he writes, "The class which entered the college at its commencement

in October 1866, it will be remembered, numbered eighteen. These all continued, with two exceptions, in connection with the class till the end of the College years." AUB.

50. *Kitab al-madrassa al-kulliyah al-suriyah al-injiliyah*, 1871, 2–4. AUB.

51. Mark Hopkins, president of Williams College (1836–1872), first published the book in 1869. It then went through numerous printings because of its popularity. Daniel Bliss used this text at SPC from at least the 1887–1888 academic year, and until he turned over the reins of the class in 1910. Mark Hopkins, *The Law of Love and Love as a Law: Moral Science, Theoretical and Practical*, 2nd ed. (New York: Charles Scribner and Company, 1869).

52. Bliss, *Reminiscences*, 74. Bliss titled his speech "Agitation" and discussed within it the context of the Fugitive Slave Law. Initially, the school refused to allow him to give this particular speech, since many alumni from the South planned to attend the ceremony, but Professor W. S. Tyler overrode the objection. The day of graduation, the local papers "praised and blamed about equally" (75).

53. Ibid., 76.

54. Ibid., 76–77.

55. Ibid., 77.

56. Ibid., 78.

57. Ibid., 204.

58. Daniel Bliss, *The Voice of Daniel Bliss* (Beirut: American Press, 1956), 67.

59. Bliss, *Reminiscences*, 205.

60. Ibid., 207.

61. Bliss, *Voice*, 57.

62. Ibid., 40.

63. Bliss, *Reminiscences*, 198. In that speech, Bliss also said, "It will be impossible for any one to continue with us long without knowing what we believe to be the truth and our reasons for that belief" (198).

64. Bliss, *Voice*, 44.

65. Ibid., 44–45.

66. Ibid., 43.

67. See A. L. Tibawi, *American Interests in Syria, 1800–1901: A Study of Educational, Literary and Religious Work* (Oxford: Clarendon Press, 1966), 147–149, and A. L. Tibawi, "The Genesis and Early History of the Syrian Protestant College," in *American University of Beirut Festival Book (Festschrift)*, edited by Fuad Sarruf and Suha Tamim (Beirut: American University of Beirut, 1967), 293–294, for a discussion of the types of texts translated into Arabic. Tibawi's analysis indicates that the school had little trouble translating medical and scientific texts into Arabic, as the native tutors on campus worked well with the American professors to produce them. The American Press, set up by missionaries to publish the Bible and school textbooks, however, made little effort to publish Arabic works of literature or English translations of Arabic literary or history texts—the texts that would have been useful for the classes first transitioned over into English.

68. Daniel Bliss to the Board of Managers of the Syrian Protestant College, July 18, 1878, in *Annual Reports to the Board of Managers, Syrian Protestant College, 1866–67–1901–1902*, 44–45. AUB.

69. Ibid., 44.

70. Ibid.

71. Ibid., 45.

72. Ibid.

73. Bayard Dodge, "An Eastern Challenge: Will Western Schools Adapt Modern Education to the Needs of the Levant?" *Asia* (December 1928), 10–11. Bayard Dodge Collection: AUB President 1923–1948, Box 3: Addresses and Articles by Him, File 3: Articles by Him, 1910s-1920s. AUB.

74. Ibid., 11.

75. Tibawi, "Genesis and Early History of the Syrian Protestant College," 281.

76. Ibid.

77. Bliss to the Board of Managers of the Syrian Protestant College, July 18, 1878, 45. AUB.

78. Tibawi, "Genesis and Early History of the Syrian Protestant College," 281.

79. For more information on the Darwin Affair, see Shafik Jeha, *Darwin and the Crisis of 1882 in the Medical Department and the First Student Protest in the Arab World in the Syrian Protestant College (Now the American University of Beirut)*, translated by Sally Kaya, edited by Helen Khal (Beirut: American University of Beirut Press, 2004); Nadia Farag, "al-Muqtataf, 1876–1900: A Study of the Influence of Victorian Thought on Modern Arab Thought" (PhD diss., St. Antony's College, Oxford University, 1969); and Donald M. Leavitt, "Darwinism in the Arab World: The Lewis Affair at the Syrian Protestant College," *The Muslim World*, vol. 71, no. 2 (April 1981), 85–98.

80. An English translation of Edwin Lewis, "Knowledge, Science and Wisdom," is included in *Annual Reports to the Board of Managers, Syrian Protestant College, 1866–67–1901–1902*, 251. AUB.

81. Roberts, 51.

82. Lewis, 251.

83. Ibid.

84. Ibid., 255.

85. Ibid.

86. Farag, "al-Muqtataf, 1876–1900," 250, and Jeha, 35–36.

87. Farag, "al-Muqtataf, 1876–1900," 250–251, and Jeha, 36. Three letters in the correspondence between William Van Dyck and Charles Darwin are identified at the Darwin Correspondence Project, http://www.darwinproject.ac.uk/darwinletters/calendar/entry-13710.html, accessed November 8, 2009. While the actual letter is not available on the site, confirmation that it was eventually published does appear. The citation reads, "On the modification of a race of Syrian street dogs,' *Proc. Zool. Soc. Lond.* 25 (1882): 367–70, published with a prefatory notice by CD; *Collected Papers* 2: 278–80."

88. Daniel Bliss Diary 1882. Daniel Bliss Collection: AUB President 1866–1902, Box 12: Diaries and Autographs. AUB.

89. Daniel Bliss to Howard S. Bliss and William T. Bliss, February 28, 1883. Bliss Family Papers, Box 1, Folder 8: Outgoing Correspondence. Amherst.

90. Daniel Bliss Diary 1882.

91. Nadia Farag, "The Lewis Affair and the Fortunes of al-Muqtataf," *Middle Eastern Studies*, vol. 8, no. 1 (January 1972), 79, and Jeha, 46.

92. Jeha, 46.

93. Farag, "The Lewis Affair and the Fortunes of al-Muqtataf," 79, and Tibawi, "Genesis and Early History of the Syrian Protestant College," 283–284.

94. See Jeha, 53–54. Except for the two initial supporters, the literary students not only stayed away from the protest but in at least one instance actively opposed what the medical students were doing. Daniel Bliss reports that after the protest had ended and the majority of students had apologized and returned to campus, the literary students expressed their disagreement with the medical students. In the most violent encounter, on May 24, 1883, "several Literary students, armed with clubs, made a sudden attack upon five or six medical students, beat and wounded them severely. The assault was so wanton and brutal that the police, being informed, took the culprits to prison." The faculty chose to expel three literary seniors because of this act and suspended two sophomores. "This prompt and decisive action seems to have rooted out the last seeds of the rebellion in the College." Daniel Bliss, "Statement 1883 by the President to the Board of Managers," July 10, 1883, in *Annual Reports to the Board of Managers, Syrian Protestant College, 1866–67–1901–1902*, 75. AUB.

95. See Jeha, 53–54.

96. Jeha, 54. After many years of negotiation, the Imperial Medical College finally agreed in 1903 to travel to Beirut to test the medical students.

97. Letter reprinted in Bliss to the Board of Managers of the Syrian Protestant College, July 10, 1883, 70.

98. Ibid., 71.

99. Letter reprinted in Jeha, 67.

100. Ibid.

101. Ibid.

102. Ibid., 68.

103. Jeha, 74–75, details how difficult it is to determine exactly how many medical students enrolled in the 1882–1883 academic year. He estimates that fifty began the year.

104. Ibid., 76–77.

105. As quoted in Thomas Philipp, *Gurgi Zaidan: His Life and Thought* (Beirut: Beiruter Texte und Studien, in Kommission bei Franz Steiner Verlag, 1979), 182.

106. See Jeha, 62–63, for a translation of the letter the students sent to the board of managers criticizing Post's attitude toward the students.

107. As quoted in Philip, 179–180.

108. Daniel Bliss to the Board of Managers of the Syrian Protestant College, 1883, in *Annual Reports to the Board of Managers, Syrian Protestant College, 1866–67–1901–1902*, 80. AUB.

109. John M. Munro, *A Mutual Concern: The Story of the American University of Beirut* (Delmar, NY: Caravan Books, 1977), 37. Penrose, Appendix J, 314–328, lists the tenures of foreign faculty starting in 1864.

110. Daniel Bliss to Mission House, ABCFM, Boston, March 18, 1862. Daniel Bliss, "A Few Reminiscences [connected with the beginnings of the Syrian Protestant College (now called the American University of Beirut), 1861–1863]." Series ABC76. Personal Papers. Houghton Library, Harvard University. Hereafter, Houghton.

111. John Wortabet initially resigned but agreed to stay on to teach pathology, at least temporarily. Wortabet resigned permanently in 1886. Faculty Minutes, Syrian Protestant College, January 8, 1883. Minutes of the Faculties, 1867–1940. AUB.

112. See Faculty Minutes, Syrian Protestant College, December 11, 1883, for a description of the offer presented to Sarruf and Nimr. Minutes of the Faculties, 1867–1940. AUB.

113. Farag, "The Lewis Affair and the Fortunes of al-Muqtataf," 80.

114. Abstract of Actions of the Board of Managers, July 1884, Faculty Minutes, Syrian Protestant College, July 28, 1884. Minutes of the Faculties, 1867–1940. AUB.

115. See Jeha, 126–136, and Tibawi, "Genesis and Early History of the Syrian Protestant College," 288, for a more extensive discussion of the reasons for the dismissals. See Marwa Elshakry, "The Gospel of Science and American Evangelism in Late Ottoman Beirut," *Past and Present*, no. 196 (August 2007), 213–214, for a discussion of how the American missionaries lost their influence over science education in Syria in the aftermath of the Darwin Affair. Arabs had generally seen the missionaries as purveyors of the most modern of scientific experimentation; after the Darwin Affair, many turned to alternative venues, such as *al-Muqtataf.*

116. See Norbert J. Scholz, "Foreign Education and Indigenous Reaction in Late Ottoman Lebanon: Students and Teachers at the Syrian Protestant College in Beirut," PhD diss., Georgetown University, 1997, 210–228, for more information on textbooks used at SPC.

117. The catalogues for the early years do not list the specific textbook used for the Arabic history class.

118. *Catalogue of the Syrian Protestant College, Beirut, Syria, 36th Year, 1901–1902*, 31. AUB.

119. Ibid.

120. Ibid.

121. *Catalogue of the Syrian Protestant College, Beirut, Syria, 39th Year, 1904–1905*, 33. AUB.
122. Ibid.
123. Tibawi, *American Interests in Syria*, 246–247.
124. Ibid., 247. Tibawi explains, "It has been little appreciated by other writers that this activity did not begin from scratch. For even competent Arabic masters like Van Dyck and Post benefited from existing books in Arabic or previous translations into that language bearing on their subjects. Moreover, they were assisted in the difficult process of preparing their works for the press by native scholars and Arabic teachers. Less proficient authors were actually mere compilers of teaching notes in English, which they put into Arabic with much assistance from native teachers and students at the college. Such was the manner of producing two books on chemistry by Lewis and one book on ancient history by Porter. Considering his own estimate of his attainments in Arabic, Bliss's book on mental philosophy was prepared for the press in a similar manner" (247).
125. Penrose, 122. Ussama Makdisi, *Faith Misplaced: The Broken Promise of U.S.-Arab Relations: 1820–2001* (New York: PublicAffairs, 2010), 90.
126. Edward F. Nickoley to Howard Bliss, June 20, 1919. Edward F. Nickoley Collection: Acting President 1920–1923, Box 1, File 3: Correspondence of Edward Nickoley with Howard Bliss and David Stuart Dodge. AUB.
127. Edward F. Nickoley to Howard Bliss, October 15, 1919. Edward F. Nickoley Collection: Acting President 1920–1923, Box 1, File 5: Correspondence of Edward Nickoley with Howard Bliss and David Stuart Dodge. AUB.
128. Edward F. Nickoley to Howard Bliss, February 18, 1920. Edward F. Nickoley Collection: Acting President 1920–1923, Box 1, File 6: Correspondence of Edward Nickoley with Howard Bliss and David Stuart Dodge. AUB.
129. Ibid.
130. Edward F. Nickoley to Howard Bliss, March 31, 1920. Edward F. Nickoley Collection: Acting President 1920–1923, Box 1, File 6: Correspondence of Edward Nickoley with Howard Bliss and David Stuart Dodge. AUB. Nickoley began the letter on March 31, 1920, and then continued it on April 1, 1920, when the vote took place.
131. Edward F. Nickoley to D. S. Dodge, August 1, 1920. Edward F. Nickoley Collection: Acting President 1920–1923, Box 2, File 2: Correspondence of Edward Nickoley with Howard Bliss and David S. Dodge. AUB.
132. Edward F. Nickoley, *Fifty-Fifth Annual Report to the Board of Trustees of the American University of Beirut, 1920–1921*, 7. AUB.
133. Samuel B. Kirkwood, *The President's Annual Report to the Board of Trustees, 1965/1966*, 2. AUB. AUB's annual reports indicate that Arab "personnel" outnumbered American or Western "personnel" by the 1930s, although no distinction is made about the particular positions these personnel held. Only in the 1965–1966 year are the professorial positions clearly indicated.
134. Daniel Bliss, *Thirty-Sixth Annual Report of the Syrian Protestant College to the Board of Managers, 1901–1902*, in *Annual Reports to the Board of Managers, Syrian Protestant College, 1866–67–1901–1902*, 227. AUB.
135. Ibid.
136. Ibid.
137. Ibid., 228.
138. Ibid.
139. The course catalogues do not always list the textbooks used in each class, so it is impossible to determine the exact year the book was last used.
140. Andrew C. Lawson, "Joseph Le Conte," *Science*, vol. 14, no. 347 (August 23, 1901), 276.
141. *Catalogue of the Syrian Protestant College, Beirut, Syria, 1891–92*, 27. AUB.
142. *Catalogue of the Syrian Protestant College, Beirut, Syria, 32nd Year, 1897–1898*, 2. AUB.

143. *Catalogue of the Officers and Students of Amherst College for the Academical Year 1881–82*, 26–31. Amherst.

144. Le Duc, 59.

145. The School of Dentistry closed in 1940.

146. Howard S. Bliss, *Forty-Sixth Annual Report of the Syrian Protestant College to the Board of Trustees, 1911–1912*, in *S.P.C. Annual Report 1898–99–1913–14*, 16. AUB.

147. Robert H. West, "Report of the Collegiate Department: 1905–'06," *Fortieth Annual Report of the Syrian Protestant College, 1905–'06*, in *S.P.C. Annual Report 1898–99–1913–14*, 24. AUB.

148. *Catalogue of the Syrian Protestant College, Beirut, Syria, 43rd Year, 1908–1909*, 17. AUB.

149. Howard Bliss, "The Modern Missionary," *Atlantic Monthly* (May 1920), 667.

150. Edward F. Nickoley, *Fifty-Fifth Annual Report to the Board of Trustees of the American University of Beirut: 1920–1921*, 5. AUB.

151. Ibid.

152. Ibid.

153. Faculty Minutes, October 26, 1920. Minutes of the General Faculty, 1920–1921. AUB.

154. *American University of Beirut, Beirut, Syria, Catalogue 1923–1924, Fifty-Eighth Year*, 40–41. AUB.

155. Bayard Dodge, *Report of the President of the American University of Beirut, Beirut, Syria, for the Fifty-Eighth Year 1923–1924*, 16. AUB.

156. George B. Stewart, Jr., "American University of Beirut School of Arts and Sciences Annual Report of the Dean 1927–1928," *Report of the Acting President of the American University of Beirut, Beirut, Syria, for the Sixty-Second Year, 1927–1928*, 2. AUB.

157. "The New 'Introduction to Social Science Course,'" *al-Kulliyah*, vol. 14, no. 1 (November 1927), 7. AUB.

158. Stephen B. L. Penrose, Jr., *President's Annual Report to the Board of Trustees, 1949/50*, 1. "New Sophs to Get Adult Approach," *Outlook*, vol. 4, no. 6 (April 21, 1951), 1. AUB.

Chapter Three

1. Daniel Bliss, *Reminiscences of Daniel Bliss, Edited and Supplemented by His Eldest Son* (New York: Fleming H. Revell Company, 1920), 222.

2. Ibid., 223.

3. Ibid.

4. Bayard Dodge, "The Syrian Protestant College," *The Presbyterian Banner* (June 10, 1920), 10–11. Bayard Dodge Collection: AUB President 1923–1948, Box 3: Addresses and Articles by Him, File 3: Articles by Him, 1910s–1920s. AUB.

5. William Hutchison, *Errand to the World: American Protestant Thought and Foreign Missions* (Chicago: University of Chicago Press, 1987), 5.

6. "An A.U.B. Man," *Handbook, 1939–1940*, 15–16, Students 1930s, Box 1, File 4: AUB Student Handbook, 1939–1940. AUB.

7. As reported in AUB's *News Highlights*, AUB sociology professor Samir Khalaf sees AUB's influence extending out into the neighboring area of Ras Beirut. He uses the phrase "to Protestantize" to describe the process whereby the residents acquired attributes of Protestantism without converting to the faith. "AUB: A Historical Accident," *News Highlights*, American University of Beirut. http://www.aub.edu.lb/news/archive/preview.php?id=114461, accessed January 9. 2011.

8. A number of these papers contain articles in more than one language; of the forty-five magazines reviewed, Arabic dominates eighteen, English twenty-six, and French one. In all, students published sixty-three separate magazines in this era.

9. John G. Cawelti, *Apostles of the Self-Made Man* (Chicago and London: University of Chicago Press), 4.

10. Peter van der Veer, ed., *Conversion to Modernities: The Globalization of Christianity* (New York and London: Routledge, 1996).

11. Daniel Bliss, *The Voice of Daniel Bliss* (Beirut: American Press, 1956), 38.

12. Ibid., 16.

13. Ibid., 19.

14. Ibid., 19 and 20.

15. Ibid., 20.

16. Daniel Bliss, Annual Report to the Board of Managers, June 27, 1872. *Annual Reports to the Board of Managers, Syrian Protestant College, 1866–67–1901–1902*, 24. AUB. Bliss explained that this method of control was in contrast to the practices used in the schools in the area. "Native schools follow the principles instituted by monks in the dark ages, keeping their pupils in subjection by penances, petty flagellation or imprisonment[,] deprivation of food, standing in disgrace in conspicuous places[,] etc.—all devised to degrade the student in his own estimation and that of others" (24).

17. See Norbert J. Scholz, "Foreign Education and Indigenous Reaction in Late Ottoman Lebanon: Students and Teachers at the Syrian Protestant College in Beirut," PhD diss., Georgetown University, 1997, 135–159, for a detailed list and examination of the many student infractions.

18. Faculty Minutes, Syrian Protestant College, April 22, 1868. Minutes of the Faculties, 1867–1920. AUB.

19. On November 24, 1879, two students were expelled for sodomy. The faculty voted that their "victim be imprisoned for a week & kept on bread & water." Faculty Minutes, Syrian Protestant College, November 24, 1879. Minutes of the Faculties, 1867–1920. AUB. Many students received punishments for using improper language on campus. In a small number of cases, students faced expulsion for bringing firearms onto campus. See, for example, Faculty Minutes, Syrian Protestant College, March 7, 1893. Minutes of the Faculties, 1867–1920. AUB.

20. Faculty Minutes, Syrian Protestant College, May 2, 1878. Minutes of the Faculties, 1867–1920. AUB.

21. Faculty Minutes, Syrian Protestant College, February 21, 1899. Minutes of the Faculties, 1867–1920. AUB.

22. Faculty Minutes, Syrian Protestant College, January 9, 1877. Minutes of the Faculties, 1867–1920. AUB. Near the end of his presidency, Bayard Dodge wrote that students sat alphabetically in chapel sessions. Bayard Dodge, *Report of the President of the American University of Beirut for the Forty-First Year 1946–1947*, 3. AUB.

23. Faculty Minutes, Syrian Protestant College, March 15, 1883. Minutes of the Faculties, 1867–1920. AUB.

24. Ibid.

25. Cited in Laurence R. Veysey, *The Emergence of the American University* (Chicago and London: University of Chicago Press, 1965), 243.

26. Julie A. Reuben, *The Making of the Modern University: Intellectual Transformation and the Marginalization of Morality* (Chicago and London: University of Chicago Press, 1996), 125 and 122.

27. George M. Marsden, "The Soul of the American University: A Historical Overview," in *The Secularization of the Academy*, edited by George M. Marsden and Bradley J. Longfield (New York and Oxford: Oxford University Press, 1992), 27.

28. Ibid., 29.

29. Bayard Dodge's father, Cleveland, was a friend of Woodrow Wilson's from their undergraduate years together at Princeton, through his tenure as president of the United

States, and as Wilson went into retirement after World War I. Wilson served as president of Princeton University (1902–1910) during Bayard Dodge's undergraduate years there.

30. Woodrow Wilson, "Princeton in the Nation's Service," in *The Papers of Woodrow Wilson*, edited by Arthur S. Link, vol. 10 (Princeton: Princeton University Press, 1971), 30.

31. The University of Chicago was founded by John D. Rockefeller in 1890. The Rockefeller Foundation served as a key donor for AUB, and particularly the medical school, throughout the 1920s and 1930s.

32. William Rainey Harper, *The Trend in Higher Education* (Chicago: University of Chicago Press, 1905), 20.

33. Ibid., 27–28.

34. Veysey, 72.

35. Richard Hofstadter, *The Age of Reform: From Bryan to F.D.R.* (New York: Alfred A. Knopf, 1955), 318.

36. "History," from Jane Addams Hull House Association Website, http://www.hull house.org/aboutus/history.html, accessed July 29, 2008.

37. Charles Howard Hopkins, *The Rise of the Social Gospel in American Protestantism: 1865–1915* (New Haven: Yale University Press, 1940), 3.

38. Howard Bliss, "Remarks before the Faculty on April 26, 1909, regarding the subject of Required Chapel and Bible Class Attendance," April 26, 1909. Students 1900s, Box 1, File 14: President Howard Bliss Remarks before the Faculty, on Chapel and Bible Class Attendance, April 26, 1909. AUB. In addition to Professors David Stuart Dodge (1860), George Post (ca. 1860), and Edwin Lewis (1869), both Howard Bliss (1887) and Bayard Dodge (1913) graduated from the Union Theological Seminary in New York. Henry Sloane Coffin, president emeritus of the school, writes in his history of the seminary that Walter Rauschenbusch's *Christianity and the Social Crisis* (1907), a key text in the Social Gospel canon, arrived at the seminary "like a gust of fresh air blowing into a stuffy room." Henry Sloane Coffin, *A Half Century of Union Theological Seminary, 1869–1945: An Informal History* (New York: Charles Scribner's Sons, 1954), 183.

39. James L. Barton, "The Modern Missionary," *Harvard Theological Review*, vol. 8, no. 1 (January 1915), 6.

40. Ibid., 15.

41. Robert T. Handy, *A Christian America: Protestant Hopes and Historical Realities* (New York: Oxford University Press, 1971), 132.

42. Quoted in Handy, 135.

43. Howard Bliss to Daniel Bliss, February 3, 1902. Bliss Family Papers, Box 1, Folder 98: Outgoing Correspondence. Amherst.

44. Ibid.

45. Howard Bliss, *Fifty-Seventh Annual Report of the Syrian Protestant College to the Board of Trustees, 1902–1903*, July 2, 1903, 7. AUB.

46. Howard Bliss, "Modern Missionary," *The Atlantic Monthly* (May 1920), 673.

47. Howard Bliss, "Unity and Uniformity," Speech delivered to the SPC "Flower of Culture" Society, May 1, 1909. Bliss Family Papers, Box 2, Folder 28: Speeches. Amherst.

48. Howard Bliss to David Stuart Dodge, May 26, 1905. Howard Bliss Collection: AUB President 1902–1920, Box 7, File 3: Correspondence from Howard Bliss to David Stuart Dodge, 1903–1904. AUB.

49. Howard Bliss, "Answers of President Howard S. Bliss of the Syrian Protestant College, Beirut, Syria, to the Questions Propounded by Commission I of the World Missionary Conference," 1. Commission I (Carrying the Gospel to All the Non-Christian World) of the World Missionary Conference, Edinburgh, June 14–23, 1910. The Archives of the Burke Library (Columbia University at Union Theological Seminary). Hereafter Burke.

50. Bliss, June 24, 1909, 1. Burke.

51. Daniel Bliss to the Board of Managers of the Syrian Protestant College. *Annual Reports to the Board of Managers, Syrian Protestant College, 1866–67–1901–1902*, July 20, 1887, 103. AUB. Daniel Bliss dates the formal establishment of the YMCA at November 1886. However, the YMCA student handbooks cite 1895 as the first year of the YMCA because before that point members considered the religious meetings informal gatherings. According to the handbook of 1904–1905, the catalyst for a formal organization came with John Mott's first visit to campus in October 1895. After that point, SPC also joined the World's Student Christian Federation. *Handbook Presented by the Young Men's Christian Association of the Syrian Protestant College, Vol. 1, 1904–05*, 10. Memorabilia, SPC. AUB.

52. *Handbook*, 9.

53. Ibid., 7–8.

54. Ibid., 14.

55. Howard Bliss to David Stuart Dodge, January 9, 1903. Howard Bliss Collection: AUB President 1902–1920, Box 7, File 2: Correspondence from Howard Bliss to David Stuart Dodge, 1902–1904. AUB. Howard Bliss to David Stuart Dodge, January 20, 1903. Howard Bliss Collection: AUB President 1902–1920, Box 7, File 2: Correspondence from Howard Bliss to David Stuart Dodge, 1902–1904. AUB.

56. Bliss, January 20, 1903.

57. Ibid.

58. Howard Bliss to David Stuart Dodge, January 27, 1903. Howard Bliss Collection: AUB President 1902–1920, Box 7, File 2: Correspondence from Howard Bliss to David Stuart Dodge, 1902–1904. AUB.

59. Howard Bliss to David Stuart Dodge, January 13, 1908. Howard Bliss Collection: AUB President 1902–1920, Box 8, File 2: Letters from Howard Bliss to David Stuart Dodge, January 7 to March 31, 1908. AUB.

60. Ibid.

61. Bayard Dodge, "America a Light to the Nations" (1924), 420–460. Bayard Dodge Collection: AUB President 1923–1948, Box 25: Articles, Speeches and Sermons by Bayard Dodge vols., 1, 2, and 3, File 3: Articles, Speeches and Sermons by Bayard Dodge, vol. 3. AUB.

62. Ibid., 433.

63. Bayard Dodge, "Article for Al-Kulliyyah: The Forward Watch" (February 28, 1923), 5. Bayard Dodge Collection: AUB President 1923–1948, Box 25: Articles, Speeches and Sermons by Bayard Dodge vols. 1, 2, and 3, File 3: Articles, Speeches and Sermons by Bayard Dodge, vol. 3. AUB.

64. Bayard Dodge, "The Syrian Protestant College," 10.

65. Ibid.

66. Bayard Dodge, "Keep Moving: President Dodge's Baccalaureate Sermon," *al-Kulliyah*, vol. 20, no. 6 (July 1, 1934), 175. AUB.

67. Ibid., 174.

68. Bayard Dodge, "Should the West Try to Help the Backward Parts of the East," 390. Bayard Dodge Collection: AUB President 1923–1948, Box 25: Articles, Speeches and Sermons by Bayard Dodge vols. 1, 2, and 3, File 3: Articles, Speeches and Sermons by Bayard Dodge, vol. 3. AUB.

69. Dodge, "America a Light to the Nations," 438.

70. Bayard Dodge, "American Contributions to Education for International Understanding and Good Will," 66. Bayard Dodge Collection: AUB President 1923–1948, Box 25: Articles, Speeches and Sermons by Bayard Dodge vols. 1, 2, and 3, File 3: Articles, Speeches and Sermons by Bayard Dodge, vol. 3. AUB.

71. Bayard Dodge, "Annual Report of the American University of Beirut," *Annual Report of the Near East College Association 1929–1930*, 11. AUB.

72. Ibid.

73. Bayard Dodge, *Report of the President of the American University of Beirut for the Eighty-First Year 1946–1947*, 8. AUB.

74. Bayard Dodge, "Inaugural Address Delivered by President Bayard Dodge at the American University of Beirut," *al-Kulliyah*, vol. 9, no. 8 (June 1923), 130. AUB.

75. Dodge, *1929–1930*, 17.

76. Laurens Hickok Seelye, "An Experiment in Religious Association," *Journal of Religion*, vol. 2, no. 3 (May 1922), 307.

77. Ibid., 308.

78. Stephen B. L. Penrose, Jr., *That They May Have Life: The Story of the American University of Beirut, 1866–1941* (Beirut: American University of Beirut, 1970), 300.

79. James Stewart Crawford, "The Religious Policy of the A.U.B." *Al-Kulliyah*, vol. 13, no. 7 (May 1927), 192–194. AUB.

80. Bayard Dodge, *Report of the American University of Beirut for the Year 1940–1941*, 19. AUB.

81. Gayatri Chakravorty Spivak uses this phrase to describe the "good society" established by the gendered separate spheres in Europe in the nineteenth century. It is used here to define all that the Americans felt they offered to the Arabs smart enough to embrace the project. Gayatri Chakravorty Spivak, "Can the Subaltern Speak?" in *Marxism and the Interpretation of Culture*, edited by Cary Nelson and Lawrence Grossberg (Houndmills, Basingstoke, Hampshire: Macmillan Education Ltd., 1988), 298–299.

82. Arabic names and titles that have been transliterated into English by the students appear as they do in those documents.

83. Nejib Yakub, "A Difficulty Facing Student Life," *Commercial Triumvirate*, no. 4 (May 18, 1906), n.p. AUB.

84. Ibid. The Kumbaz is a long, loose robe.

85. K.S.J., "And Who Is This?" *al-Kulliyah Review*, vol. 1, no. 6 (March 3, 1934), 5. AUB.

86. Ibid.

87. Ibid.

88. Ibid.

89. Yakub, n.p.

90. Ibid.

91. Selim A. Haddad, "Syrian Youth or an Appeal to Syrian Youngmen," *Commercial Triumvirate*, no. 2 (March 2, 1906), 64. AUB.

92. Ibid., 65.

93. Ibid.

94. Ibid., 67.

95. Ibid., 68.

96. Ibid., 69.

97. Mishil Samaʿaiyya Sawayya, "Ahlam al-shabab," *al-Thamarah*, vol. 1, no. 2 (February 24, 1914), 7. AUB.

98. "Health Hints," *Students' Union Gazette*, vol. 8 (January and February 1913), 23. AUB.

99. Ibid.

100. "Bi-l-saʿi umm bi-l-saʿd," *Thamarat al-Adhan*, no. 12 (May 31, 1900), 3. AUB.

101. Abdus Sattar El-Khairi, "The Master-Key to Success," *Light*, vol. 1, no. 1 (January 1906), 11. AUB.

102. Abdus Sattar El-Khairi, "How to Make a Determination," *Light*, vol. 1, no. 4 (April 1906), 12. AUB.

103. "A Plain Talk," *Anchor* (March 1924), 51. AUB.

104. "al-Muʿamala al-hasana wa ma laha min al-taʾthir," *al-Hadiqa*, vol. 3, no. 5 (April 22, 1902), 11. AUB.

105. "al-Muqaddima," *al-Manara*, no. 10 ([1906]), 2. AUB.

106. "Reference," *Students' Union Gazette* (1923), 48. AUB.

107. J. M. Weidberg, "A Biography: Leland Stanford," *Commercial Review*, vol. 1, no. 1 (April 1906), 5. AUB.

108. Ibid.

109. Ibid., 20.

110. Ibid., 21.

111. Ibid., 22.

112. J. M. Weidberg, "Abraham Lincoln," *University Times* (May 1908), 26. AUB.

113. Ibid.

114. H.A., "Abraham Lincoln," *University*, no. 9 (December 21, 1927), 18. AUB.

115. Stephan, "Ambition, Its Weal and Woe," *Review Organ of the Freshman School* ([1927]), 5. AUB.

116. Ibid.

117. "Miscellaneous: The Mainspring of Greatness," *Commercial Triumvirate*, no. 4 (May 18, 1906), n.p. AUB.

118. Ibid.

119. Stephan, 4.

120. Ibid.

121. A. Shimshirsian, "What Napoleon Did to Europe," *Happy Days*, vol. 2, no. 3 (March 1, 1905), 48. AUB.

122. Ibid., 49.

123. Mohammed Hajjar, "Who Is the Greatest Man." *Sub-Freshman Star*, no. 3 (June 1926), 27. AUB.

124. "The Oriental Hero, Ghengis [*sic*] Khan," *Happy Days*, vol. 2, no. 1 (January 1, 1905), 15. AUB.

125. Y. Behlis, "One of the Great Men in the East. General Nogi," *Pioneers of the S.P.C.*, vol. 2, no. 4 (1906), 17. AUB. General Nogi commanded the Japanese Army at Port Arthur, succeeding in wresting the port away from the Russians between 1904 and 1905.

126. A. Abu Hussein, "No Pains No Gains," *Sub-Freshman Star*, no. 2 (May 17, 1926), 48–49. AUB.

127. Hasan Balyuzi, "Ghandi [*sic*]: The Prophet of Satyagraha," *Students' Union Gazette* (February 1931), 85. AUB.

128. Yusuf M. Abs, "Who Is the True Gentleman of the S.P.C.?" *Students' Union Gazette* ([1916]), 398. AUB.

129. Ibid.

130. Ibid., 399–400.

131. Ibid., 400–401.

132. Ibid., 402.

133. Erik J. Zürcher, *Turkey: A Modern History* (London: I. B. Tauris, 2009), 86.

134. Ibid.

135. Abdulhamid II failed in his countercoup of 1909; the Young Turks deposed him and placed his brother, Mehmet V, on the Ottoman throne.

136. Howard Bliss, *Forty-Third Annual Report of the Syrian Protestant College to the Board of Trustees, 1908–1909*, 3. AUB.

137. Ibid., 4.

138. For more information on the Muslim Controversy of 1909, see John M. Munro, *A Mutual Concern: The Story of the American University of Beirut* (Delmar, NY: Caravan Books, 1977), 52–60.

139. Bliss, *1908–1909*, 6–7.

140. Franklin Moore, January 25, 1909, 10. Students 1900s, Box 1, File 11: Report of Remarks Made Subsequent to a Paper Read by Dr. Franklin Moore, January 25, 1909. AUB.

141. Ibid., 9.

142. Ibid.

143. Edward F. Nickoley to Howard Bliss, January 20, 1909. Students 1900s, Box 1, File 9. AUB.

144. "The Christian student body is thus far solid behind the Faculty. To this there seem to be only a few isolated exceptions." Ibid.

145. "Report of the 'Strike' from the Students' Point of View," February 5, 1909, 6. Students 1900s, Box 1, File 12. AUB. Franklin Moore to Howard Bliss, February 6, 1909, states that Professor William Hall prepared the report. Students 1900s, Box 1, File 13: Correspondence Addressed to Dr. Howard Bliss, February 5–11, 1909. AUB. In the last years of Abdulhamid II's reign, he assumed the old title of "caliph," or deputy or successor to the Prophet.

146. No student magazines were published during the spring 1909 semester since the faculty suspended all activities of the student associations during the crisis. When the papers returned in fall 1909, no article mentioned the previous semester's conflict.

147. "Report of the 'Strike' from the Students' Point of View."

148. Moore, January 25, 1909. AUB.

149. "The Beirut College and Islam," *Lewa* (Egypt), January 24, 1909. Students 1900s, Box 1, File 15. AUB. Dr. Harvey Porter translated all the articles appearing in this file. He also transliterated the newspaper's title.

150. See Faculty Minutes, Syrian Protestant College, January 26, 1909, and February 11, 1909, Minutes of the Faculties, 1867–1920. AUB. Faculty Minutes, 1908–1917.

151. Howard Bliss, *Fiftieth Annual Report of the Syrian Protestant College, 1915–1916*, 9. AUB.

Chapter Four

1. Layla Shuayb, "Senior Calls Slam at Coeds 'Lament' for Dead Customs, Decries Writers' 'Idealism'," *Outlook*, November 9, 1957, 4. AUB.

2. Ibid.

3. Ibid.

4. Ibid.

5. Ibid.

6. Ibid.

7. The American Woman's Board of Missions of the Congregational Church began teaching girls in Istanbul in the Home School in 1871. The school became the American College for Girls at Constantinople, colloquially known as the Constantinople Women's College, in 1890. At that time, it was chartered by the Massachusetts legislature and offered courses for its students leading to a BA. A medical department opened in 1920. In 1971, the school merged with Robert Academy to form Robert College, a coeducational secondary school. At the same time, the campus of the old Robert College became Boğaziçi University, a public university. For more information, see Mary Mills Patrick, *A Bosporus Adventure: Istanbul (Constantinople) Woman's College, 1871–1924* (Stanford: Stanford University Press, 1934), 29, 31, and 93–94; John Freely, *A History of Robert College: The American College for Girls, and Boğaziçi (Bosphorus University)*, vol. 1 (Istanbul: Yapi Kredi Yayınları, 2000), 11; and John Freely, *A History of Robert College: The American College for Girls, and Boğaziçi (Bosphorus University)*, vol. 2 (Istanbul: Yapi Kredi Yayınları, 2000), 190 and 192. Jean Said Makdisi reports that the American College for Girls, opened on March 28, 1910, was the first school in Egypt to offer higher education for women. Jean Said Makdisi, *Teta, Mother, and Me: Three Generations of Arab Women* (New York: W. W. Norton & Company, 2006), 196. Cairo University admitted a small group of women to a coeducational program in 1929, the same year the first public secondary school for girls, Shubra Secondary School, graduated its first

class. Margot Badran, *Feminists, Islam, and Nation: Gender and the Making of Modern Egypt* (Princeton: Princeton University Press, 1995), 148.

8. Barbara Miller Solomon, *In the Company of Educated Women: A History of Women and Higher Education in America* (New Haven: Yale University Press, 1985), 102.

9. Faculty Minutes, Syrian Protestant College, December 11, 1917. Minutes of the Faculties, 1867–1920. AUB.

10. Mrs. Edward Nickoley, Untitled, Women at AUB, Box 1, File 2: Women at AUB, 1930s–1960s. "March 1967" is written at the bottom of the document. AUB.

11. For additional information on coeducation at AUB, see Aleksandra Majstorac Kobiljiski, "Women Students at the American University of Beirut from the 1920s to the 1940s," in *Gender, Religion and Change in the Middle East: Two Hundred Years of History*, edited by Inger Marie Okkenhaug and Ingvild Flaskerud (Oxford and New York: Berg, 2005).

12. Edward Nickoley to Howard Bliss, February 1, 1920. Edward F. Nickoley Collection: Acting President 1920–1923, Box 1, File 6: Correspondence of Edward Nickoley to Howard Bliss and David S. Dodge. AUB.

13. Ibid.

14. Ibid. Nickoley mentions to Bliss that the British had already voiced complaints about the curriculum and the religious training at SPC and AUB and that these differences had catalyzed the missionaries to build a different kind of school. No colleges materialized from these plans.

15. Mrs. Edward Nickoley.

16. American missionaries established the Beirut Female Seminary in 1835, renaming it the American School for Girls (ASG) in 1904. In 1927, the American Junior College for Women (AJCW) split off from the ASG. It used this title until 1948–1949, when the school became the Beirut College for Women (BCW), offering a four-year BA program. Named the Beirut University College (BUC) in 1973, the school began admitting male students in 1975. Finally, in 1994, the school became the Lebanese American University (LAU). For more information, see Ellen L. Fleischmann, "'Under an American Roof': The Beginnings of the American Junior College for Women in Beirut," *Arab Studies Journal*, vol. 17, no. 1 (Spring 2009), 62–84.

17. Faculty Minutes, Executive Committee of the American University of Beirut, February 24, 1927. Minutes of the Faculties, 1920–1956. AUB.

18. Edward F. Nickoley, "Higher Education for Women," *al-Kulliyah*, vol. 13, no. 6 (April 1927), 157. AUB.

19. Ibid., 158.

20. Barbara Sicherman, "College and Careers: Historical Perspectives on the Lives and Work Patterns of Women College Graduates," in *Women and Higher Education in American History: Essays from the Mount Holyoke College Sesquicentennial Symposia*, edited by John Mack Faragher and Florence Howe (New York and London: W. W. Norton and Company, 1988), 154; Marie Aziz Sabri, *Pioneering Profiles: Beirut College for Women* (Beirut: Khayat Book and Publishing Company, 1967), 31; Ellen L. Fleischmann, "Lost in Translation: Home Economics and the Sidon Girls' School of Lebanon, c. 1924–1932," *Social Sciences and Missions*, vol. 23, no. 1 (2010), 33–34. "Style Show," *al-Kulliyah Review*, vol. 3, no. 13 (May 9, 1935), 3, and "Junior College Reception," *al-Kulliyah Review*, vol. 4, no. 3 (November 14, 1936), 2, both identify a "Home Economics Club" and classes existing at AJCW by the 1930s. AUB.

21. Fleischmann, "Lost in Translation," 34.

22. Nadya Sbaiti, "Lessons in History: Education and the Formation of National Society in Beirut, Lebanon, 1920–1960s," PhD diss., Georgetown University, 2008, 255.

23. Margaret A. Lowe, *Looking Good: College Women and Body Image, 1875–1930* (Baltimore and London: Johns Hopkins University Press, 2003), 135.

24. Charlotte Williams Conable, *Women at Cornell: The Myth of Equal Education* (Ithaca and London: Cornell University Press, 1977), 114.

25. Ibid., 115.

26. Nickoley, "Higher Education for Women," 157.

27. "To Hold What We Have," *News Letter: Robert College at Constantinople, Syrian Protestant College at Beirut*, vol. 1, no. 5 (October 1920), 1. AUB.

28. "News from the Colleges: Syrian Protestant College," *News Letter: Robert College at Constantinople, Syrian Protestant College at Beirut*, vol. 1, no. 3 (June 1920), 4. AUB.

29. Nickoley, "Higher Education for Women," 159.

30. Numbers calculated from president's annual reports, 1921–1959. See Edward F. Nickoley, *Fifty-Sixth Annual Report of the American University of Beirut, 1921–1922*, 4–5; George B. Stewart, Jr., *Report of the Acting President of the American University of Beirut, Beirut, Syria, for the Sixty-Second Year 1927–1928*, Appendix; and J. Paul Leonard, *Report of the President Covering the Years 1957–58 and 1958–59*, Appendixes A and H. AUB.

31. Leonard, *1957–58 and 1959*, Appendix I. AUB.

32. "Co-Acting," *al-Kulliyah Review*, vol. 5, no. 4 (November 20, 1937), 2. AUB.

33. Minutes of the Executive Committee, American University of Beirut, May 12, 1942. Minutes of the Faculties, 1920–1956. AUB.

34. Minutes of the University Senate, American University of Beirut, May 9, 1944. Minutes of the Faculties, 1920–1956. AUB.

35. "Report of the Student Committee," *al-Kulliyah*, vol. 9 (Commencement 1945), 38. AUB.

36. Bayard Dodge, "American Contributions to Education for International Understanding and Good Will" (December 3, 1927), 66. Bayard Dodge Collection: AUB President 1923–1948, Box 25: Articles, Speeches and Sermons by Bayard Dodge, vols. 1, 2, and 3. File 3: Articles, Speeches and Sermons by Bayard Dodge, vol. 3. AUB.

37. Bayard Dodge, "The Awakening of the Near East," 275. Bayard Dodge Collection: AUB President 1923–1948, Box 25: Articles, Speeches and Sermons by Bayard Dodge, vols. 1, 2, and 3. File 3: Articles, Speeches, and Sermons by Bayard Dodge, vol. 3. AUB.

38. Bayard Dodge, *Annual Report of the Near East College Association, 1929–1930*, 11. AUB.

39. Bayard Dodge, *Report of the President of the American University of Beirut for the Forty-First Year 1946–1947*, 3. AUB.

40. Ibid.

41. Ibid.

42. Ibid.

43. Stuart C. Dodd, *Social Relationships in the Near East: A Civics Textbook of Readings and Projects for College Freshmen* (Beirut: American University of Beirut, 1931), i. The acknowledgments indicate that Mrs. George Shahla prepared part of the chapter on the status of women as a lecture. Her contributions are not specifically marked, so it is impossible to determine whether she or Stuart Dodd provided the quotes cited here.

44. Ibid., 42–43.

45. Ibid., 44–49.

46. Ibid., 51.

47. Ibid., 47.

48. See Leila Ahmed, *Women and Gender in Islam: Historical Roots of a Modern Debate* (New Haven and London: Yale University Press, 1992), for an analysis of the hypocrisies presented by such writings, given the poor legal, economic, and political status of women in Western countries. Also, this paradigm harks back to Gayatri Chakravorty Spivak's now famous statement, "White men are saving brown women from brown men"; the Americans saw themselves bringing a better society to the Arabs because they could

not initiate the change on their own. The Americans, in the case of SPC and AUB, unconditionally accepted the trope of Western society's goodness, and the concomitant respect and dignity allowed to women within it. Gayatri Chakravorty Spivak, "Can the Subaltern Speak?" In *Marxism and the Interpretation of Culture*, edited by Cary Nelson and Lawrence Grossberg (Houndmills, Basingstoke, Hampshire: Macmillan Education Ltd., 1988), 296 and 298.

49. I. Matar, "Women of Turkey," *University*, no. 1 (October 19, 1927), 42. AUB.

50. Students glued postcards on to many pages of these magazines. They were so plentiful they must have been readily available to the students, and part of their everyday consumption patterns. Very few have Arab motifs; the scenes almost always depict a European or American scene. Hundreds of them included images of women, running the gambit from beautiful Western women to the faithless wife and girlfriend.

51. "Cats on the Mat," *Outlook*, vol. 1, no. 3 (November 25, 1949), 2. A longer version of this same "Element" appears in "Women! Women! Women!," *Focus*, no. 2 (May 1965), 15. AUB.

52. "Cats on the Mat," 2. AUB.

53. Abu Fuad, "Thoughts behind Farewell," *Outlook* (Commencement 1950), 3. AUB.

54. A.L., "Courtesy on the Tennis Courts," *al-Kulliyah Review*, vol. 1, no. 2 (January 5, 1934), 4. AUB.

55. Ibid.

56. Ibid.

57. X.Y., "Courtesy," *al-Kulliyah Review*, vol. 1, no. 3 (January 20, 1934), 4. AUB.

58. Ibid.

59. Rostom, "Confessions," *al-Kulliyah Review*, vol. 8, no. 2 (February 1, 1944), 9. AUB.

60. Ibid.

61. Ibid.

62. Ibid.

63. Ibid., 20.

64. Ibid.

65. T.N.M., "Tragedy on the Campus," *al-Kulliyah Review*, vol. 8, no. 2 (February 1, 1944), 19. AUB.

66. Howard Bliss, "Baccalaureate Sermon," *al-Kulliyah*, vol. 2, no. 8 (June 1911), 270. AUB.

67. I do not use quotation marks for the phrase *making women* to call attention to the fact that the phrase was not used at the school. The making of women was subsumed in the "making men" program.

68. Fleischmann, "Under an American Roof," 74.

69. Mary Robinson, "Mary Robinson, Dean of Women," *Focus*, vol. 1, no. 1 (February 1962), 8. AUB.

70. Lila Abu-Lughod, ed., *Remaking Women: Feminism and Modernity in the Middle East* (Princeton: Princeton University Press, 1998). For similar studies, see Mona L. Russell, *Creating the New Egyptian Woman: Consumerism, Education, and National Identity, 1863–1922* (New York: Palgrave Macmillan, 2004); Omnia El Shakry, "Schooled Mother and Structured Play: Child Rearing in Turn-of-the-Century Egypt," in *Remaking Women: Feminism and Modernity in the Middle East*, edited by Lila Abu-Lughod (Princeton: Princeton University Press, 1998); Akram Fouad Khater, *Inventing Home: Emigration, Gender, and the Middle Class in Lebanon, 1870–1920* (Berkeley and Los Angeles: University of California Press, 2001); and Badran, *Feminists, Islam, and Nation.*

71. Lila Abu-Lughod, "Introduction: Feminist Longings and Postcolonial Conditions," in *Remaking Women: Feminism and Modernity in the Middle East*, edited by Lila Abu-Lughod (Princeton: Princeton University Press, 1998), 9.

72. Ibid., 8–9.

73. Beth Baron, *The Women's Awakening in Egypt: Culture, Society, and the Press* (New Haven: Yale University Press, 1994), 140.

74. Ibid., 141.

75. Hala Ramez Dimechkie, "Julia Tu'mi Dimashqiyi and *al-Mar'a al-Jadida*: 1883–1954," MA thesis, American University of Beirut, 1998, 111–112.

76. Elizabeth Thompson, *Colonial Citizens: Republican Rights, Paternal Privilege, and Gender in French Syria and Lebanon* (New York: Columbia University Press, 2000), 98.

77. Ibid., 99.

78. Ibid., 142.

79. Ibid., 144.

80. Ibid., 215.

81. Elsa R. Kerr, "To the Women Graduates," *al-Kulliyah Review* (Commencement 1946), 61. AUB.

82. Mrs. S. E. Kerr, "Coeducation in the A.U.B.," *al-Kulliyah Review*, vol. 22, no. 2 (March 1947), 6–7. AUB.

83. Margaret Avery, "The Ladies' Luncheon," *al-Kulliyah*, no. 9 (June 1928), 244. AUB.

84. "Ladies' Reception," *al-Kulliyah*, vol. 19, no. 6 (July 1, 1933), 176.

85. Mary Robinson, "Women Students of Our Campus," *Focus*, no. 1 (1964), 16–17. AUB.

86. Lily A. Hawie, "Brotherhood Questionnaire Replies: A Girl Majoring in Science! OH!!," *al-Kulliyah Review*, vol. 3, no. 6 (January 11, 1936), 5. AUB.

87. Ibid.

88. Ibid.

89. Asma Najjar, "al-Mar'a al-ʿarabiyah," *al-ʿUrwa al-Wuthqa*, vol. 2, no. 4 (June 1937), 71. AUB.

90. Jane E. Van Zandt, "The Trained Nurse in Syria," *al-Kulliyah*, vol. 8, no. 7 (May 1922), 103. AUB.

91. Ibid.

92. "Higher Education of Women," *al-Kulliyah*, vol. 16, no. 4 (February 1930), 88. AUB.

93. "The Ladies' Reception," *al-Kulliyah Review*, vol. 20, no. 6 (July 1, 1934), 184. AUB.

94. Kerr, "To the Women Graduates," 67.

95. "Women—Today & Tomorrow," *al-Kulliyah Review*, vol. 7, no. 4 (February 1940), 12. AUB.

96. Wadad Cortas, "Women's Education," *al-Kulliyah Review*, vol. 22, no. 8 (November 1947), 6. AUB.

97. Ibid.

98. Zahiyah Qadura and Shams al-Din Najm, "Risalat al-mar'a li-hayatina al-qawmiyah," *al-ʿUrwa al-Wuthqa*, vol. 3, no. 3 (May 1938), 68. AUB.

99. Fatima al-ʿAskari, "al-Shabab al-ʿarabi wa-l-mar'a. 1—al-Mushkila ka-ma yaraha al-shabb," *al-ʿUrwa al-Wuthqa*, vol. 6, no. 2 (March 1941), 47. AUB.

100. Fatima al-Husseini, "Mushkilat al-bayt al-ʿarabi," *al-ʿUrwa al-Wuthqa*, vol. 5, no. 3 (April 15, 1940), 5. AUB.

101. Ibid., 6.

102. Ibid.

103. Balqis ʿIwad, "al-Mar'a al-ʿarabiyah fi ʿasrina al-hadir," *al-ʿUrwa al-Wuthqa*, vol. 13, no. 4 (May 1948), 19–23. AUB.

104. Ibid., 19.

105. Ibid.

106. Ibid., 21.

107. Alia Solh, "First AUB Woman Student Was Also First Woman Medic," *Outlook*, vol. 6, no. 12 (May 31, 1952), 2. AUB.

108. Cortas, "Women's Education," 4–5. AUB.

109. Wadad Makdisi Cortas, *A World I Loved: The Story of an Arab Woman* (New York: Nation Books, 2009), 43.

110. Cortas, "Women's Education," 5.

111. Cortas, *A World I Loved*, 44.

112. Cortas, "Women's Education," 5.

113. Ibid.

114. Marie Aziz Sabri, "Dr. Jamal (Karam) Harfouche," in *Pioneering Profiles: Beirut College for Women* (Beirut: Khayat Book and Publishing Company, 1967), 175.

115. Ibid.

116. Ibid.

117. Ibid.

118. Leila Khairallah, "Coeds Considered Civilizing Influence Back in '33: Dr. Salwa Nassar, 1st Physics PhD Here, Remembers," *Outlook*, March 22, 1958, 18. AUB.

119. Ibid.

120. Ibid.

121. Marie Aziz Sabri, "Angela (Jurdak) Khoury," in *Pioneering Profiles: Beirut College for Women* (Beirut: Khayat Book & Publishing Co., 1967), 194–195.

122. Ibid., 195–196.

123. Wadad Bulus quoted in Faruq Saʿd Abu-Jabir, ed., *Dhikrayat fi al-jamiʿa al-amirkiyah fi bayrut* ([Amman]: Matbaʿat al-Aswaq, 1998), 59.

124. Ibid., 60.

125. Ibid.

126. Ibid.

127. Ibid.

128. John Waterbury, "Women at AUB: Today and Yesterday," October 7, 2002. American University of Beirut, http://www.aub.edu.lb/news/archive/preview.php?id=29015, accessed August 28, 2006.

129. Ibid.

130. Ibid.

Chapter Five

1. "AUB School of Revolution Planned: 'We Make Rebels' to Be New Campus Ideal," *Lookout*, vol. 6, no. 6 (March 29, 1952), 1. AUB. Parts of this chapter appeared in an earlier version as "Voices of Protest: The Struggle over Freedom at the American University of Beirut (AUB)," *Comparative Studies of South Asia, Africa and the Middle East*, vol. 28, no. 3 (2008), 390–403.

2. "AUB School of Revolution Planned," 1.

3. Ibid., 4.

4. "Important Notice," *Lookout*, vol. 6, no. 6 (March 29, 1952), 3. AUB.

5. Israel Gershoni, "Rethinking the Formation of Arab Nationalism in the Middle East, 1920–1945: Old and New Narratives," in *Rethinking Nationalism in the Arab Middle East*, edited by James Jankowski and Israel Gershoni (New York: Columbia University Press, 1997), 13.

6. See Amjad Deeb Ghanma, *Jamiʿat al-ʿUrwa al-Wuthqa* (Beirut: Riad El-Rayyes Books: 2002), 35–40, for the confusion surrounding the year of the club's official establishment.

7. Bayard Dodge, "The Awakening of the Near East" (1935), 270. Bayard Dodge Collection: AUB President 1923–1948, Box 25: Articles, Speeches and Sermons by Bayard Dodge vols. 1, 2, and 3, File 3: Articles, Speeches and Sermons by Bayard Dodge, vol. 3. AUB.

8. Ibid..

9. Ibid., 271.

10. Ibid.

11. Ibid.

12. Ibid.

13. Ibid., 272.

14. J. Somerville, "The Tour around the World," *Students' Union Gazette* (Christmas 1914), 31. AUB. The exhibit for the United States represented a skit with "a boot-black, two niggers, a china [*sic*] man and a U.S.A. police-man" (36). No exhibit on American culture appears to have been presented at any of the following university nights over the next few years.

15. Laurens H. Seelye, "Inter-racial Night," *al-Kulliyah*, vol. 8, no. 4 (February 1922), 59. AUB.

16. Ibid.

17. Ibid., 59–60.

18. Ibid., 60.

19. Ibid.

20. Ibid.

21. "Cosmopolitan Night," *al-Kulliyah*, vol. 9, no. 8 (June 1923), 141. AUB.

22. Ibid., 141–142.

23. Ibid., 142.

24. Ibid.

25. "Halatuna," *al-Mabda' al-Sahih*, no. 2 (May 25, 1899), 1. AUB.

26. Ibid.

27. al-Asayf Habib Khalil Tayigh, "Wafat al-sharq," *Sada al-Isti'dadiyah*, no. 3 (February 3, 1902), 2. AUB.

28. Ibid., 4.

29. "Mubahatha fi hal naf'at al-muhajaramin biladina am akhratahu," *Sada al-Isti'dadiyah*, vol. 1, no. 3 (May 4, 1906), 5–6. AUB.

30. Yusuf Abs, "Our Needs," *Students' Union Gazette*, no. 1 (November 1915), 185. AUB.

31. "Our Future Men," *Students' Union Gazette* (Easter 1924), 146. AUB.

32. Iskandar Afandi Ya'qub, "Matami' al-awriawbin," *al-'Asr*, vol. 1, no. 2 (April 9, [1900]), 2–3. AUB.

33. "Bab al-muqabalat hujum 'ala al-sharq," *al-Hadiqa*, vol. 3, no. 1 (January 31, 1902), 2 and 5. AUB.

34. E. Mirshak, "East and West," *Sub-Freshman Star*, no. 2 (May 17, 1926), 46. AUB.

35. "al-'Arabiyah wa-l-'arab," *al-Hadiqa*, vol. 3, no. 6 (May 6, 1902), 1. AUB.

36. H. Abdulmajid, "The Iraquian Students' First Social Gathering," *University*, no. 6 (November 30, 1927), 14a, and "The Speech of Professor Khûry in Chapel," *University*, no. 10 (January 4, 1928), 3. AUB. The surname "Khawri" might be misspelled; no professor by that name is listed in the school catalogues of the late 1920s. Professor Khûry could have been Jurjus Ilyas Khûry or Anis Ilyas Khûry.

37. "Arab Poets during the Abbasside [*sic*] Dynasty," *al-Kulliyah*, vol. 17, no. 2 (December 15, 1930), 41. AUB.

38. "A Memorandum to the Trustees and Faculty from the Arabic-Speaking Students Committee on the Revival of Instruction in Arabic in the American University of Beirut." Students 1920s, Box 1, File 6: Petition from Arabic-Speaking Students of the AUB for Revival of Instruction in Arabic, July 1923. AUB.

39. Ibid., 17.

40. Ibid., 5.

41. Ibid.

42. Ibid., 6.

43. Ibid., 10.

44. Ibid.

45. Mahatma Gandhi, *Men Are Brothers: Life and Thoughts of Mahatma Gandhi as Told in His Own Words*, compiled and edited by Krishna Kripalani (Paris: UNESCO, 1969), 154.

46. Ngugi wa Thiong'o, *Decolonising the Mind: The Politics of Language in African Literature* (London: James Currey, 1997), 18.

47. Edward F. Nickoley to Bayard Dodge, August 13, 1923. Edward F. Nickoley Collection: Acting President 1920–1923, Box 2, File 5: Correspondence between Edward Nickoley and Bayard Dodge. AUB.

48. Nickoley to Howard Bliss, January 14, 1920. Edward F. Nickoley Collection: Acting President 1920–1923, Box 1, File 6: Correspondence of Edward Nickoley to Howard Bliss and David S. Dodge. AUB.

49. Ibid.

50. Bayard Dodge, Dodge Personal Letters 1922, July 12, 1922. Bayard Dodge to Family, July 12, 1922. Bayard Dodge Collection: AUB President, 1923–1948, Box 7, File 5: Personal Letters, 1922. AUB.

51. Saʿd Nimri quoted in Faruq Saʿd Abu-Jabir, ed., *Dhikrayat fi al-jamiʿa al-amirkiyah fi bayrut* ([Amman]: Matbaʿat al-Aswaq, 1998), 53.

52. Hala Sakakini, *Jerusalem and I: A Personal Record* (Amman: Economic Press Company, 1990), 97. Hisham Sharabi, by contrast, became disillusioned. As a student during World War II, he joined an Arab nationalist cell of students. "To this day, I don't know who was behind this organization. Later on, it was recognized as one of several nuclei of the Arab Nationalists' Movement. Our cell consisted of a number of students from the freshman and sophomore classes. We met once a week in one of the dorm rooms and discussed different topics under the leadership of the person responsible for the cell. The meetings were long and the discussions boring. I became fed up after a short while." He later joined the Syrian Social Nationalist Party of Antun Saʿadeh. Hisham Sharabi, *Embers and Ashes: Memoirs of an Arab Intellectual*, translated by Issa J. Boullata (Northampton, MA: Olive Branch Press, 2008), 49.

53. Sakakini, 97.

54. A selection of their books includes Philip Hitti, *History of the Arabs* (London: Macmillan, 1937); Constantine Zurayq, *The Meaning of the Disaster*, translated by R. Bayly Winder (Beirut: Khayat's College Book Cooperative, 1956); Zeine N. Zeine, *The Struggle for Arab Independence: Western Diplomacy and the Rise and Fall of Faisal's Kingdom in Syria* (Beirut: Khayat's, 1960); and Anis al-Khuri Makdisi, *al-Ittijahat al-Adabiyah fi al-ʿAlam al-ʿArabi al-Hadith, wa-Hiya Dirasat Tahliliyah lil-ʿAwamil al-Faʿalah fi al-Nahda al-ʿArabiyah al-Hadithah wa-li-Zawahiriha al-Adabiyah wa-Raʾisiyah* (Beirut: Dar al-ʿIlm lil-Malayin, 1963).

55. George Habash established the Arab Nationalist Party in Jordan in the 1950s and then formed the Popular Front for the Liberation of Palestine (PFLP) in 1967. For more information, see Yezid Sayigh, *Armed Struggle and the Search for State: The Palestinian National Movement, 1949–1993* (Oxford: Oxford University Press, 1997).

56. Anis Sayigh, "Introduction," in Ghanma, 15–16.

57. Mahi al-Din Nusuli, "Risalat al-ʿurwa," *al-ʿUrwa al-Wuthqa*, vol. 1, no. 2 (March 1, 1936), 1. AUB.

58. Ibid., 2. The term *qawmiyah* is used throughout *al-ʿUrwa al-Wuthqa* to denote the larger pan-national Arab nationalism. Writers typically used *wataniyah* and *watan* throughout *al-ʿUrwa al-Wuthqa* to define a localized nationalism associated with a state, such as Syria, Palestine, or Jordan.

59. Matta Akrawi, "wa-l-Dhikrayat," *al-ʿUrwa al-Wuthqa*, vol. 2, no. 1 (December 1936), 1. AUB.

60. A large number of articles discuss relationships with women, and the students wrote many love poems. One report details a debate in 1922 asking, "Is it necessary to have equality

of women with men?" After much discussion, the majority of participants voted in favor of equality. Ghanma, 66.

61. Mahi al-Din Yusuf, "al-Nahda al-ʿiraqiyah," *al-ʿUrwa al-Wuthqa*, vol. 2, no. 1 (January 1925), 21–25. AUB.

62. Until the early 1950s, students used the term *umma* to denote the Arab nation almost exclusively. *Umma* often refers to a religious nation or community, but the student writers of *al-ʿUrwa al-Wuthqa* used the term in a secular sense. It means, in almost all instances, a secular pan-Arab nation.

63. Mahi al-Din Yusuf, "Tajanus al-ʿaqliyyat," *al-ʿUrwa al-Wuthqa*, part 1 (1925–1926), 16–17. AUB.

64. Shawqi Dandashi and Mudrik ʿIlmi, "Hal yumkin ijad wahda ʿarabiyah," *al-ʿUrwa al-Wuthqa*, part 1 (1925–1926), 33–38. AUB.

65. "Bawaʾith li-istimar," *al-ʿUrwa al-Wuthqa* (June 1928), 43–46. AUB.

66. Hisham Sharabi presents a counternarrative: "The most lethal intellectual weapon in the hands of our professors was sarcasm, and they did not hesitate to use it whatever the occasion. How easy it was for a professor to destroy all in the classroom who disagreed with his beliefs and feelings. All my professors at the American University of Beirut practiced the style of sarcasm and mockery—it didn't matter what subjects they taught. Some of them practiced sarcasm in a direct and obvious way, others in an indirect and subtle manner." They were not, Sharabi felt, open to opposing ideas or philosophies. "What our professors liked most was for us to ask questions on the topics they were speaking about. We used to submit to their ideas and repress whatever we thought contradicted them." Sharabi also criticized the professors for providing only excerpts of philosophical writings. Sharabi, 21–22, 25.

67. Ghanma, 60.

68. ʿAziz al-ʿAzmah, *Qustantin Zurayq: ʾArabi lil-qarn al-ʿishrin* (Beirut: Muʾassasat al-Dirasat al-Filastiniyah, 2003), 42–43. AUB.

69. ʿAzmah, 48–49, uses 1935 for the founding and 1937 for the establishment of the society's governing council, 50. Shafik Jeha, *al-Haraka al-ʿarabiyah al-sirriyah jamaʿat al-kitab al-ahmar* (Beirut: al-Furat li-l-nashr, 2004), 7, confirms the date of 1935.

70. Shadid, cited in Ghanma, 141–142.

71. I would like to thank Samir Seikaly for engaging in a helpful discussion with me about these topics.

72. For a full reprint of The Red Book, see Jeha, 383–431, and al-ʿAzmah, 120–137.

73. al-ʿAzmah, 120.

74. Almost the only verb the student writers use for the Arab struggle for the nation is *jahada*. In Islam, jihad contains three elements: a personal struggle, a verbal struggle, and a physical struggle. In *al-ʿUrwa*, the students primarily use the term to mean a struggle to understand the elements of Arab nationalism and the obstacles in the way of Arab unity.

75. al-ʿAzmah, 122.

76. Ibid., 125.

77. Ibid., 130.

78. Ibid., 47.

79. "Tasdir," *al-ʿUrwa al-Wuthqa*, vol. 11, no. 1 (1945), 2. AUB.

80. "Kalimat tamhid," *al-ʿUrwa al-Wuthqa*, vol. 6, no. 2 (March 1941), 4. AUB.

81. Khalil Ayntabi, "al-Intaj al-fikri fi-l-sharq wa-l-gharb wa mawqif al-shabab minhi," *al-ʿUrwa al-Wuthqa*, vol. 6, no. 2 (March 1941), 14–22. AUB.

82. Ibid., 14.

83. Idmun al-Bawi, "Masʾuliyyat al-talib al-ʿarabi," *al-ʿUrwa al-Wuthqa*, vol. 13, no. 1 (December 1947), 36. AUB.

84. Ibid., 36–37.

85. Ibid., 37.

86. Ibid.

87. Abd al-ʿAziz Sawwaf, "al-Thawra ʿala al-waqiʿ," *al-ʿUrwa al-Wuthqa*, vol. 11, no. 2 (April 1946), 56–62. AUB.

88. Ibid., 56.

89. Ibid.

90. Ibid., 57.

91. Ibid., 59.

92. Ibid., 60.

93. Riyad al-Azhari, "Shartan li-najah al-dimuqratiyah," *al-ʿUrwa al-Wuthqa*, vol. 14, no. 4 (June 1949), 51–56.

94. Ibid., 51.

95. "Al-Taʾmim huwa al-khatwa al-thaniyah," *al-ʿUrwa al-Wuthqa*, vol. 17, no. 2 (February 1952), 2. AUB.

96. "Al-Taʾmim wa-l-ishtirakiyah," *al-ʿUrwa al-Wuthqa*, vol. 17, no. 2 (February 1952), 22. AUB.

97. "Al-Taʾmim fi-l-watan al-ʾarabi," *al-ʿUrwa al-Wuthqa*, vol. 17, no. 2 (February 1952), 25. AUB.

98. "Al-Istiqlal wa-l-sharikat," *al-ʿUrwa al-Wuthqa*, vol. 17, no. 2 (February 1952), 36. AUB.

99. Until the late 1940s, the term *dawla* appears rarely in *al-ʿUrwa al-Wuthqa* because the Arab *umma* is the primary actor. By the late 1940s, students use *dawla* to denote the state structure within each of the Arab nations.

100. Announcement, *al-ʿUrwa al-Wuthqa*, vol. 17, no. 3 (April 1952), 2. AUB.

101. "Qawmiyah wa-l-ishtirakiyah," *al-ʿUrwa al-Wuthqa*, vol. 17, no. 2 (February 1952), 4–5. AUB.

102. Ibid., 5.

103. Ibid., 7.

104. Ibid.

105. Heather Sharkey reports that 1948 marked a moment of change for the American missionaries in Egypt and the founders of the American University in Cairo (AUC). "The first big rupture in the missionaries' relationship with the U.S. government came when President Harry S. Truman recognized the state of Israel in 1948. This was also the first time that the American Presbyterians found themselves uncomfortable as Americans in Egypt, and the first time that they felt obligated to speak out against U.S. policy." Heather J. Sharkey, *American Evangelicals in Egypt: Missionary Encounters in an Age of Empire* (Princeton: Princeton University Press, 2008), 229.

106. Nihad Haykal, "al-Hiyad darura qawmiyah," *al-ʿUrwa al-Wuthqa*, vol. 16, nos. 4–5 (1951), 56–59. AUB.

107. Stephen Penrose worked for the Office of Strategic Services (OSS) in Cairo and as chief of secret intelligence in Washington, DC, and in Europe during World War II. After the war, Penrose worked as special assistant to Secretary of Defense James Forrestal. "Guide to the Stephen B. L. Penrose, Jr. Papers: 1908–1990," Northwest Digital Archives, http://nwda-db.wsulibs.wsu.edu/findaid/ark:/80444/xv75253, accessed January 23, 2010.

108. Stephen B. L. Penrose, Jr., *The Palestinian Problem—Retrospect and Prospect* (Beirut: World Council of Churches, 1951), 11. Penrose also made loans and scholarships available to AUB's Palestinian students.

109. Bayard Dodge, "Must There Be War in the Middle East?" *Reader's Digest* (April 1948), 45. Bayard Dodge Collection: AUB President 1923–1948, Box 3: Addresses and Articles by Him, File 4: Articles by Him, 1930s–1940s. AUB.

110. Trygve Lie to Bayard Dodge, December 2, 1948. Bayard Dodge Collection: AUB President 1923–1948, Box 5, File 5: Correspondence with the Secretary General of United Nations (Trygve Halvdan Lie), on Palestinian Refugees, December 2, 1948. AUB.

111. Amin Sharif, "Arab Women and Political Rights," *al-Kulliyah Review*, vol. 10, no. 1 (January 1946), 32. AUB.

112. Habiba Shaʿaban Yakun, "Amnahu al-marʾa haquqaha al-siyasiyah," *al-ʿUrwa al-Wuthqa*, vol. 14, no. 2 (February 1949), 6–9. AUB.

113. Ibid., 7.

114. Ibid.

115. Ibid.

116. Ibid., 8.

117. Ibid.

118. Ibid.

119. "Ansatuna yatahaddathna," *al-ʿUrwa al-Wuthqa*, vol. 15, no. 4 (May 1950), 54–58. AUB.

120. Ibid., 54.

121. Ibid., 54–55.

122. Hasan Saʿb, "Akhbarna," *al-ʿUrwa al-Wuthqa*, vol. 13, no. 1 (December 1947), 51. AUB.

123. "The Student Council Utilizes Five Historical Days," *al-Kulliyah Review*, vol. 22, no. 9 (December 1947), 3 and 5.

124. Elie A. Salem, *Violence and Diplomacy in Lebanon: The Troubled Years, 1982–1988* (London: I. B. Tauris, 1995), 15; and author interview with Elie Salem, Balamand University, Lebanon, July 25, 2005. AUB. Fawzi al-Qawuqji led the Arab Liberation Army (ALA) that arrived in Palestine in spring 1948.

125. Hasan Saʿb, "Tanzim al-diʿayya li-l-jihad al-qawmi al-ʿarabi fi filastin," *al-ʿUrwa al-Wuthqa*, vol. 13, no. 2 (January 1948), 8. AUB.

126. Morocco achieved independence in March 1956.

127. "al-ʿUrwa wa marrakish," *al-ʿUrwa al-Wuthqa*, vol. 16, no. 3 (May 1951), 58. AUB.

128. "Students Attack French Monument: March on Legations in Protest Strike," *Outlook*, vol. 4, no. 3 (March 10, 1951), 1. AUB.

129. "al-ʿUrwa wa marrakish," 59.

130. Mushin, "Ghadbat al-shabab al-ʿarab min ajli marrakish," *al-ʿUrwa al-Wuthqa*, vol. 16, no. 3 (May 1951), 3. AUB.

131. "SA Strike, Demand Military Training," *Outlook*, vol. 5, no. 9 (December 22, 1951), 1. AUB.

132. "SA Protest Action of Gov; Student Release," *Outlook*, vol. 5, no. 10 (January 12, 1952), 1. AUB.

133. See Constantine Zurayq to Stephen Penrose, April 1, 1954, attached to Minutes of the University Senate, American University of Beirut, March 29, 1954, for details of the events of that day. AUB.

134. Minutes of the University Senate, American University of Beirut, May 11, 1954. AUB.

135. An appointed Student Council existed as of 1943.

136. "Rise and Fall of the Student Council," *Outlook*, vol. 21, no. 13 (May 16, 1966), 1. AUB.

137. Ibid., 6.

138. Ibid.

139. "Nationalists Sweep Elections," *Outlook*, vol. 2, no. 10 (May 5, 1950), 1. AUB.

140. "Rise and Fall of the Student Council," 6. AUB.

141. Ibid.

142. Ibid.

143. Michael Madonian, "MSS, Urwa Boycott Plan; Other Societies Reject Coordinating Committee on Student Affairs," *Outlook*, vol. 7, no. 3 (November 8, 1952), 1. AUB.

144. Ibid.

145. Ibid.

146. Ibid.

147. John Racy, "Of Ideals, Buildings, and a Mound of Sand," *Outlook*, vol. 7, no. 4 (November 15, 1952), 2. AUB.

148. "Friday Meeting Major Issue," *Outlook*, vol. 11, no. 11 (January 22, 1955), 4. AUB.

149. "Suspended Trio Appeals; Gains [Readmittance]," *Outlook*, vol. 6, no. 4 (March 15, 1952), 1. AUB.

150. Ibid.

151. Minutes of the Executive Committee, American University of Beirut, August 7, 1952. AUB.

152. Ibid.

153. Stephen B. L. Penrose, *Annual Report of Dr. Stephen B. L. Penrose, Jr., 1950–1951*, 11. AUB. He reports that the Communist literature declared, "The imperialist powers are forging new chains for the Arab people, seeking to enslave them and force them to fight on their behalf against the peace-loving nations of the world, at the head of which is the Soviet Union" (12). AUB.

154. S. B. L. Penrose, "From the President to YOU," *Outlook*, vol. 9, no. 1 (October 17, 1953), 1. AUB.

155. Abdul Fattah Jandali, "Urwa Misunderstood, Jandali Explains Aims," *Outlook*, vol. 5, no. 8 (December 15, 1951), 1. AUB.

156. John Racy, "Degrees & Politics," *Outlook*, vol. 4, no. 7 (May 5, 1951), 2. AUB.

157. "We Want to Learn," *Outlook*, vol. 12, no. 4 (November 19, 1955), 2. AUB.

158. Najwa Khayrallah, "Right Paths and Blind Alleys," *Outlook* (January 18, 1958), 2. AUB.

Chapter Six

1. "Guerrilla U," *Newsweek*, vol. 6, no. 15 (October 5, 1970), 68. Earlier versions of this chapter appeared as "Voices of Protest: The Struggle over Freedom at the American University of Beirut (AUB)," *Comparative Studies of South Asia, Africa and the Middle East*, vol. 28, no. 3 (2008): 390–403; and "September 1970 and the Palestinian Issue: A Case Study of Student Politicization at the American University of Beirut (AUB)," *Civil Wars*, vol. 10, no. 3 (September 2008): 261–280.

2. Gill Potter and Nadia Hijab, "Strike Paralyzes AUB for a Week," *Outlook*, vol. 25, no. 8 (January 11, 1969), 3. AUB.

3. After the 1967 war, Palestinian fedayeen groups moved many of their military operations from Jordan to southern Lebanon and the border between the two countries became the sight of numerous attacks between Israel and the Palestinians. The Israeli attack on the Beirut airport in December came in retaliation for a Palestinian attack on an Israeli airliner in Athens two days earlier. In Beirut, the Israelis destroyed thirteen Lebanese planes and caused a crisis inside the Lebanese government because of the army's failure to repel the attack. See Yezid Sayigh, *Armed Struggle and the Search for State: The Palestinian National Movement, 1949–1993* (Oxford: Oxford University Press, 1997), 188–190.

4. Potter and Hijab, 2.

5. Halim Barakat, *Lebanon in Strife: Student Preludes to the Civil War* (Austin and London: University of Texas Press, 1977), 139.

6. Ahmed Abdalla, *The Student Movement and National Politics in Egypt: 1923–1973* (London: Al Saqi Books, 1985), 127.

7. Ibid., 149.

8. Ibid., 152.

9. Haggai Erlich, *Students and University in Twentieth-Century Egyptian Politics* (London: Frank Cass, 1989), 193.

10. Robert Cohen, "The Many Meanings of the FSM: In Lieu of an Introduction," in *The Free Speech Movement: Reflections on Berkeley in the 1960s*, edited by Robert Cohen and Reginald E. Zelnik (Berkeley and Los Angeles: University of California Press, 2002), 17.

11. Muscatine quoted in David Lance Goines, *The Free Speech Movement: Coming of Age in the 1960s* (Berkeley: Ten Speed Press, 1993), 187–188. The Special Select Committee on Education (SCOE) was tasked by the university senate with preparing an educational reform program addressing student concerns.

12. List provided in E. G. Williamson and John L. Cowan, *The American Student's Freedom of Expression: A Research Appraisal* (Minneapolis: University of Minnesota Press, 1966), 7.

13. Julie A. Reuben, "The Limits of Freedom: Student Activists and Educational Reform at Berkeley in the 1960s," in *The Free Speech Movement: Reflections on Berkeley in the 1960s*, edited by Robert Cohen and Reginald E. Zelnik (Berkeley and Los Angeles: University of California Press, 2002), 488.

14. Ibid.

15. Ibid.

16. Ibid.

17. Williamson and Cowan, 29–36.

18. Ibid., 89–102.

19. Mario Savio, quoted in Williamson and Cowan, 88.

20. Edward Shils, "Dreams of Plentitude, Nightmares of Scarcity," in *Students in Revolt*, edited by Seymour Martin Lipset and Philip G. Altbach (Boston: Houghton Mifflin Company, 1969), 5.

21. Barakat, 76.

22. Ibid., 183–184.

23. Shils, 12.

24. Art Goldschmidt, "Can-Can on Earth: Engineers First to Reach Moon, Make It on 1 Stage," *Outlook* (May 9, 1958), 12. AUB.

25. Ibid.

26. "'Sock Hop' a Wonderful Experience," *Outlook*, vol. 15, no. 12 (January 26, 1957), 1 and 6. AUB.

27. Herman Hoecke and Najwa Khairallah, "AUB Coeds, Growing Minority, Make Mark as Scholars as Attitudes toward Coeducation Change in Near East," *Outlook* (March 22, 1958), 12. AUB. "Women Head Honor List," *Outlook*, vol. 22, no. 2 (October 24, 1964), 7. AUB.

28. Rudolph Nassar, "Miss AUB: Garden Party's Popular Attraction Remains: New Election Procedures Add Dignity to Contest," *Outlook*, vol. 13, no. 18 (April 25, 1959), 4. AUB. "Campus News," *al-Kulliyah Review*, vol. 1, no. 9 (May 5, 1934), 1, reports, "A Beauty Contest has been suggested to determine the real beauty on our campus. Perhaps this idea arose from the 'Sleeping Beauties' posted by the Athletic Department." AUB. No action seems to have been taken on this suggestion. On May 1, 1937, the university night organizers awarded one of the female students the title of May Queen while recognizing a male participant with the title of "*stage* May Queen." Both received flowers at their coronations. "The University Night," *al-Kulliyah Review*, vol. 4, no. 13 (May 15, 1937), 4. AUB. No other beauty contests appear in the AUB written record until the inauguration of the Miss AUB contest in 1950.

29. Nadya Sbaiti identifies the 1929 Miss Syria/Lebanon pageant as the first to choose a female representative for the area. The winner was chosen in Paris from a cohort of Syrian and Lebanese women. The point of the exercise was for hoteliers and journalists to generate interest in tourism to Lebanon. By 1933, local pageants occurred all over Mt. Lebanon, with the winners competing for the title of Miss Lebanon. See Nadya Sbaiti, "Land, Tourism and Pageantry in 1930s Lebanon," paper presented at the World Congress for Middle East Studies (WOCMES), Barcelona, Spain, July 2010.

30. Colleen Ballerino Cohen and Richard Wilk, with Beverly Stoeltje, note that "whether the competition is for the title of Miss Universe or the Crooked Tree Cashew Queen, these

contests showcase values, concepts, and behavior that exist at the center of a group's sense of itself and exhibit values of morality, gender, and place." Colleen Ballerino Cohen and Richard Wilk, with Beverly Stoeltje, "Introduction," in *Beauty Queens on the Global Stage: Gender, Contests, and Power*, edited by Colleen Ballerino Cohen and Richard Wilk, with Beverly Stoeltje (New York and London: Routledge, 1996), 2.

31. "Miss Trip," *Outlook*, vol. 10, no. 12 (June 5, 1954), 1. AUB.

32. For example, in 1962, students nominated thirty-eight women for Miss AUB, but only thirteen ultimately chose to run for the crown. A small number had academic "blemishes" on their record and so could not compete; four others who agreed to be interviewed by *Outlook* gave a number of explanations, ranging from a fear of losing the competition to questions about whether Miss AUB stressed beauty far more than academic achievement. Imad Shehadeh, "Miss AUB: The Behind-the-Scenes Story," *Outlook*, vol. 17, no. 21 (May 19, 1962), 3. AUB.

33. Events, Activities, Clubs and Societies, *Outlook* (Commencement 1955), n.p. AUB.

34. Karen W. Tice, "Queens of Academe: Campus Pageantry and Student Life," *Feminist Studies*, vol. 31, no. 2 (Summer 2005), 251. A survey of issues of the *Boston University News* from 1950 to 1960 confirms this finding. The names and photographs of women students appeared on the first page of the paper when they entered the many campus queen contests; they received this honor for few other activities.

35. Ibid.

36. Vladimir Tamari, "Beauty, Character and Activity Determine Choice of Miss AUB," *Outlook*, vol. 16, no. 11 (May 13, 1961), 1. AUB.

37. "Jury Elects Miss AUB," *Outlook*, vol. 13, no. 19 (May 2, 1959), 1. AUB.

38. Ibid.

39. "Right Girl—Wrong Title," *Outlook*, vol. 14, no. 20 (May 14, 1960), 2. AUB.

40. Ibid.

41. "Miss AUB," *Outlook*, vol. 16, no. 12 (May 27, 1961), 5. AUB.

42. Shehadeh, "Miss AUB," 3.

43. Huda Akil, "CWL Corner: New Procedure for Miss AUB," *Outlook*, vol. 21, no. 12 (April 30, 1966), 3. AUB.

44. "Of These Candidates Elect Your Centennial Queen," *Outlook*, vol. 21, no. 14 (May 27, 1966), 2–3. AUB. That year, Miss AUB became Centennial Queen in honor of the school's anniversary.

45. "Nine Candidates Vie for Miss AUB Title: Five Answer Outlook Queries," *Outlook*, vol. 27, no. 12 (April 27, 1971), 8–9. AUB. "Three More Candidates for Miss AUB Title Answer Outlook Queries," *Outlook*, vol. 27, no. 13 (May 4, 1971), 11. AUB.

46. Imad Shehadah, "Boys Count Coeds, Find Coeds Count," *Outlook*, vol. 17, no. 5 (November 4, 1961), 3. AUB.

47. Ibid.

48. "Wearing Slacks: New Girls' Rules Will Be Effective Next Year," *Outlook*, vol. 22, no. 23 (April 29, 1967), 1. AUB. According to the article, new regulations allowed women, starting the following year, to wear slacks on Saturday, Sunday, and holidays in the residence halls. They could also wear slacks while on any private outdoor car trips. At this time, women also received extended curfew hours.

49. "Are Girls Necessary at AUB?" *Outlook*, vol. 21, no. 11 (April 1, 1966), A. AUB.

50. Ibid.

51. Nabih Khuri, "Students Respond to Egypt's Support," *Outlook*, vol. 15, no. 4 (November 3, 1956), 1. AUB. In October 1956, Israel, Britain, and France attacked Egypt in retaliation for the Egyptian nationalization of the Suez Canal. The three quickly gained territory

in the Sinai and bombarded Cairo. The fighting ended when the United States and the Soviet Union persuaded the three allies to pull back their troops.

52. "Magnificent Response to Call for Duty," *Outlook*, vol. 15, no. 5 (November 10, 1956), 1. AUB.

53. "Military Trainees Return Today," *Outlook*, vol. 15, no. 6 (November 17, 1956), 1. AUB.

54. "Dean Weidner Outlines Principles to Follow for Civil Defense," *Outlook*, vol. 15, no. 5 (November 10, 1956), 3. AUB.

55. "University Disciplinary Committee Acts on Events of February 21: 11 Students Put on Special Probation," *Outlook*, vol. 13, no. 13 (March 7, 1959), 1. AUB.

56. "13 Students Suspended by Disciplinary Committee," *Outlook*, vol. 15, no. 1 (November 5, 1960), 1. AUB.

57. Vladimir Tamari, "AUB Demonstration Facts Revealed," *Outlook*, vol. 15, no. 2 (November 19, 1960), 1 and 8. AUB.

58. Vladimir Tamari, Samia Hissen, and Peter Shebay'a, "Feb. 22: Events Before and After," *Outlook*, vol. 16, no. 8 (March 11, 1961), 10. AUB.

59. Ibid.

60. "New President Indicates Need for Responsible Student Gov't: He Calls Self-Control First Step," *Outlook* (October 26, 1957), 1. AUB.

61. "AUB Student Government Takes Giant Step Forward as President, 70 Campus Leaders Discuss Problems of Self Rule in Three Hour Marquand House Confab," *Outlook* (November 16, 1957), 7. AUB.

62. Ibid.

63. Ibid.

64. Hilda Khoury, "Question of Veto Delays Student Group 6 Months," *Outlook* (April 26, 1958), 4. AUB.

65. Ibid.

66. "Burns Invites Students to Sit on Student Life Committee," *Outlook*, vol. 18, no. 14 (May 11, 1963), 1. AUB. See also Representatives of Student Societies, "Announcement to AUB Students," May 10, 1963, Students 1960s, Box 3, File 1: Political Affiliations: Statements, Student Council Statements, 1963–1966. AUB.

67. Norman Burns, *1961–1965 Annual Report of the President and Administration, American University of Beirut*, 42. AUB.

68. Ibid.

69. "Apathy on Campus Investigated," *Outlook*, Special Spring Issue, 1964, 28–29. AUB.

70. Saleh Mounir Nsuli, "Professors Have Their Word: 'General Apathy of Students Exaggerated,'" *Outlook*, vol. 22, no. 23 (April 29, 1967), 3. AUB.

71. Samuel B. Kirkwood, *The President's Annual Report to the Board of Trustees 1965–1966*, 4. AUB.

72. Peter Dodd, "Refugee Report: "Just Like a Dream—As if We'd Never Been There," *Outlook*, vol. 23, no. 3 (November 4, 1967), 2. AUB. The camp was situated 45 kilometers south of Amman.

73. "On Twentieth Anniversary: Students Protest U.N. Partition of Palestine," *Outlook*, vol. 23, no. 6 (December 2, 1967), 1. AUB.

74. Ibid.

75. Ibid.

76. Majida Muashsher, "Inter-University Panel Debates on 'The Role of [the] Student after June 5,'" *Outlook*, vol. 23, no. 12 (February 24, 1968), 6. AUB.

77. Ibid.

78. Ibid.

79. Ibid.

80. "'For Academic Freedom': Students Stage Peaceful Strike," *Outlook*, vol. 23, no. 15 (March 23, 1968), 12. AUB.

81. Organization of Arab Students at A.U.B., May 9, 1968. Students 1960s, Box 3, File 2: Political Affiliations: Statements, Student Council Statements, 1967–1969. AUB. Moshe Dayan was Israeli defense minister during and after the June 1967 war. Abba Eban was the Israeli foreign minister.

82. Ibid.

83. Ibid.

84. *al-Anwar*, November 11, 1968, 3.

85. Ibid., 4.

86. "60% of Student Body Supports Strike," *Outlook*, vol. 25, no. 2 (November 9, 1968), 1. AUB.

87. "In Its First Survey, Outlook Polls Students on Strike," *Outlook*, vol. 25, no. 2 (November 9, 1968), 3. AUB.

88. Samuel B. Kirkwood, "Statement to the Faculty, Students and Staff of the AUB," January 14, 1969. Students 1960s, Box 3, File 2: Political Affiliations: Statements, Student Council Statements, 1967–1969. AUB.

89. "AUB Strike in Its Second Week," *Outlook*, vol. 25, no. 9 (January 18, 1969), 3. AUB.

90. Ibid.

91. Habib Hammam, "As a Lebanese," *Outlook*, vol. 25, no. 9 (January 18, 1969), 2. AUB.

92. Ibid.

93. Ibid.

94. See, for example, a statement to the students by the AUB Student Societies, January 8, 1969. Students 1960s, Box 3, File 2: Political Affiliations: Statements, Student Council Statements, 1967–1969. AUB.

95. "AUB Students Launch Constructive Projects," *Daily Star* (January 15, 1969), n.p. Students 1960s, Box 4, File 2: AUB Students Protest: Press Clippings, 11–15 January 1969. AUB.

96. "Classes Resume Today Following Eleven Hectic Days," *Outlook*, vol. 25, no. 16 (May 3, 1969), 1, AUB.

97. Fawwaz Traboulsi, *A History of Modern Lebanon* (London: Pluto Press, 2007), 154.

98. Barakat, *Lebanon in Strife*, 124.

99. Halim Barakat, "Social Factors Influencing Attitudes of University Students in Lebanon toward the Palestinian Resistance Movement," *Journal of Palestine Studies*, vol. 1, no. 1 (Autumn 1971), 90.

100. Ibid., 91.

101. Ibid., 94.

102. Rima Najjar, "'Speakers' Corner' to Fight Apathy on Campus," *Outlook*, vol. 26, no. 2 (November 17, 1969), 4. AUB.

103. For more information about Black September, see "The Jordanian Civil War: A Retrospective Analysis," a special issue of *Civil Wars*, vol. 10, no. 3 (September 2008).

104. Nadia Hijab, "Speakers' Corner," *Outlook*, vol. 27, no. 1 (October 27, 1970), 6. AUB.

105. Ibid.

106. Ibid.

107. Ibid.

108. "Girl Commando Leila Khaled at AUB Balfour Anniversary," *Daily Star* (November 2, 1969), n.p. Students 1960s, Box 3, File 6: Civil Commando Leila Khaled at AUB on Balfour Anniversary: Press Clippings, 1969. AUB. Leila Khaled hijacked a TWA plane flying from Rome to Athens on August 29, 1969, and unsuccessfully attempted to hijack an El Al plane on September 6, 1970, flying from Amsterdam to New York. During the second

attempt, she was arrested and imprisoned in London until an October 1 prisoner exchange allowed for her release. Leila Khaled, *My People Shall Live: The Autobiography of a Revolutionary*, edited by George Hajjar (London: Hodder and Stoughton, 1973).

109. "Commando at Speaker's [*sic*] Corner: Leila Khaled: Let's Build Wahadat!" *Outlook*, vol. 27, no. 2 (November 3, 1970), 12. AUB.

110. Ibid.

111. Ibid.

112. During a January 14, 1971, session of the Speakers' Corner, the students spent ninety minutes attacking the policies of the Jordanian government. Only one student extended praise for Jordanian governmental decisions, saying that all human beings are capable of mistakes and that the Jordanian regime was not bent on liquidating the Palestinian revolution. "At Speaker's [*sic*] Corner: Jordan Regime Rapped for 90 Minutes Running," *Outlook*, vol. 27, no. 8 (January 19, 1971), 3. AUB. Halim Barakat conducted a new poll with Jordanian students in fall 1970 and found that only 22 percent now "strongly supported" the Palestinian commandos, 22 percent "did not support them," and 56 percent "supported them with reservation." Barakat, "Social Factors," 91, n. 3.

113. For more information on the Rogers Plan, see William B. Quandt, *Peace Process: American Diplomacy and the Arab-Israeli Conflict Since 1967*, rev. ed. (Washington, DC: Brookings Institute Press and Berkeley and Los Angeles: University of California Press, 2001), and Robert J. Pranger, *American Policy for Peace in the Middle East 1969–1971: Problems of Principle, Maneuver and Time*, Foreign Affairs Study 1 (Washington, DC: American Enterprise Institute for Public Policy Research, April 1971).

114. "Fateh Leader at AUB: 'We Cannot Lay Down Our Arms for We Would Be Giving up Our Lives; Jordan Massacres Are Part of Rogers Plan,'" *Outlook*, vol. 27, no. 7 (January 12, 1971), 1. AUB.

115. Ibid.

116. Ibid.

117. Ibid.

118. *al-Hayat*, January 12, 1971, 5.

119. "'Voice of Student' Reverberates New Clashes in Jordan," *Outlook*, vol. 27, no. 7 (January 12, 1971), 1. AUB.

120. Ibid.

121. "AUB Strikes against Jordan 'Lackeys,'" *Outlook*, vol. 27, no. 8 (January 19, 1971), 1. AUB.

122. Ibid., 12.

123. Ibid.

124. "The Free University—What It Is," *Outlook*, vol. 27, no. 7 (January 12, 1971), 6. AUB.

125. Namir Cortas, "For Change," *Outlook*, vol. 28, no. 1 (November 16, 1971), 2. AUB.

126. Ibid.

127. Free University Collective, "Sadeq Al-Azm's Comeback: Free University Challenges AUB Educational Initiative," *Outlook*, vol. 27, no. 8 (January 19, 1971), 9. AUB.

128. Julie A. Reuben, "Reforming the University: Student Protests and the Demand for a 'Relevant' Curriculum," in *Student Protest: The Sixties and After*, edited by Gerard J. deGroot (London and New York: Longman, 1998), 155.

129. Ibid.

130. Nicely Student Council Action Committee, "An Appeal to the Silent Majority," *Outlook*, vol. 28, no. 2 (November 30, 1971), 7. AUB.

131. Ibid.

132. Samuel B. Kirkwood, *Annual Report of the President, American University of Beirut: 1970–1971*, 5. AUB.

133. AUB Student Council, "Bulletin 1," *Outlook*, vol. 27, no. 15 (May 25, 1971), 11. AUB.

134. "Academic Program Is Suspended Following 'No Vote' to Proposals and Occupation of Jessup, Fisk Halls, including Office of the Dean; Masri: 'It's Just What We Expected!'" *Outlook*, vol. 27, no. 15 (May 25, 1971), 1. AUB.

135. Ibid.

136. Ibid.

137. Samuel B. Kirkwood, *The President's Annual Report to the Board of Trustees*, 1970–1971, 4. AUB.

138. Edwin T. Prothero, Memo to All Members of the University Community, May 31, 1971. Students 1970s, Box 1, File 1: General, 1971–1979. AUB.

139. Barakat, *Lebanon in Strife*, 175–176.

140. Samuel B. Kirkwood, Memo to All Members of the AUB Community, July 26, 1971. Students 1970s, Box 1, File 3: Letters and Statements by AUB President Samuel Kirkwood; Letters to AUB President Samuel Kirkwood, 1971–1975. AUB.

141. Samuel B. Kirkwood, "An Open Letter to AUB Faculty, Students and Staff," October 29, 1971. Students 1970s, Box 1, File 3: Letters and Statements by AUB President Samuel Kirkwood; Letters to AUB President Samuel Kirkwood, 1971–1975. AUB.

142. Kirkwood, The President's Annual Report to the Board of Trustees, 1970–1971, 24.

143. On October 6, 1973, Egypt and Syria attacked Israel and immediately moved their forces across the 1967 cease-fire lines and into the Sinai Peninsula and the Golan Heights. Within a week, Israel counterattacked with US military aid. The fighting ended without any land changing hands.

144. "A.U.B. at War: General Assemblies," *Outlook*, vol. 20, no. 1 (October 19, 1973), 4. AUB.

145. Mohammad Matar to the Faculty, May 21, 1974. Students 1970s, Box 2, File 1: Student Council: General, 1970–1974. AUB.

146. Ibid.

147. "The Aims Are Clear," *Outlook*, vol. 20, no. 9 (March 4, 1974), 2. AUB.

148. "Strike . . . ," *Outlook*, vol. 20, no. 11 (March 18, 1974), 2. AUB.

149. Makram Rabah, *A Campus at War: Student Politics at the American University of Beirut, 1967–1975* (Beirut: Dar Nelson, 2009), 106. For more information on the fragmentation of the student movement in the last couple of years, see Rabah, 75–106.

150. Ibid., 106.

151. Ibid., 94 and 104.

152. John M. Munro, *A Mutual Concern: The Story of the American University of Beirut* (Delmar, NY: Caravan Books, 1977), 177.

153. Ibid.

154. "Interview with Mohammed Dajani, President of AUB's Student Council," *al-Kulliyah* (Spring 1972), 1. AUB.

155. Barakat, *Lebanon in Strife*, 183.

Chapter Seven

1. "Mission, Vision and Core Values," Middle States Commission on Higher Education, http://www.msche.org/?Nav1=ABOUT&Nav2=MISSION, accessed August 23, 2010.

2. "Chapter 12: General Education," 148, in American University of Beirut, Institutional Self-Study Commission on Higher Education, Middle States Association of Colleges and Schools, http://www.aub.edu.lb/accreditation/Documents/SS%20Chap%2012%20Jan%20 19%2004.pdf, accessed January 17, 2010.

3. "AUB Mission Statement," American University of Beirut, http://www.aub.edu.lb/about/mission.html, accessed September 26, 2009.

4. "The Historical Development of AUB Mission Statement," 11, in American University of Beirut, Institutional Self-Study Commission on Higher Education, Middle States Association of Colleges and Schools. Appendix F 1-1, http://www.aub.edu.lb/accreditation/Documents/Appendix%20F%20%20Jan%2019%2004.pdf, accessed January 17, 2010.

5. Interview with President John Waterbury, 18, in American University of Beirut, Institutional Self-Study Commission on Higher Education, Middle States Association of Colleges and Schools. Appendix F 1-4 A, http://www.aub.edu.lb/accreditation/Documents/Appendix%20F%20%20Jan%2019%2004.pdf, accessed January 17, 2010.

6. Peter F. Dorman, "Presidential Inaugural Address of Peter Dorman," May 4, 2009, 3. American University of Beirut, http://staff.aub.edu.lb/~webinfo/public/inaug_dorman/dorman_speech.pdf, accessed September 26, 2009.

7. For more information on the Lebanese civil war, see Fawwaz Traboulsi, *A History of Modern Lebanon* (London: Pluto Press, 2007); Tabitha Petran, *The Struggle over Lebanon* (New York: Monthly Review Press, 1987); and Robert Fisk, *Pity the Nation: The Abduction of Lebanon* (New York: Touchstone, 1990).

8. John M. Munro, *A Mutual Concern: The Story of the American University of Beirut* (Delmar, NY: Caravan Books, 1977), 185–186.

9. Author interview with Huda Zurayq, Beirut, Lebanon, January 12, 2006. AUB. Huda Zurayq is the daughter of Constantine Zurayq.

10. See author interview with Kamal Salibi, Beirut, Lebanon, June 30, 2005; author interview with Nabil Dajani, Beirut, Lebanon, July 7, 2005; and author interview with Ibrahim Salti, Beirut, Lebanon, July 13, 2005. AUB.

11. Fisk, 284.

12. Author interview with Dajani; author interview with Salti; and author interview with Zurayq. AUB.

13. Munro, 186.

14. Elie A. Salem, *Violence and Diplomacy in Lebanon: The Troubled Years, 1982–1988* (London: I. B. Tauris, 1995), 1.

15. Fisk, 284.

16. Ibid., 314. The SPC School of Medicine opened in 1867; in 1887, its faculty made an arrangement to use the facilities at the Prussian Hospital for Clinical Teaching. In 1902, SPC's administration bought land across the street from the main campus and this became the foundation for the American University Hospital (AUH). "American University of Beirut Medical Center," American University of Beirut, http://www.aubmc.org/users/subpage.asp?id=3, accessed August 22, 2010.

17. Fisk, 300.

18. Nathaniel David George cites letters in which US government officials in the 1970s explicitly claim AUB as a government asset. Furthermore, they made it clear that future government money would be tied to administration efforts to curtail the AUB student movement. Nathaniel David George, "United States Imperialism in the Middle East and the Lebanese Crisis of 1973," MA thesis, American University of Beirut, 2010. Despite the content of these letters, it is impossible to determine how much influence the US government had over the AUB administration. In terms of the student movement, both organizations shared the same goal of limiting its activities.

19. "Minutes of the University Senate Meetings," April 20, 1970. Students 1970s, Box 1, File 5: Minutes of the University Senate Meeting; Minutes of the Meetings of the Faculty of Arts and Sciences, 1970–1974. AUB. A note on the file indicates that the Organization of Student Struggle made the minutes available to the students.

20. "Interview with Mohammed Dajani, President of AUB's Student Council," *al-Kulliyah* (Spring 1972), 1. AUB.

21. Author interview with Muhammed Dajani Daoudi, Beirut, Lebanon, December 21, 2005. AUB.

22. Author interview with Salibi; Ann Zwicker Kerr, *Come with Me from Lebanon: An American Family Odyssey* (Syracuse: Syracuse University Press, 1994), 3 and 5.

23. Salibi interview.

24. Ibid.

25. Ussama Makdisi, *Faith Misplaced: The Broken Promise of U.S.-Arab Relations: 1820–2001* (New York: PublicAffairs, 2010), 2.

26. I would like to thank Makram Rabah for his help in acquiring information about the current system of student government.

27. Makram Rabah, "Activism in the Y Generation," *Main Gate*, vol. 4, no. 3 (Spring 2006), 37. AUB.

28. "AUB Relives Student Activism in Hyde Park Event," *AUB Bulletin Today*, vol. 10, no. 8 (July 2009), http://staff.aub.edu.lb/~webbultn/v10n8/article38.htm, accessed January 31, 2010.

29. Ibid.

30. Ibid.

Bibliography

Archive Collections

American University of Beirut/Library Archives

Annual Reports by the Presidents to the Boards of Managers and Trustees, Syria Protestant College, 1866–1920.
Annual Reports by the Presidents to the Board of Trustees, American University of Beirut, 1920–1928, 1932–1972.
Annual Reports of the Near East College Association, 1928–1931.
Course Catalogues, Syrian Protestant College, 1871–1920.
Course Catalogues, American University of Beirut, 1920–1957.
Daniel Bliss Collection: AUB President 1866–1902.
Howard Bliss Collection: AUB President 1902–1920.
Bayard Dodge Collection: AUB President 1923–1948.
Edward F. Nickoley Collection: Acting President 1920–1923.
Memorabilia, Syrian Protestant College.
Minutes of the Faculties, Syrian Protestant College, 1867–1940.
Minutes of the Faculties, American University of Beirut, 1920–1956.
Minutes of the University Senate and Executive Council, American University of Beirut, 1920–1956.

Students 1900s–1970s

Women at AUB

Newspapers, Magazines, and Journals of the Syrian Protestant College and American University of Beirut

The Anchor
al-'Asr
Brotherhood Bulletin
Business Man
Cedar
Chemical and Industrial Gazette
The Commercial Review
Commercial S.P.C. Editor
The Commercial Triumvirate
al-Daira
Faculty Bulletin
Fifth Form Crescent
Focus
Ghadat al-Fikr
al-Hadiqa
Happy Days of the S.P.C.
al-Hazz
al-Iffah

I.O.U. Five Minutes
al-Kinanah
al-Kulliyah [Arabic; 1899]
al-Kulliyah
al-Kulliyah Review
Life of Service
Light
Lookout
L'Orient
al-Mabda' al-Sahih
Main Gate
al-Manara
Middle East Forum
The Miltonian
News Letter: Robert College at Constantinople, Syrian Protestant College at Beirut [Later
       called *Near East Colleges News Letter: Robert College, Constantinople; American Uni-
       versity of Beirut, Syria; Constantinople Woman's College; International College, Smyrna;
       American College of Sofia, Bulgaria; Athens College, Greece*]
Outlook
Pioneers of the S.P.C.
Prep. Progress
The Review Organ of the Freshman School
Sada al-Isti'dadiyah
Seniors of SPC
SPC Torch Gazette
Students' Union Gazette
Sub-Freshman Star
Syria
al-Thamarah
Thamarat al-Adhan
The University
University Times
al-'Urwa al-Wuthqa
Zaharat al-Kulliyah

Amherst College

Bliss Family Papers
Catalogue of the Officers and Students of Amherst College, 1847–1852
Catalogue of the Officers and Students of Amherst College for the Academical Year 1881–82

Burke Library, Columbia University at Union Theological Seminary

Commission I (Carrying the Gospel to All the Non-Christian World) of the World Mis-
       sionary Conference, Edinburgh, June 14–23, 1910.

Houghton Library, Harvard University

Daniel Bliss, Personal Papers

Published Sources

Abdalla, Ahmed. *The Student Movement and National Politics in Egypt: 1923–1973*. London: Al Saqi Books, 1985.

Abu-Jabir, Faruq Saʿd, ed. *Dhikrayat fi al-jamiʿa al-amirkiyah fi bayrut* [Amman]: Matbaʿat al-Aswaq, 1998.

Abu-Lughod, Lila. "Introduction: Feminist Longings and Postcolonial Conditions." In *Remaking Women: Feminism and Modernity in the Middle East*, edited by Lila Abu-Lughod. Princeton: Princeton University Press, 1998.

———, ed. *Remaking Women: Feminism and Modernity in the Middle East*. Princeton: Princeton University Press, 1998.

Ahmed, Leila. *Women and Gender in Islam: Historical Roots of a Modern Debate*. New Haven and London: Yale University Press, 1992.

Altbach, Philip G. "Perspectives on Student Political Activism." In *Student Political Activism: An International Reference Handbook*, edited by Philip G. Altbach. New York and Westport, CT: Greenwood Press, 1989.

———, ed. *Student Political Activism: An International Reference Handbook*. New York and Westport, CT: Greenwood Press, 1989.

Anderson, Betty S. "September 1970 and the Palestinian Issue: A Case Study of Student Politicization at the American University of Beirut (AUB)." *Civil Wars*, vol. 10, no. 3 (September 2008), 261–280.

———. "Voices of Protest: The Struggle over Freedom at the American University of Beirut (AUB)." *Comparative Studies of South Asia, Africa and the Middle East*, vol. 28, no. 3 (2008), 390–403.

———. "Writing the Nation: Textbooks of the Hashemite Kingdom of Jordan." *Comparative Studies of South Asia, Africa and the Middle East*, vol. 21, nos. 1 and 2 (2001), 5–14.

Anderson, Rufus. *Foreign Missions: Their Relations and Claims*. New York: Charles Scribner and Company, 1869.

———. *Report to the Prudential Committee of a Visit to the Missions in the Levant*. Boston: American Board of Commissioners for Foreign Missions, Printed by T. R. Marvin, 1844.

Axtell, James. *The Making of Princeton University: From Woodrow Wilson to the Present*. Princeton: Princeton University Press, 2006.

al-ʿAzmah, ʿAziz. *Qustantin Zurayq: ʿArabi lil-qarn al-ʿishrin*. Beirut: Muʿassasat al-Dirasat al-Filastiniyah, 2003.

Badran, Margot. *Feminists, Islam, and Nation: Gender and the Making of Modern Egypt*. Princeton: Princeton University Press, 1995.

Barakat, Halim. *Lebanon in Strife: Student Preludes to the Civil War*. Austin and London: University of Texas Press, 1977.

———. "Social Factors Influencing Attitudes of University Students in Lebanon toward the Palestinian Resistance Movement." *Journal of Palestine Studies*, vol. 1, no. 1 (Autumn 1971), 87–112.

Baron, Beth. *The Women's Awakening in Egypt: Culture, Society, and the Press*. New Haven: Yale University Press, 1994.

Barton, James L. "The Modern Missionary." *Harvard Theological Review*, vol. 8. no. 1 (January 1915), 1–17.

Bliss, Daniel. *Reminiscences of Daniel Bliss, Edited and Supplemented by His Eldest Son*, edited by Frederick Jones Bliss. New York: Fleming H. Revell Company, 1920.

———. *The Voice of Daniel Bliss*. Beirut: American Press, 1956.

Bliss, Howard S. "The Modern Missionary." *The Atlantic Monthly* (May 1920), 664–675.

Callcott, George H. *History in the United States, 1800–1860: Its Practice and Purpose*. Baltimore: Johns Hopkins Press, 1970.

Cawelti, John G. *Apostles of the Self-Made Man*. Chicago and London: University of Chicago Press, 1965.

Coffin, Henry Sloane. *A Half Century of Union Theological Seminary, 1869–1945: An Informal History*. New York: Charles Scribner's Sons, 1954.

Cohen, Colleen Ballerino, Richard Wilk, and Beverly Stoeltje. "Introduction." In *Beauty Queens on the Global Stage: Gender, Contests, and Power*, edited by Colleen Ballerino and Richard Wilk, with Beverly Stoeltje. New York and London: Routledge, 1996.

Cohen, Robert, and Reginald E. Zelnik. "The Many Meanings of the FSM: In Lieu of an Introduction." In *The Free Speech Movement: Reflections on Berkeley in the 1960s*, edited by Robert Cohen and Reginald E. Zelnik. Berkeley and Los Angeles: University of California Press, 2002.

———, eds. *The Free Speech Movement: Reflections on Berkeley in the 1960s*. Berkeley and Los Angeles: University of California Press, 2002.

Conable, Charlotte Williams. *Women at Cornell: The Myth of Equal Education*. Ithaca and London: Cornell University Press, 1977.

Cortas, Wadad Makdisi. *A World I Loved: The Story of an Arab Woman*. New York: Nation Books, 2009.

Davison, Roderic H. "Westernized Education in Ottoman Turkey." *Middle East Journal*, vol. 15, no. 3 (Summer 1961), 189–301.

DeGroot, Gerard J., ed. *Student Protest: The Sixties and After*. London and New York: Longman, 1998.

Deringil, Selim. *The Well-Protected Domains: Ideology and the Legitimation of Power in the Ottoman Empire, 1876–1909*. London: I. B. Tauris, 1998.

Devlin, John F. *The Ba'th Party: A History from Its Origins to 1966*. Stanford, CA: Hoover Institution Press, 1976.

Dodge, Bayard. *The American University of Beirut: A Brief History of the University and the Lands Which It Serves*. Beirut: Khayat's, 1958.

Eliot, Charles William. *Academic Freedom: An Address Delivered before the New York Theta Chapter of the Phi Beta Kappa Society at Cornell University, May 29, 1907*. Ithaca, NY: Press of Ithaca and Church, 1907.

Elshakry, Marwa. "The Gospel of Science and American Evangelism in Late Ottoman Beirut." *Past and Present*, vol. 196, no. 1 (August 2007), 173–214.

El Shakry, Omnia. "Schooled Mother and Structured Play: Child Rearing in Turn-of-the-Century Egypt." In *Remaking Women: Feminism and Modernity in the Middle East*, edited by Lila Abu-Lughod. Princeton: Princeton University Press, 1998.

Eppel, Michael. "Notes and Comments: Note about the Term *Effendiyya* in the History of the Middle East." *International Journal of Middle East Studies*, vol. 41 (2009), 535–539.

Erlich, Haggai. *Students and University in Twentieth-Century Egyptian Politics*. London: Frank Cass, 1989.

Farag, Nadia. "The Lewis Affair and the Fortunes of al- Muqtataf." *Middle Eastern Studies*, vol. 8, no. 1 (January 1972), 73–83.

Fisk, Robert. *Pity the Nation: The Abduction of Lebanon*. New York: Touchstone, 1990.

Fleischmann, Ellen L. "Lost in Translation: Home Economics and the Sidon Girls' School of Lebanon, c. 1924–1932." *Social Sciences and Missions*, vol. 23, no. 1 (2010), 32–62.

———. "'Under an American Roof': The Beginnings of the American Junior College for Women in Beirut." *Arab Studies Journal*, vol. 27, no. 1 (Spring 2009), 62–84.

Fortna, Benjamin C. *Imperial Classroom: Islam, the State, and Education in the Late Ottoman Empire*. Oxford: Oxford University Press, 2003.

Freely, John. *A History of Robert College: The American College for Girls, and Boğaziçi (Bosphorus University)*. Vols. 1 and 2. Istanbul: Yapi Kredi Yayınları, 2000.

Fuess, Claude Moore. *Amherst: The Story of a New England College*. Boston: Little, Brown, and Company, 1935.

Gandhi, Mahatma. *Men Are Brothers: Life and Thoughts of Mahatma Gandhi as Told in His Own Words*, compiled and edited by Krishna Kripalani. Paris: UNESCO, 1969.

Geiger, Roger. "Introduction." In *The American College in the Nineteenth Century*, edited by Roger Geiger. Nashville: Vanderbilt University Press, 2000.

Gelvin, James L. "The Other Arab Nationalism: Syrian/Arab Populism in Its Historical and International Contexts." In *Rethinking Nationalism in the Arab Middle East*, edited by James Jankowski and Israel Gershoni (New York: Columbia University Press, 1997).

General Education in a Free Society. Cambridge: Harvard University Press, 1945.

Gershoni, Israel. "Rethinking the Formation of Arab Nationalism in the Middle East, 1920–1945: Old and New Narratives." In *Rethinking Nationalism in the Arab Middle East*, edited by James Jankowski and Israel Gershoni. New York: Columbia University Press, 1997.

Ghanma, Amjad Deeb. *Jami'at al-'Urwa al-Wuthqa*. Beirut: Riad El-Rayyes Books, 2002.

Göçek, Fatma Müge. *Rise of the Bourgeoisie, Demise of Empire: Ottoman Westernization and Social Change*. New York and Oxford: Oxford University Press, 1996.

Goines, David Lance. *The Free Speech Movement: Coming of Age in the 1960s*. Berkeley: Ten Speed Press, 1993.

"Guerrilla U." *Newsweek*, vol. 6, no. 15 (October 5, 1970), 68 and 70.

Handy, Robert T. *A Christian America: Protestant Hopes and Historical Realities*. New York: Oxford University Press, 1971.

Hanssen, Jens. *Fin de Siècle Beirut: The Making of an Ottoman Provincial Capital*. Oxford: Oxford University Press, 2005.

Harper, William Rainey. *The Trend in Higher Education*. Chicago: University of Chicago Press, 1905.

Hitti, Philip. *History of the Arabs*. London: Macmillan, 1937.

Hofstadter, Richard. *The Age of Reform: From Bryan to F.D.R.* New York: Alfred A. Knopf, 1955.

Hofstadter, Richard, and Wilson Smith, eds. *American Higher Education: A Documentary History*. Vol. 2. Chicago: University of Chicago Press, 1961.

Hollinger, David A. "Inquiry and Uplift: Late Nineteenth-Century American Academics and the Moral Efficacy of Scientific Practice." In *The Authority of Experts: Studies in History and Theory*, edited by Thomas L. Haskell. Bloomington: Indiana University Press, 1984.

Hopkins, Charles Howard. *The Rise of the Social Gospel in American Protestantism: 1865–1915*. New Haven: Yale University Press, 1940.

Hourani, Albert. *Arabic Thought in the Liberal Age: 1798–1939*. Cambridge: Cambridge University Press, 1983.

———. "Ottoman Reform and the Politics of Notables." In *The Modern Middle East: A Reader*, edited by Albert Hourani, Philip S. Khoury, and Mary C. Wilson. Berkeley and Los Angeles: University of California Press, 1993.

Hutchison, William R. *Errand to the World: American Protestant Thought and Foreign Missions*. Chicago: University of Chicago Press, 1987.

Jankowski, James P. *Nasser's Egypt, Arab Nationalism, and the United Arab Republic*. Boulder, CO: Lynne Rienner Publishers, 2002.

Jeha, Shafik. *Darwin and the Crisis of 1882 in the Medical Department and the First Student Protest in the Arab World in the Syrian Protestant College (Now the American University of Beirut)*, translated by Sally Kaya, edited by Helen Khal. Beirut: American University of Beirut Press, 2004.

———. *al-Haraka al-ʿarabiyya al-sirriyya jamaʿat al-kitab al-ahmar.* Beirut: al-Furat li-l-nashr, 2004.

"The Jordanian Civil War: A Retrospective Analysis." Special issue of *Civil Wars*, vol. 10, no. 3 (September 2008).

Kassab, Elizabeth Suzanne. *Contemporary Arab Thought: Cultural Critique in Comparative Perspective.* New York: Columbia University Press, 2010.

Kerr, Ann Zwicker. *Come with Me from Lebanon: An American Family Odyssey.* Syracuse: Syracuse University Press, 1994.

Khaled, Leila. *My People Shall Live: The Autobiography of a Revolutionary*, edited by George Hajjar. London: Hodder and Stoughton, 1973.

Khater, Akram Fouad. *Inventing Home: Emigration, Gender, and the Middle Class in Lebanon, 1870–1920.* Berkeley and Los Angeles: University of California Press, 2001.

Khoury, Philip S. "The Paradoxical in Arab Nationalism: Interwar Syria Revisited." In *Rethinking Nationalism in the Arab Middle East*, edited by James Jankowski and Israel Gershoni. New York: Columbia University Press, 1997.

———. *Syria and the French Mandate: The Politics of Arab Nationalism, 1920–1945.* Princeton: Princeton University Press, 1987.

Kobiljiski, Aleksandra Majstorac. "Women Students at the American University of Beirut from the 1920s to the 1940s." In *Gender, Religion and Change in the Middle East: Two Hundred Years of History*, edited by Inger Marie Okkenhaug and Ingvild Flaskerud. Oxford and New York: Berg, 2005.

Lawson, Andrew C. "Joseph Le Conte." *Science*, n.s., vol. 14, no. 347 (August 23, 1901), 273–277.

Leavitt, Donald M. "Darwinism in the Arab World: The Lewis Affair at the Syrian Protestant College." *The Muslim World*, vol. 71, no. 2 (April 1981), 85–98.

Le Duc, Thomas. *Piety and Intellect at Amherst College: 1865– 1912.* New York: Arno Press and The New York Times, 1969.

Lindsay, Rao Humpherys. *Nineteenth Century American Schools in the Levant: A Study of Purposes.* University of Michigan Comparative Education Dissertation Series, no. 5. Ann Arbor: University of Michigan School of Education, 1965.

Lipset, Seymour Martin, and Philip G. Altbach, eds. *Students in Revolt.* Boston: Houghton Mifflin, 1969.

Lowe, Margaret A. *Looking Good: College Women and Body Image, 1875–1930.* Baltimore and London: Johns Hopkins University Press, 2003.

Makdisi, Anis al-Khuri. *al-Ittijahat al-Adabiyah fi al-ʿAlam al-ʿArabi al-Hadith, wa-Hiya Dirasat Tahliliyah lil-ʿAwamil al-Faʿalah fi al-Nahda al-ʿArabiyah al-Hadithah wa-li-Zawahiriha al-Adabiyah al-Raʾisiyah.* Beirut: Dar al-ʿIlm lil-Malayin, 1963.

Makdisi, Jean Said. *Teta, Mother, and Me: Three Generations of Arab Women.* New York: W. W. Norton & Company, 2006.

Makdisi, Ussama. *Artillery of Heaven: American Missionaries and the Failed Conversion of the Middle East.* Ithaca and London: Cornell University Press, 2008.

———. *The Culture of Sectarianism: Community, History, and Violence in Nineteenth-Century Ottoman Lebanon.* Berkeley and Los Angeles: University of California Press, 2000.

———. *Faith Misplaced: The Broken Promise of U.S.-Arab Relations: 1820–2001.* New York: PublicAffairs, 2010.

Marsden, George M. "The Soul of the American University: A Historical Overview." In *The Secularization of the Academy*, edited by George M. Marsden and Bradley J. Longfield. New York and Oxford: Oxford University Press, 1992.

Munro, John M. *A Mutual Concern: The Story of the American University of Beirut*. Delmar, NY: Caravan Books, 1977.

Ngugi wa Thiong'o. *Decolonising the Mind: The Politics of Language in African Literature*. London: James Currey, 1997.

Patrick, Mary Mills. *A Bosporus Adventure: Istanbul (Constantinople) Woman's College, 1871–1924*. Stanford: Stanford University Press, 1934.

Pendergast, Tom. *Creating the Modern Man: American Magazines and Consumer Culture, 1900–1950*. Columbia: University of Missouri Press, 2000.

Penrose, Stephen B. L., Jr. *The Palestinian Problem—Retrospect and Prospect*. Beirut: World Council of Churches, 1951.

———. *That They May Have Life: The Story of the American University of Beirut, 1866–1941*. Beirut: American University of Beirut, 1970.

Petran, Tabitha. *The Struggle over Lebanon*. New York: Monthly Review Press, 1987.

Philipp, Thomas. *Gurgi Zaidan: His Life and Thought*. Beirut: Beiruter Texte und Studien, in Kommission Bei Franz Steiner Verlag, 1979.

Pranger, Robert J. *American Policy for Peace in the Middle East, 1969–1971: Problems of Principle, Maneuver and Time*. Foreign Affairs Study 1. Washington, DC: American Enterprise Institute for Public Policy Research, 1971.

Provence, Michael. "Late Ottoman State Education." In *Religion, Ethnicity and Contested Nationhood in the Former Ottoman Space*, edited by Jørgen S. Nielsen. Leiden: Brill, forthcoming.

Quandt, William B. *Peace Process: American Diplomacy and the Arab–Israeli Conflict Since 1967*. Rev. ed. Washington, DC: Brookings Institution Press; Berkeley and Los Angeles: University of California Press, 2001.

Rabah, Makram. *A Campus at War: Student Politics at the American University of Beirut, 1967–1975*. Beirut: Dar Nelson, 2009.

al-Razzaz, Munif. "Munif al-Razzaz Yatadhakkar: Sanawat al- Jami'ah." *Akhar Khabar* (January 3–4, 1994).

Reid, Donald Malcolm. *Cairo University and the Making of Modern Egypt*. Cambridge: Cambridge University Press, 1990.

Reuben, Julie A. "The Limits of Freedom: Student Activists and Educational Reform at Berkeley in the 1960s." In *The Free Speech Movement: Reflections on Berkeley in the 1960s*, edited by Robert Cohen and Reginald E. Zelnik. Berkeley and Los Angeles: University of California Press, 2002.

———. *The Making of the Modern University: Intellectual Transformation and the Marginalization of Morality*. Chicago and London: University of Chicago Press, 1996.

———. "Reforming the University: Student Protests and the Demand for a 'Relevant' Curriculum." In *Student Protest: The Sixties and After*, edited by Gerard J. DeGroot. London and New York: Longman, 1998.

Richard, Carl J. *The Golden Age of the Classics in America: Greece, Rome, and the Antebellum United States*. Cambridge: Harvard University Press, 2009.

Roberts, Jon H. *Darwinism and the Divine in America: Protestant Intellectuals and Organic Evolution, 1859–1900*. Madison: University of Wisconsin Press, 1988.

Roberts, Jon H., and James Turner. *The Sacred and the Secular University*. Princeton: Princeton University Press, 2000.

Russell, Mona L. *Creating the New Egyptian Woman: Consumerism, Education, and National Identity, 1863–1922*. New York: Palgrave Macmillan, 2004.

Sabri, Marie Aziz. "Angela (Jurdak) Khoury." In *Pioneering Profiles: Beirut College for Women*. Beirut: Khayat Book & Publishing Co., 1967.

———. "Dr. Jamal (Karam) Harfouche." In *Pioneering Profiles: Beirut College for Women*. Beirut: Khayat Book and Publishing Company, 1967.

————. *Pioneering Profiles: Beirut College for Women*. Beirut: Khayat Book and Publishing Company, 1967.

Sakakini, Hala. *Jerusalem and I: A Personal Record*. Amman: Economic Press Company, 1990.

Salem, Elie A. *Violence and Diplomacy in Lebanon: The Troubled Years, 1982–1988*. London: I. B. Tauris, 1995.

Sayegh, Fayez A. *Arab Unity: Hope and Fulfillment*. New York: Devin-Adair Company, 1958.

Sayigh, Yezid. *Armed Struggle and the Search for State: The Palestinian National Movement, 1949–1993*. Oxford: Oxford University Press, 1997.

Schulze, Reinhard. "Mass Culture and Islamic Cultural Production in Nineteenth-Century Middle East." In *Mass Culture, Popular Culture, and Social Life in the Middle East*, edited by Georg Stauth and Sami Zubaida. Frankfurt: Campus Verlag, 1987.

Seelye, Julius. "Progressive Apprehension of Divine Truth." *American Presbyterian and Theological Review*, no. 20 (October 1867), 592–604.

Seelye, Laurens Hickok. "An Experiment in Religious Association." *The Journal of Religion*, vol. 2, no. 3 (May 1922), 303–309.

Sharabi, Hisham. *Embers and Ashes: Memoirs of an Arab Intellectual*, translated by Issa J. Boullata. Northampton, MA: Olive Branch Press, 2008.

Sharkey, Heather J. *American Evangelicals in Egypt: Missionary Encounters in an Age of Empire*. Princeton: Princeton University Press, 2008.

Sheehi, Stephen. *Foundations of Modern Arab Identity*. Gainesville: University Press of Florida, 2004.

Shils, Edward. "Dreams of Plentitude, Nightmares of Scarcity." In *Students in Revolt*, edited by Seymour Martin Lipset and Philip G. Altbach. Boston: Houghton Mifflin Company, 1969.

Sicherman, Barbara. "College and Careers: Historical Perspectives on the Lives and Work Patterns of Women College Graduates." In *Women and Higher Education in American History: Essays from the Mount Holyoke College Sesquicentennial Symposia*, edited by John Mack Faragher and Florence Howe. New York and London: W. W. Norton and Company, 1988.

Smith, Lacey Baldwin. "A Study of Textbooks on European History during the Last Fifty Years." *Journal of Modern History*, vol. 23, no. 3 (September 1951), 250–256.

Solomon, Barbara Miller. *In the Company of Educated Women: A History of Women and Higher Education in America*. New Haven: Yale University Press, 1985.

Somel, Selçuk Akşin. *The Modernization of Public Education in the Ottoman Empire, 1839–1908: Islamization, Autocracy and Discipline*. Leiden: Brill, 2001.

Spivak, Gayatri Chakravorty. "Can the Subaltern Speak?" In *Marxism and the Interpretation of Culture*, edited by Cary Nelson and Lawrence Grossberg. Houndmills, Basingstoke, Hampshire: Macmillan Education Ltd., 1988.

Tejirian, Eleanor H., and Reeva Spector Simon, eds. *Altruism and Imperialism: Western Cultural and Religious Missions in the Middle East*. Occasional Papers no. 4. New York: Middle East Institute, Columbia University, 2002.

Thompson, Elizabeth. *Colonial Citizens: Republican Rights, Paternal Privilege, and Gender in French Syria and Lebanon*. New York: Columbia University Press, 2000.

Tibawi, A. L. *American Interests in Syria, 1800–1901: A Study of Educational, Literary and Religious Work*. Oxford: Clarendon Press, 1966.

————. "The Genesis and Early History of the Syrian Protestant College." In *American University of Beirut Festival Book (Festschrift)*, edited by Fuad Sarruf and Suha Tamim. Beirut: The American University of Beirut, 1967.

Tice, Karen W. "Queens of Academe: Campus Pageantry and Student Life." *Feminist Studies*, vol. 31, no. 2 (Summer 2005), 250–283.

Traboulsi, Fawwaz. *A History of Modern Lebanon*. London: Pluto Press, 2007.

Veer, Peter van der, ed. *Conversion to Modernities: The Globalization of Christianity*. New York and London: Routledge, 1996.

Veysey, Laurence R. *The Emergence of the American University*. Chicago and London: University of Chicago Press, 1965.

Watenpaugh, Keith David. *Being Modern in the Middle East: Revolution, Nationalism, Colonialism, and the Arab Middle Class*. Princeton and Oxford: Princeton University Press, 2006.

Waterbury, John. *The Egypt of Nasser and Sadat: The Political Economy of Two Regimes*. Princeton: Princeton University Press, 1983.

Williamson, E. G., and John L. Cowan. *The American Student's Freedom of Expression: A Research Appraisal*. Minneapolis: University of Minnesota Press, 1966.

Wilson, Woodrow. "Princeton in the Nation's Service." In *The Papers of Woodrow Wilson*, edited by Arthur S. Link. Vol. 10. Princeton: Princeton University Press, 1971.

Zeine, Zeine N. *The Struggle for Arab Independence: Western Diplomacy and the Rise and Fall of Faisal's Kingdom in Syria*. Beirut: Khayat's, 1960.

Zurayq, Constantine. *The Meaning of the Disaster*, translated by R. Bayly Winder. Beirut: Khayat's College Book Cooperative, 1956.

———. "More Than Conquerors." In *More Than Conquerors: Selected Addresses Delivered at the American University of Beirut, 1953–1966*. Beirut: American University Press, 1968.

Zürcher, Erik J. *Turkey: A Modern History*. London: I. B. Tauris, 2009.

Textbooks

Dodd, Stuart C. *Social Relationships in the Near East: A Civics Textbook of Readings and Projects for College Freshmen*. Beirut: American University of Beirut, 1931.

Hopkins, Mark. *The Law of Love and Love as a Law: Moral Science, Theoretical and Practical*. 2nd ed. New York: Charles Scribner and Company, 1869.

Robinson, James Harvey. *An Introduction to the History of Western Europe*. Vol. 2. Boston: Ginn and Company, 1904.

Tarr, Ralph S., and Frank M. McMurry. *Elementary Geography*. New York: Macmillan and Company, Ltd., 1907.

Interviews

Nabil Dajani, Beirut, Lebanon, July 7, 2005.

Muhammed Dajani Daoudi, Beirut, Lebanon, December 21, 2005.

Elie Salem, Balamand University, Lebanon, July 25, 2005.

Kamal Salibi, Beirut, Lebanon, June 1, 2005, and June 30, 2005.

Ibrahim Salti, Beirut, Lebanon, July 13, 2005.

Huda Zurayq, Beirut, Lebanon, January 12, 2006.

Dissertations and Unpublished Works

Dimechkie, Hala Ramez. "Julia Tu'mi Dimashqiyi and al-Mar'a al-Jadida: 1883–1954." MA thesis, American University of Beirut, 1998.

Farag, Nadia. "*al-Muqtataf*, 1876–1900: A Study of the Influence of Victorian Thought on Modern Arab Thought." PhD diss., St. Antony's College, Oxford, 1969.

George, Nathaniel David. "United States Imperialism in the Middle East and the Lebanese Crisis of 1973." MA thesis, American University of Beirut, 2010.

Sbaiti, Nadya. "Land, Tourism and Pageantry in 1930s Lebanon." Paper presented at the World Congress for Middle East Studies (WOCMES), Barcelona, Spain, July 2010.

———. "Lessons in History: Education and the Formation of National Society in Beirut, Lebanon, 1920–1960s." PhD diss., Georgetown University, 2008.

Scholz, Norbert J. "Foreign Education and Indigenous Reaction in Late Ottoman Lebanon: Students and Teachers at the Syrian Protestant College in Beirut." PhD diss., Georgetown University, 1997.

Newspapers

al-Anwar, Beirut
Boston University News, Boston
Daily Star, Beirut
al-Hayat, Beirut
al-Muqtataf, Beirut and Cairo
an-Nahar, Beirut

Web Sources

American University of Beirut. Institutional Self-Study Commission on Higher Education, Middle States Association of Colleges and Schools. American University of Beirut. http://www.aub.edu.lb/accreditation/Documents/Accreditation%20Self%20Study%20Intro%20Jan%2019%2004.pdf.

"American University of Beirut Medical Center." American University of Beirut. http://www.aubmc.org/users/subpage.asp?id=3.

"AUB: A Historical Accident." *News Highlights*. American University of Beirut. http://www.aub.edu.lb/news/archive/preview.php?id=114461.

"AUB Mission Statement." American University of Beirut. http://www.aub.edu.lb/about/mission.html.

"AUB Relives Student Activism in Hyde Park Event." *AUB Bulletin Today*, vol. 10, no. 8 (July 2009). http://staff.aub.edu.lb/~webbultn/v1on8/article38.htm.

Cross, Timothy P. "An Oasis of Order: The Core Curriculum." Columbia University. http://www.college.columbia.edu/core/oasis.

Darwin Correspondence Project. http://www.darwinproject.ac.uk/darwinletters/calendar/entry-13710.html.

"Directory of AUB Faculty, Staff, and Officers, 1880–." American University of Beirut. http://www.aub.edu.lb/cgi-bin/asc-directory.pl?.

Dorman, Peter F. "Inauguration of Peter Dorman." American University of Beirut. http://staff.aub.edu.lb/~webinfo/public/inaug_dorman/dorman_speech.pdf.

"Guide to the Stephen B. L. Penrose, Jr. Papers: 1908–1990." Northwest Digital Archives. http://nwda-db.wsulibs.wsu.edu/findaid/ark:/80444/xv75253.

"History." Jane Addams Hull House Association Website. http://www.hullhouse.org/aboutus/history.html.

"Mission, Vision and Core Values." Middle States Commission on Higher Education. http://www.msche.org/?Nav1=ABOUT&Nav2=MISSION.

"Reports on the Course of Instruction in Yale College; by a Committee of the Corporation, and the Academical Faculty, 1828." http://collegiateway.org/reading/yale-report-1828/.

Waterbury, John. "Women at AUB: Today and Yesterday," October 7, 2002. American Univsersity of Beirut. http://www.aub.edu.lb/news/archive/preview.php?id=29015.

Index

CPSIA information can be obtained at www.ICGtesting.com
Printed in the USA
BVOW07s2311030814

361135BV00001B/18/P